IN THE VALLEY OF THE PANG

edited by *Dick Greenaway &*

In the Valley of The Pang

edited by *Dick Greenaway & Dorcas Ward*

THE FRIENDS OF THE PANG
AND KENNET VALLEYS

Reading 2002

Published by
The Friends of the Pang and Kennet Valleys
The Cottage
Ashampstead Common
Reading RG8 8QT

ISBN 0-9543597-0-4

Designed by Jessica Clarke and Chris Goodwin
undergraduate students in the Department of Typography &
Graphic Communication, The University of Reading.

The copy-editing style of this book represents the intentions of its editors
and authors, which its printer has followed. The book was typeset in
Monotype Dante and printed in the Department of Typography &
Graphic Communication, The University of Reading.

Front cover photograph
The Pang Valley around Stanford Dingley
supplied by UK Perspectives Ltd, Axbridge, Somerset
(telephone 01934 732 122)

Contents

Acknowledgements

We would like to thank most sincerely all of those who contributed to these chapters. They have given of their time and knowledge most generously and delivered against often unrealistic deadlines. The opinions expressed in the essays are, in each case, the author's own and for which we, the editors, bear no responsibility. Each author has given us permission to publish their work but they retain the individual copyright. 'The Sources of the River' by Linnet McMahon was first published in *The Story of Compton*. The book would not have been possible without the generous financial support of the Heritage Lottery Fund–Local Heritage Initiative, the Nationwide Building Society and the Countryside Agency. This has allowed us to aim for a standard of publication which would otherwise have been beyond our reach. We are duly grateful for this award and we hope that the donors consider their money well spent. Our grateful thanks are also due to the Friends of the Pang and Kennet Valleys for their financial and project management support and in particular to Rob Prinn their treasurer.

All maps are based on the Ordnance Survey mapping of the Pang Valley and their copyright is individually acknowledged with each map. The photographs came from many sources and are individually acknowledged. The largest contributions came from the Rural History Centre of The University of Reading and from the Greenaway collection. Many of these photographs originated from residents in the villages along the valley and, where possible, their approval has been obtained to publish. Old photographs pass through many hands and it is very difficult to establish the owner of the original copyright. If we have infringed anyone's copyright we hope they will accept our apologies.

We gratefully acknowledge the support all our authors have received from libraries and record offices and in particular from the Berkshire Record Office.

The chapter opening illustrations were drawn by Dorcas Ward as were the flower illustrations – both black and white and coloured. The maps and diagrams are based on original drawings by Dick Greenaway.

Dedicated to Felicity Palmer of Coombe Farm, Frilsham:
Farmer, Natural Historian and Scholar

Introduction

This is not a guidebook, nor is it a local history. It is intended instead as a celebration of place by people who either live in the Pang Valley or who are fascinated by it. The project to produce the book started at a memorial service for a remarkable woman – Felicity Palmer of Frilsham – who had lived in, worked in, studied and loved the valley and its people for more than half her life. Her friends decided to produce a book of essays on the subjects close to her heart and this is the result.

Once started the book grew and the difficulty was to know where to stop, what to leave out. Readers living in the lower valley may feel that they have been neglected, as may those living along the southern edge at Bucklebury. Our only excuse is that those areas have been celebrated in print already by their own people, as has Compton.

Our ambition for this book is that it will stir an interest in the valley in anyone opening it. It is a book to dip into. Some pieces are longer and more challenging, others are shorter and lighter. We are looking for the 'ah, yes!' factor – for the spark of recognition of a name, a picture or a place that builds an understanding of the landscape and turns a mere location into a home.

We hope that, as our readers move around the valley, they will recognise the names and the places and the whole landscape will start to grow in meaning for them. If the reader is encouraged to search out but one of the sites or read but one of the other books mentioned, we will feel that we have succeeded.

Dick Greenaway & Dorcas Ward

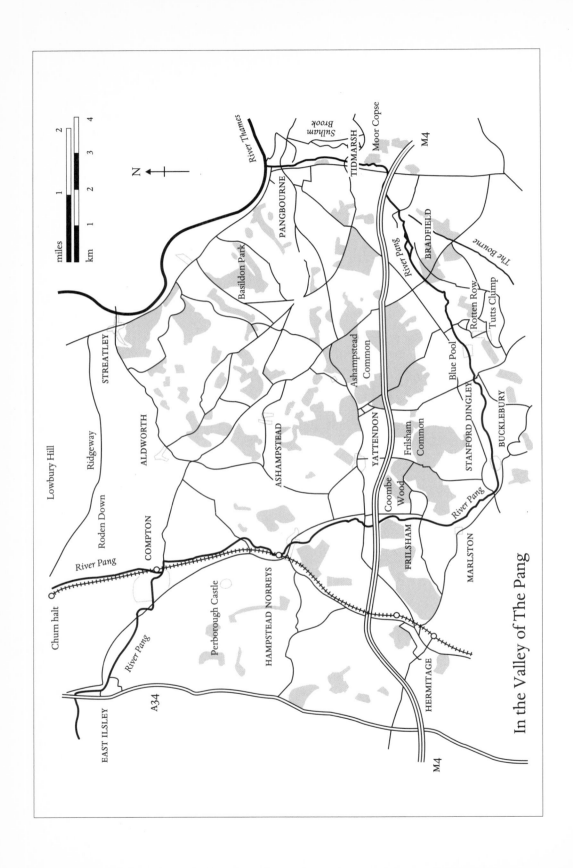

In the Valley of The Pang

The People

1 Felicity Palmer of Frilsham

Sukey Johnson

COOMBE FARM.

This short summary of a long and particularly valuable life is based on an address given at the memorial service for Felicity Palmer at Yattendon on Sunday 17 September 2000.

When I was in Frilsham earlier in the year, shortly after Felicity's death in April 2000, many of her friends asked me if anything was being arranged to celebrate her life. Repeatedly I was told how much she contributed during her many years living in Frilsham.

Felicity was born in South Kensington in 1913 the second of four sisters. However, most of her childhood was spent in the country at Exning near Newmarket. Her elder sister Sue told me that, as the biggest and bossiest of the four, she was in charge of organising the games. These could be anything from tennis to performances for the grandparents. The performances were arranged strictly in teams of blondes and brunettes. Sue and my mother Gillian Pilkington were blondes and Fel and Rachel were brunettes.

Felicity was always a little different from her more extrovert sisters, slightly reserved and highly strung. Somewhat accident prone in childhood, she was the one who fell off her bicycle on a stony bit of road while the others fell comfortably on the grassy verges.

By the age of twelve or so she was well on the way to becoming an intellectual. Her father Joe – much loved in Yattendon in later life – was a writer and from him Felicity inherited a love of books which was to become a passion. Another great influence on her childhood was her governess Miss Hardy. Miss Hardy was a keen naturalist and she started Felicity off on her life long interest in the countryside.

In her teens Felicity attended Burgess Hill PNEU (Parents' National Education Union) School in Sussex and then went on

Felicity Palmer
© Sukey Johnson

to Bedford College London where she took a first in Modern Languages. She travelled to Italy with her sisters, spent six months at the Sorbonne in Paris and some months in Vienna learning German.

It was then time to find a job. She found it difficult to secure anything appropriate experiencing the discrimination encountered by many intellectual women in the thirties. After being refused employment with Huntley & Palmers in Reading – apparently due to a lack of lavatories for women accessible from the Board Room – she found a post in 1937 working for the League of Nations in Geneva. She found the Swiss countryside stunning to explore but the organisation was unimaginative, bureaucratic and unsupportive and Felicity was not at all happy. After two years she resigned and returned to London just before the beginning of World War Two.

During the war the Palmer family moved into the Grange at Yattendon. Food shortages were already a problem and Felicity turned her energies to re-organising the garden, turning it over entirely to vegetables. She grew more than the family could eat and there were people in the towns hungry for beans and onions. Fel formed a small village co-operative and made weekly trips to the Women's Institute stall in Reading with her car loaded with surplus vegetables. She also grew soft fruit and helped with the milking at Yattendon Manor Farm.

In 1947 Coombe Farm and its small farmhouse at Frilsham was for sale and with the rural skills she had acquired she felt it was time to graduate to her own farm. The farm was a small mixed holding which she ran very successfully, working it by herself with one helper. At this time her sister Sue also bought a small farm – Fir Tree Farm at Hampstead Norrys – and became passionate about the benefits of organic farming. Although Felicity was more traditional in her farming methods, they both shared a love and respect for their animals and this deep mutual interest in farming matters was the basis for another fifty years of often heated discussion.

Life for Felicity, though, was always about much more than farming. She took a deep interest in every aspect of life in Yattendon and Frilsham and became a fund of local knowledge and history. She was particularly interested in the rural trades. She researched and published the *Blacksmith's Ledgers* – an account of the foundry at Bucklebury – and a scholarly history of *Frilsham and the Floyd Family*. She was an expert on local politics and always well primed with village news, much of it gleaned through editing the parish magazine *The Broadsheet*. Consequently she could report accurately on anything from the state of the church roof to the new lunch menu at the pub!

Felicity loved every aspect of nature. Her final project was the co-ordination of 'The Countryside in Frilsham 2000'. This was a project close to her heart, a survey and record of the wildlife in Frilsham. Her co-ordinating role was an appropriate legacy as she died a week before the opening of the exhibition displaying the results of the project.

On many occasions when staying with Felicity, I was driver and counter of hedgerow species. Each species to be meticulously recorded and compared with the records she had kept since the 1950s. Her delight came from fostering and encouraging interest in others and she was acutely aware of the need to include the younger generation if the local countryside was to be safeguarded. I find this book of essays by her friends and colleagues on the subjects so close to her heart a wonderful tribute to her memory and to the work she did on so many aspects of the Pang Valley.

Her garden was a sanctuary. There were more wild flowers than hybrids. The April view from her sitting room was a path of primroses leading through an arching avenue of hazelnut trees. No such nonsense as a laburnum tunnel. Weeds were not discouraged and a large part of her garden was unmown meadow. Her vegetables were prolific and grown organically. She kept chickens that laid eggs with lovely deep yellow yolks. She kept bees and her garden was a paradise for small birds. Some local angel must have shot the magpies! The dawn chorus, now faint in many country gardens, roared its head off at Coombe Farmhouse.

Although Felicity lived a quiet life after retiring from farming, rarely travelling far, she had many friends who were always welcome. With two of her sisters living close by, Gillian at Frilsham and Sue at Hampstead Norreys, she was always involved and in touch with the rest of the family and – more recently – with her six great nieces and nephews wherever they were in the world. She was exceedingly well informed on a wide variety of topics, and took every opportunity to broaden the viewpoint of the younger generation. Hence, for most of the years I have lived in Australia, the *Guardian Weekly* was sent to me by Felicity. She was a great believer in the importance of young people and their contribution to village life and she involved herself in any project to make it possible for them to stay. She had definite political opinions yet was very interested in an alternative point of view. However, her intellectual and spiritual needs were fulfilled by two principal interests – books and the natural world. She read and read, persuading the travelling library to procure the most obscure books. She would telephone literary friends in the evening, just to talk about books for fifteen minutes or more. Literature from a diverse range of world charities poured into her house and she gave to them all generously, keenly interested in their objectives. On my last visit, however, she told me she was concentrating on local issues as she felt it was here that she could be most effective. Her mind was focused and sharp to the very end.

Felicity lived simply, believing in the Quaker philosophy. She was tolerant and non judgemental. Although she did not like the modern world, she did not fight it. She simply chose to be uncompetitive, to use her considerable gifts to enjoy, to chronicle and cultivate small things.

2 'Thomas Paty in Yattenden'
A Seventeenth-Century
Yattendon Grocer

Jill Greenaway

Thomas Paty was born in Yattendon in 1634 and was baptised in
Yattendon Church on 29 March. He was the third son and sixth
child of William and Annis Paty who had married in Yattendon
Church on 23 April 1621. Yattendon baptismal register records
seven children of William and Annis, six of whom, Joane (Johana),
Ann, William, John, Thomas and Edward survived into adulthood.

A Thomas Paty and a John Paty were listed as tenants of John
Norys in 1522 and the study of this family in the sixteenth and
seventeenth centuries offers fascinating insights into the social
and economic life of a rural community at this time.

Schoolchildren today would be delighted by the flexibility
of the spelling of the time. The Paty family name was variously
spelt Paty, Patey, Patye or Patie. The difference in the spelling
is not significant and does not indicate a separate branch of the
family. Henry Patey of 'Evrington', whose burial in Yattendon is
recorded for 9 December 1559, described himself in his will as
Henry Patie. He left a brass pot, a dish, a 'bushell' of barley and a
sheep to his daughter Joan Patye, a coffer, a platter, two 'bushells'
of barley and three sheep to his daughter Alice Paty and the
residue of his goods to his wife Helen and his son William Paty.
Spelling was irrelevant for Henry, as it was throughout the period,
but our Thomas consistently signed himself as Paty.

During this period, when a death occurred all the deceased's
goods and chattels – everything other than land – had to be listed

and valued on oath by two appraisers, usually neighbours, for probate. These inventories are often very detailed and provide information about the size of the house and the standard of living within it. The surviving Yattendon wills and inventories of the Paty family reflect a life of comfortable prosperity and indicate that some members of the family could be regarded as wealthy. The inventory of Edward Paty(e)'s goods taken on 28 December 1619 valued them at £13 10s 5d; that of another Edward Patye on 20 June 1631 was £111 4s 0d. The goods of William Paty were valued at £40 6s 11d on 28 March 1662, when Thomas was one of the appraisers. Edward Paty, Thomas's brother, died in 1685 and his goods were valued at £111 2s 7½d on 28 March 1685. Against this comfortable background Thomas Paty's inventory taken on 27 July 1675 stands out. His goods were valued at the remarkable sum of £533 13s 6d, nearly five times that of his brother who died almost ten years later. This was at a time when the average wage for an agricultural labourer was 11 pence a day for a six day week.

Why then was Thomas Paty so much wealthier than other members of his family? In what way was he different? All the Yattendon Patys whose wills and inventories survive for this period are described as tailors, the sole exception being Henry whose occupation is not given. Thomas, however, was a grocer. His name appears on documents and inventories and he was literate, always signing his own name, whereas many of his contemporaries witnessed documents with their mark. At the time of the baptism of the first of his three children on 7 May 1664 he is described in the register as a churchwarden. These activities were typical of a respected and prosperous member of the community. However, he was unusual in that he was the only Yattendon businessman who struck his own token coinage.

Between 1649 and 1672 there was a national lack of coins of small denomination which were necessary small change for everyday use and many local traders issued their own token coins to supply this need. The majority of the token coins issued by traders throughout the country were copper farthings and this is the denomination that Thomas Paty issued in Yattendon. His token coin on one side reads 'THOMAS PATY IN' around a sugar loaf; and on the other side 'YATTENDEN BERKS' around 'PTE' with the TE below the P. The initial P is for Paty, whilst the initials T and E are for Thomas and his wife Elizabeth. The circulation of these tokens would have been restricted to the area served by Thomas Paty's business because only he was obliged to redeem them. They would have been used to buy goods directly from him or from other traders who in their turn could use the tokens in their dealings with him.

Thomas died in 1675, three years after a royal proclamation
made it illegal to use such tokens. He was buried in Yattendon
on 28 May. He was forty-one years old and his children were aged
fifteen, nine and five. He left no will so his death is likely to have
been unexpected and sudden, and the administrator's account of
the payments from his estate reveal a thriving and wide ranging
trade. He was obviously buying produce locally and exporting it,
as well as importing goods from elsewhere to sell locally. Perhaps
it is significant that the discharge list in the administration
account itemises payments to two bargemasters. The inventory
of his possessions reveals the commodities in which he was
trading. The contents of the shop and warehouse are an amazing
mixture of necessities and more exotic goods. He stocked
woollen cloth to the value of £49 2s 3d, fustion, calico, canvas
and sheepskin; but he also had five pounds of silk and two boxes
of buttons which were valued together at £16 16s 6d, as well as
ribbon, cotton, lace, four and a half pounds of whalebone and
a quantity of hooks and eyes. He had spices for the kitchen,
including cloves, mace and cinnamon, ginger, mustard seed and
pepper; raisins, currants, treacle, rice, sugar and brandy were
listed along with the more prosaic soap, starch, cheese and hops.
He had pins, knives, earthen jugs and bottles, whipcord, powder
horns, gunpowder, seeds and raddle, but also eight hundred
pound of tobacco, valued at £29 14s 0d, one hundred and thirty
pounds of loose tobacco worth £4 11s 0d, a tobacco engine and a
stock of tobacco pipes, stockings and eight bibles. With this range
of merchandise for a variety of customers, it is not surprising
that Thomas Paty felt the need to issue his own token coins.
Some of the contents of his shop and warehouse came from as

far afield as the East and West Indies and America. It would have taken months in a slow sailing ship to carry these to England where Thomas Paty could buy them. He was owed £68 11s 2d in 'hopeful debts', but the problems of this kind of trading is highlighted by the 'desparate debts' of £52 16s 1d.

The life style that this thriving business supported was comfortable but not opulent, although the house was large. He was still a farmer with a cow and two hogs, corn upon the ground and in the barn, and dung upon the land; cheese was pressed in his milkhouse whilst beer was brewed and bacon salted in his kitchen. His cellar contained two hogsheads and ten small barrels. His food was cooked at the fire in the hall and this room also contained his one little silver dish, his twenty-nine pewter dishes, three flagons, one bowl and three pint pots, his wooden platters and spoons, his brass pot and his warming pan. No doubt he ate his food at the table sitting on one of the five joint stools or eight chairs and perhaps sometimes he leant against one of the three cushions and looked at one of the books in his parcel of small books. Four chambers were well furnished with beds and bedding, all of which is listed. The only surprising omission in the domestic part of this inventory is that no horse is listed in his stable although it contained saddles, bridle and harness. One wonders whether the absence of a horse could be connected with his death.

Thomas Paty lived in comfort and ran a business which supplied the community with a range of commodities, the scale and variety of which would justify regarding him as a merchant, rather than a grocer. He supplied the everyday items needed by his rural neighbours but also the more exotic luxury items for the wealthy. His sudden death left his widow with a large business to run and three young children to raise. Three years later, on 2 June 1679 she married John Nullis and she and the three children receive legacies in Edward Paty's will in 1685. It will be interesting to expand this research to follow the fortunes of Thomas Paty's widow and children and trace what happened to his business after his death.

3 Frilsham and the Floyds

Felicity Palmer

In 1800, in the middle of the long and costly wars against France and Napoleon, Robert Hayward bought the manors of Frilsham and Eling from a gentleman in Herefordshire. It may seem a humdrum event, but it was, in fact, to be a landmark in our village's history. From Domesday onwards, the owners of the land had lived elsewhere. For about a hundred years the Norreys had been close by at Yattendon. But in Elizabeth's time they had moved away to Rycote and later to Wytham, leaving Frilsham in probably very welcome obscurity, a small village at the farthest edge of a large estate. In 1764 the land had been sold out of the family altogether, to another absentee.

There would always have been a manor farm. In the middle ages this would have been managed by a bailiff on behalf of the lord, and in later periods it would be let to a tenant farmer. But the nearest any of the villagers came to the landowner was probably only the twice yearly visit of his steward to collect the rents.

This was about to change. Robert Hayward came from the Vale of the White Horse and, although for a while in legal documents he is referred to as 'of East Ginge', he quite soon becomes 'Robert Hayward Esq of Frilsham'. He became churchwarden here and a tablet in the church records his burial here, leaving no doubt that this became his home. His home was not in the present Manor House, which was still to be built, but was in the old farmhouse of which sadly no print survives.

In the village he came to in 1800 an Elizabethan villager would have found much that was familiar. There were new crops in the fields and he would have noted that farmers had greater freedom to follow their own devices. But he would have felt at home in a

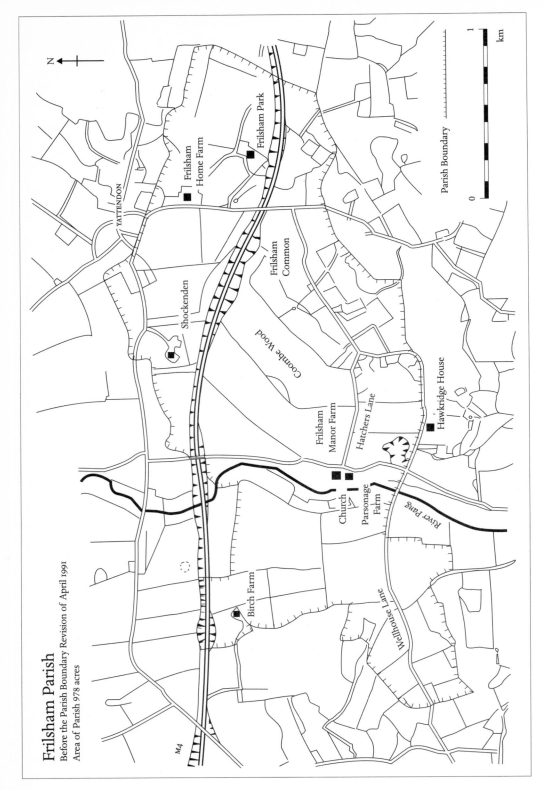

Frilsham Parish

Before the Parish Boundary Revision of April 1991
Area of Parish 978 acres

N

YATTENDON

Frilsham
Home Farm

Frilsham Park

Shockenden

Frilsham
Common

Coombe Wood

Frilsham
Manor Farm

Hatchers Lane

Hawkridge House

Church

Parsonage
Farm

River Pang

Wellhouse Lane

Birch Farm

M4

Parish Boundary

km

0

1

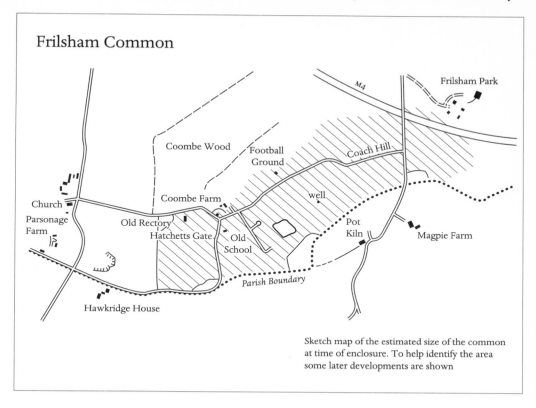

Frilsham Common

Sketch map of the estimated size of the common at time of enclosure. To help identify the area some later developments are shown

community coping with the well-known problems of weeds and weather, where life still moved to its old agricultural rhythm. It was still an almost self-sufficient neighbourhood, building with local bricks and timber, its tools hand or blacksmith made, its energy needs supplied by human muscle and by horse and water power. For most it must have been a hard life but not without its jollities for the traditional festivities were still alive, – the May Day procession, the harvest feast, the Christmas mummers* to add to the church festivals at Easter and Christmas.

To its 181 inhabitants (the first census was taken in 1801) the war, still largely a naval war, would have seemed very distant, but, with Newbury a regular staging post for the Royal Mail, news would certainly have reached the neighbourhood. Villages, too, along with towns, would have been affected by the periodic calling up of the local militia, which had begun as early as 1793, in the very first year of the war. (The *Reading Mercury*, in February of that year reported that a contingent of the Berkshire militia had been ordered to the coasts of Kent and Sussex to relieve 'such of the regulars as are destined for other causes').†

We can get some picture of the farming scene when Robert Hayward took over from the valuation made of the estate when the Abingdons sold it in 1764. At this time there were ten tenants

* They survived, if only as shadows of their former selves, to nearly the end of the century. See *Yattendon School logbooks* and Miss Waterhouse's 'Memories' in *The Broadsheet*.

† The names of those called on to serve were drawn by ballot. In his *Record of the History of Hampstead Norreys Parish* Roger Chapman gives details of the ballot there in 1806.

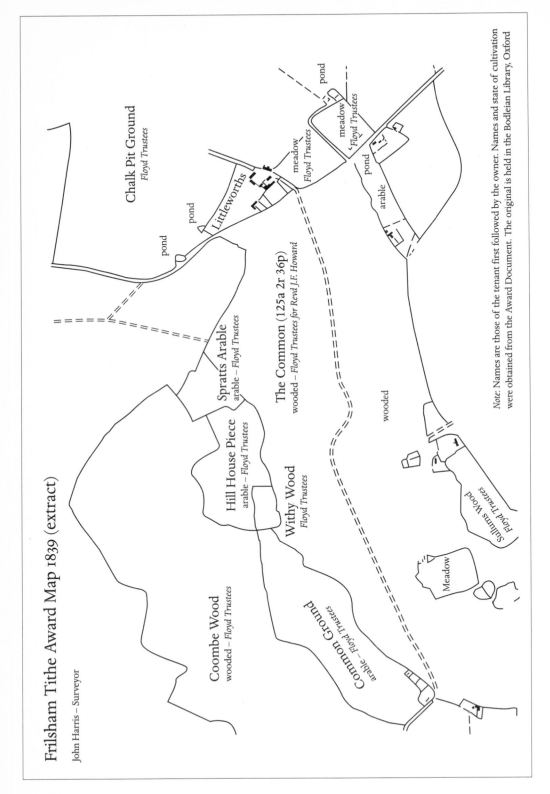

Frilsham Tithe Award Map 1839 (extract)

John Harris – Surveyor

Chalk Pit Ground
Floyd Trustees

pond

pond

pond

Littleworths

meadow
Floyd Trustees

meadow
Floyd Trustees

pond

meadow
Floyd Trustees

pond

arable

Spratts Arable
arable – *Floyd Trustees*

The Common (125a 2r 36p)
wooded – *Floyd Trustees for Revd J.F. Howard*

Hill House Piece
arable – *Floyd Trustees*

Withy Wood
Floyd Trustees

wooded

Coombe Wood
wooded – *Floyd Trustees*

Common Group
arable – *Floyd Trustees*

Sullums Wood
Floyd Trustees

Meadow

Note: Names are those of the tenant first followed by the owner. Names and state of cultivation were obtained from the Award Document. The original is held in the Bodleian Library, Oxford

Manderley was once a farmhouse on the edge of Frilsham Common. It was built in the seventeenth century, possibly replacing an earlier, smaller dwelling. The farmer or husbandman who lived here could have been a copyholder of the manor, paying a low fixed rent, who had prospered with the rising prices and the expanding market for all farm produce. It is a reasonable guess, too, that with good clay so close and plenty of wood for firing, the bricks came from near at hand.

under various agreements. Robert Coster at the manor farm with 225 acres and Richard Matthew with 40 acres were 'tenants at will'. So was the miller with his two closes. (These were tenancies which could be terminated or the rent altered annually). The other seven, who between them farmed 100 acres, held leases for 'one or two lives', paying very low fixed rents but liable to pay a lump sum when a new life was added or an old one removed from the agreement.

Most of these smaller holdings are described as 'a house and lands'. A Board of Agriculture report in 1808 described Frilsham farmland as 'partly enclosed'. It seems to me virtually certain that the 'lands' were in the unenclosed part of the parish, very possibly in the field stretching from Frilsham church towards Yattendon. An 18th century map of Yattendon shows an open field beside the Yattendon–Hermitage road with the medieval strips joined together into more workable blocks which still lay side by side, somewhat like a series of outsize allotments. The field in Frilsham probably looked much the same. One can also guess that the small tenants themselves – Thomas Awbury, Alexander Smallbones, Mary Wiggins and the rest – lived with their livestock on the 200 acres of common, following a way of life which had become much freer over the centuries but which, in other ways, had not greatly altered.

As well as the tenants, the valuation also gives the names of six freeholders and five cottagers. The annual return from the woodlands is estimated and there is the following reference to the common: 'The pasturage of Frilsham Common belongs to the parishioners but the wood and timber with liberty of

Frilsham House, the residence of Captain Bertie's widow till her death in 1833. It was originally known as Cooke's Farm but was renamed Frilsham House probably by the previous occupants, the Peregrine Berties. One can see that in the pre-enclosure days the Common stretched almost to the front door. (The above print is published, with acknowledgements, from *Yattendon and its Church* by the Revd Smith-Masters.)

After Sir Cameron Gull bought the farm he pulled down the farmhouse and built his much larger country seat which many people will remember. That in its turn was demolished after the coming of the M4. The site is now occupied by the Frilsham Park houses.

planting at pleasure to the Lord of the Manor'. The size of the estate is given as 487 acres, so that it only included about half the parish.

Robert Hayward, the new owner, was not long in adding to his property. He bought – from John Cooke of Whitchurch – Cooke's Farm (Frilsham Home Farm) and later three more. His last buy was in 1818 and on this deed of sale the name of Robert Floyd appears as witness and Hayward's signature is described as 'shaky'. Robert Floyd was the son of Hayward's niece, from Frilford near Wantage.

Robert Hayward died in 1820, five years after Waterloo and his long will shows him to have been a wealthy man. He was apparently unmarried; nearly all his legacies went to members of his large extended family living in his home neighbourhood of White Horse Vale. His Frilsham land he left to Robert Floyd – who may already have been living here – with the charge that he was to provide £1000 for each of his three sisters. Eling Farm was left separately to two other cousins, William and John Aldworth, and money was also left for three charities to benefit the village. Two of these were for the Frilsham old and poor and one for the education of the village children. I imagine it went to the parish clerk, traditionally the schoolmaster, to buy readers. Nowadays it buys books for the school every year.

So at the age of twenty-seven Robert Floyd became the new squire of Frilsham. He probably married soon after for his first child, to be named Robert Hayward Floyd, was born in 1822. One hopes that domestic happiness helped to compensate for the bleak times that the countryside was going through; the longed for peace had not brought prosperity – on the contrary, prices fell but taxes to pay for the enormous cost of the war did not. There were reports of many farmers going bankrupt or absconding, and of counties where hundreds of acres were left derelict.

William Cobbett riding through southern England in the 1820s noted the steep fall in the price of nearly all farm produce and spoke to many despairing farmers. He was particularly moved to pity and indignation by the plight of the labourers. To their struggle to keep a family on wages of 8 or 9 shillings a week (40–45 pence) was now added the threat of unemployment. It was the advent of threshing machines which would deprive them of much needed winter work, which finally led to the machine riots of 1830. In that winter, in Berkshire, bands of labourers roamed the countryside demanding a wage of 12 shillings a week and attacking the hated machines. In this area machines in Bucklebury, Bradfield and Stanford Dingley were burnt. Labourers from Yattendon, Frilsham and Hampstead Norreys joined together to confront local farmers and demand a rise in pay. Many were later rounded up by soldiers from Reading and will have been lucky if they escaped the harsh sentences handed down by frightened magistrates. One man from Kintbury was hanged despite a widespread appeal for clemency, others were sentenced to transportation to Australia. The neighbourhood must have passed anxious years.

Nevertheless there is reason to believe that the hard times here were not quite so hard as in many other places. William Cobbett, who near Salisbury had seen four or five households sharing a fire to boil a kettle, was in no doubt that the labourers in wooded country, which provided fuel as well as work in winter, suffered less than those on the bare downland farms (*see* note 2). And there are indications that Robert Floyd was not as short of funds as some farmers. It is never easy to date farm buildings but the stable block at the manor farm may have been built in his day; and according to the church history building work went on there too. In 1834 the wooden bell turret was replaced by the present brick tower and a south porch was added. Like his predecessor, Robert Floyd was churchwarden. As such, and as the patron and landowner, it is hard to believe that he was not the chief funder and one of the moving spirits behind the work. Somewhat earlier the wooden rails around the churchyard had been replaced by the present iron railings, cast in Hedges' foundry at Bucklebury. Another hint to the Floyds' close involvement is the inclusion of the third little gate, near the barn, for the people at the manor farm.

Unlike his predecessor Robert Floyd barely added to his estate. His only recorded acquisition is of a 10 acre smallholding which the owner Joseph Chamberlain exchanged for a cottage. It sounds

as though the small holding was mortgaged. Robert Floyd under-
took to repair the cottage, dig a well and add some outbuildings.
It was expressly stated that Joseph should keep his right to put
stock on the common. ('Two horses, two cows, geese, ducks
and pigs'). This was in 1833.

Robert Floyd died in 1837 at the age of forty-four, leaving a
widow and five children – the oldest now a boy of fifteen – and
the estate was for a while in the hands of trustees. It is fortunate
that the old Tithe Commutation Map of 1839 still survives. It
shows all the houses in the parish with the names of their occupants and owners and, taken together with the census notebook
of 1851, it gives quite a detailed picture of the village this new
generation of Floyds was growing up in.

The population of 182 souls hardly differs from what it was in
1800 but the farming scene is very different. The handful of freeholders are still there, owning their houses and small adjoining
paddocks, but the tenants – lease-holders and tenants at will –
have all vanished, their holdings absorbed into the manor farm.
The great majority of the working population of men and boys
are described as agricultural labourers – that convenient blanket
term covering so many skills. Certainly there must have been a
good many landless farm workers in earlier days and it is more
than likely that some of the small-holders were used to working
part-time for their larger neighbours. Nevertheless the final break
with the open field tradition, the disappearance of the last peasant
farmers, must have seemed then, as it does now, a watershed.
The change to larger enclosed farms, so ardently preached by the
agricultural improvers and already spreading through most of the
country, would result in greater production of food. At the same
time it set English farming and village life on a course very
different from the rest of Europe with consequences that we
still see today.

In 1851 the farm labourers, two shepherds and five farm
servants together make up a total of sixty-one, a figure which
corresponds very closely with the fifty-seven entered as employed
on the Floyds' two farms, Manor Farm and Home Farm. Even
this probably underestimates the number at work in busy times.
Only one woman is listed as a farm worker but memories going
back to later in the century show that many took on seasonal jobs
such as stone picking and hay making. And in the arduous weeks
of harvest, when every hand was needed, entire villages turned
out as they must always have done.

We know from contemporary accounts that it was quite
common for a family to undertake to reap a certain area at piece
work rates and at such times even young hands were valuable.
The needs of schooling had to take second place and the school

What is now Hill Cottage was for many years the village shop. It was probably started by William Toms in the 1860s and carried on after his death for many years by his daughter Annie. It had a bakehouse where bread was baked twice a week and we have memories of it from early in the last century when it was probably little changed. At that time Annie's nephew, Percy Lailey, came over from Stanford Dingley to help her with the baking and delivery. As well as groceries the shop sold oil and household articles such as saucepans, kettles and brooms. It also sold dairy produce for along with the shop Annie had inherited her father's five Jersey cows. In hot weather the butter and cream were packed into a large bucket and lowered down the well. Arthur Creasey, Annie's husband, ran the shop after she died until it finally closed in the 1960s.
(Another print from one of Mr Ward's photographs)

* Since the Elizabethan Poor Law it had been the duty of each parish to support its own poor and infirm members. The new Poor Law Act of 1834 directed that they should be sent to workhouses, serving several parishes. It was a harsh measure that Dickens was to get his teeth into. It is therefore reassuring to discover that here, as late as 1851, there were still people getting help at home. It was not, of course, until 1906 that the Lloyd George government introduced old age pensions.

logbook shows the school holiday arranged to suit the season, starting sometimes in July, sometimes in August and equally variable in length. Even after term had begun a full class could not be relied on. An entry for September 1885 reads: 'Children irregular, gleaning not yet being quite over'. (It must have been about this time that Mr Wilkins' mother could remember taking the family gleanings down to the mill to be ground).

Going back to the 1851 census, we find among the few who were not farm workers two shoemakers, (one of them William Toms, a freeholder living in what later became Appledown), and three sawyers. There was one potter's labourer, one mole-catcher, one blacksmith, Briant, (probably working in Yattendon), a clerk John Werrell (evidently the parish clerk) and an errand boy. Ten of the villagers, most of them widows, were on parish relief *

At the other end of the age scale, the census shows a village alive with children, fifty of them twelve years old or under. One boy of twelve was already a farm worker, thirteen children are entered as 'scholars', probably having lessons from the clerk or perhaps attending school in Yattendon. Yattendon, at this time, was much better provided with not only a schoolmistress but also a butcher, a grocer, blacksmith's shop, saddler, carpenters and a wheelwright. For many services and resources Frilsham must have depended on its neighbour.

What Frilsham had was the common, a provider not only of space and grazing for the commoners' livestock but also of fuel, bracken for bedding, materials for fencing and building rough shelters, and so on, benefits which could make life considerably less hard at a time when the labourer's wage had to be stretched to buy the basic necessities. Not only that, but proceeds from livestock on the common, long before social insurance had been thought of, could help to tide a family over times of accident and sickness.

The map on page 13 shows how the common may have looked in the 1850s. It began at the Old Rectory park and stretched eastwards to include the field at the bottom of Coach Hill by the motorway. In the other direction it took in part of Coombe Farm and part of the Potkiln meadow with the wood-land in between, which must have been much less dense than it is now.

It was on the common that most of the villagers lived. The old map of 1839 shows two dozen or so cottages, singly or in small groups, scattered over it or around its edges, their siting largely determined, it would seem, by nearness to water. Part of the map reproduced here shows Frideswide, Hatchets Gate, a group of cottages, and a chapel where the Four Cottages are now. Further to the east is Richard Werrell's freehold and more scattered cottages near the well and Potkiln Lane. Some have a successor on the same site today but others have vanished entirely. Probably most were built of wattle and daub with thatched roofs like those that Mr Wilkins remembers from the early 1900s – picturesque but primitive. Very likely many originated as squatters dwellings but all, apart from the freeholds, are put down as owned by the Floyds.

Down in the valley, separate from the rest of the village, lay the church, the parsonage, the manor farm and mill and a row of four cottages. It seems so likely that this was the site of the original village that the question has often been asked, why and when did the migration up to the common take place? Flooding and the Black Death have been put forward as reasons. However, an almost identical shift took place at Bucklebury and it may simply be that commons tended to act as honeypots. They did, after all, provide many resources, fuel in particular, and – perhaps no less important – the opportunity of adding a few yards to the boundary of the homestead without anyone taking very much notice.

At the manor farm in 1851 were living Mary Floyd, Robert's widow and four of her children, Robert Hayward, Martha, Thomas and Elizabeth. The youngest son, George, may have been away at school. Also living in were two women servants and eight unmarried young farm labourers, the latter dossing down probably in attics and outhouses and eating in the farmhouse kitchen. This was still the old farmhouse but one can guess that the new house was being planned and that big alterations had already been made to the farmyard. After the hard times, agriculture was prospering again. The dire consequences which landowners had forecast when the Corn Laws were repealed in 1846 had not materialised and the rapidly growing town population meant an expanding market for food. Better livestock and more scientific knowledge were making their way onto farms. The Royal Agricultural Society of England was founded in 1839 and, among other things, was encouraging design of more efficient farm buildings. For the first time, (perhaps as a sweetener to the landed interest) the Government was offering grants for farm improvements of various kinds, from drainage to the improvement of buildings and farmhouses.

Of the old buildings at the manor only the great barn nearest to the house was left. The rest is typical of Victorian farming with its orderly layout of bullock yards, stalls, food store, bull pen and so on, all under one roof, very different from the higgledy-piggledy collection of sheds one sees in pictures of earlier farm yards.

Village tradition has it that the bricks for the rebuilding came from Coombe Wood. There are a number of pits and hollows near the wood edge and the 1839 map shows a brick kiln in the nearby corner of the Rectory park. With good clay near at hand, it would certainly have made sense to cart the bricks downhill rather than up from the Potkiln, but it could have been the Potkiln brickmakers that carried out the work.

Brickmaking is an ancient craft in this part of Berkshire, and local skills are seen to great advantage in the brickwork at the Manor. Mr Floyd clearly took great trouble in his choice of bricks, and it seems too that he used to go round with a watering can making sure that the mortar was damp enough. This little anecdote – handed down in the Wyatt family – suggests that, as one might have expected, they were the carpenters on the job. A young William Wyatt did in fact carve his name on the tie-beams in two of the barns, together with the date, 1845. The mill was probably the last of the group to be rebuilt. There is no mention of a miller in either of the censuses of 1841 or 1851, which is odd since we know there had been one earlier and there was one again in the 1880s. Perhaps the building had fallen into a bad state of repair. At any rate, the new building is made of the same bricks as the Manor but with slates for the roof. (With the coming of the railways Welsh slate must have been able to compete with local tiles.)

In the census of 1851 Robert Hayward Floyd is described as a farmer of 600 acres employing forty men. This is much larger than the Manor Farm acreage and I think he may also have been farming his cousin's land at Eling. The ample bullock yards at the farm and the two shepherds show that he kept a good head of livestock, and the late Harry Chamberlain, whose grandfather was head carter at the Manor, remembered being told that in those days (around 1870 perhaps) the farm kept nine three-horse teams.

The planning of the new buildings suggest that young Mr Floyd was greatly interested in the new ideas. It seems to me quite likely that he knew of the work being done on the Pusey estate in the Vale of the White Horse. (It was, after all, the Floyd heartland where members of the family were still living). Philip Pusey, a scientist himself, was a founder member of the Royal Agricultural Society and one of the pioneer farmers of the day. Chemists and botanists visited him for lectures and discussions to which neighbouring farmers were invited so that knowledge of the Pusey experiments, successful or otherwise, became widely spread.

We know so little about this Floyd brother that it is worth repeating a story of Harry Chamberlain's in which he is mentioned. It really concerns Mr Pain, a tenant farmer who took over when the Floyds left.

One morning he rebuked the head carter for not taking the teams out in the pouring rain. His men in Hampshire hadn't minded a little rain. 'Time's time, you know Chamberlain.' No prizes for guessing that this was unwise. One afternoon, knocking off time came when there was half an acre of barley left to drill. Chamberlain ordered the men to unhitch, in spite of Mr Pain's remonstrances that surely they weren't going to leave that little corner. 'If time's time for you, sir, so it is for us!' 'And that night', said Harry 'it *rained*, and time they got onto that field again the corn was *that* high up in the drill. Of course, if it'd been Mr Floyd, they'd have gone on and finished it.'

I imagine the greatest sorrow the Robert Hayward Floyds experienced during their years at the Manor, was the death in infancy of their two children, Emily and Robert, recorded on a tablet in the church. But another blow must have been the great agricultural depression which set in in the 1870s, and in which the prosperity and optimism of the mid-century slowly drained away. It began with a run of wet summers and severe winters, which played havoc with crop yields, but the lasting damage was done by the rising tide of imports, not only of corn, but of other food. (Readers of *Lark Rise* may remember the appearance in the 1880s of tins of Canadian salmon and Australian meat even in that remote hamlet.)

Whether it was financial trouble that caused the R. H. Floyds to leave Frilsham there is no means of telling. What is certain is that by 1883, the farm and the Manor House had been let to John Pain. The Floyds moved to Reading where Robert Hayward Floyd died

in 1889 leaving the Manor to his wife. As far as is known, she
never came back and in 1903 the Manor was sold.

Thomas, the second brother, was eleven when his father died,
leaving him the inheritor of Cooke's Farm with its 300 acres and
the Georgian farmhouse which had been the home of Peregrine
Bertie and which he had re-christened Frilsham House. In 1851 a
bailiff was still living there but Thomas probably moved in soon
afterwards.

His elder brother may have been a progressive farmer; but what
we know of Thomas suggests a lover of the old ways. In the 1881
census he describes himself as a 'yeoman' and the chief memory
he left in the minds of those who were village boys in the 1880s
was that he was the last farmer to plough with oxen. Several
old residents had clear memories of the five red animals with
spreading horns stabled in Magpie Barn. To a wider neighbourhood he was known as a passionate rider to hounds. It was said
that nobody knew the South Berks country like he did and that
successive masters and huntsmen welcomed his advice 'for, if
anyone knew where a fox was to be found, it was Tommy Floyd.'
He was also an excellent rifle shot, the County Challenge Cup one
of many trophies on his sideboard. Away from the sporting scene
he was a leading supporter of the Yattendon Benefit Club. In
politics, it need hardly be added he was a staunch Conservative.

A stable full of hunters can be an expensive hobby and perhaps
he was not good at counting the pennies. At any rate in 1864 he
took out a mortgage for £4000 (from the Misses Dewe of
Hampstead Norreys) and in 1876 another for £3000 from a
Martha Floyd in Reading. The earlier mortgage was redeemed
but not the later one, and in 1886 when the agricultural depression had struck deep, he took out a larger mortgage, for £8000,
from outsiders. Seven years later he sold his house and land to
Sir Cameron Gull for £13000, and he and his wife went to live
in Hermitage.

There are several memories of him in these later years. He
never lost his devotion to the hunt and would walk many miles
to attend the meet where, so we are told, 'his genial, cheery
presence was as warmly welcomed as in his palmy days.' A small
girl in Yattendon saw him often on Frilsham Common whenever
the hunt met nearby. 'He looked' she said 'like a character out of
Dickens.'

Robert Bridges, for many years a neighbour at Yattendon
Manor, invited him to visit the family's new home near Oxford
and included a sonnet in which he wrote of 'the stubborn thews
and ageless heart of Floyd.' And he could still impress a farm-
worker with his keen and knowledgeable eye. When Harry
Chamberlain was drilling roots on Wellhouse Farm, old Mr Floyd

had walked across to him. He had picked up a handful of seed and earth and was tossing it up and down in his hand muttering 'turnips, turnips.' 'No sir' I says 'swedes.' 'Swedes?' he says. 'Yes, sir' I says 'Umph' he says 'And blow me if that corner of the field didn't come up turnips!' The boy Harry had sent for some more seed had gone to the wrong bag.

Thomas Floyd's American born wife, Charlotte died in 1912 and he himself in 1914 at the age of eighty-seven. It is said he died insolvent. Very many of his friends among the local farmers and gentry, including Robert and Mrs Bridges and several members of the Waterhouse family from Yattendon, gathered in Frilsham churchyard for his interment.

George, the youngest of the three brothers, was educated at Marlborough College and at Caius College, Cambridge. Coming from a family so closely connected with the church, and with his oldest brother patron of the living, there were probably hopes that he would enter the ministry. He was in fact ordained at Norwich in 1858, served as a curate in Norfolk and elsewhere before he was inducted as rector of Frilsham in 1869 when he was 36. John Flory Howard, the rector of Yattendon, resigned the living to make way for him.

At this time the village had not had a resident parson for well over a hundred years. The old Parsonage, (now Parsonage Farm) near the church on the far side of the river, had been turned into two farm cottages. In any case it is doubtful if it would have fitted the Victorian idea of a rectory. A new site was chosen near the top of the hill, on land which had only become glebe since the enclosure of the common. It was much further from the church but a good deal nearer to the rector's scattered flock and – what may also have been a consideration – nearer to what was to become the Church of England school. Getting this started must have been an early preoccupation for, with the passing of the 1870 Education Act, schooling for all five- to twelve-year-olds would become compulsory. Some Frilsham children were already being taught in Mary Werrell's little school at Hatchets Gate or in the Yattendon Parish School, but it is unlikely that either of these could have coped with all the children of school age. The Government was offering grants towards school buildings and teachers' salaries, and in the event it was decided to add a largish room to the cottage, later to become Coombe Farm.

The first register of admissions, dated 1869, contains just one name and only a trickle for the next few years. There is then a big jump to twenty-one in 1876. Coping with such an intake of children of various ages, many of them new to school and probably unenthusiastic, would surely have taxed even an experienced teacher and these were hard to find. Poor Mary Chislett lasted

The Frilsham Church of England School in 1895 when it was still at Coombe Farmhouse. The head teacher was then, I think, Mrs Lane who an ex-pupil remembers as 'kind and nice' in spite of her rather forbidding look. The figure on the left must be the monitoress, one of the older girls who stayed on to act as assistant. She must have been badly needed with forty children of all ages to deal with. The one classroom must also have been very crowded and the move to the new school with its two rooms more than welcome. This was to happen in the spring of 1899 and there seems to have been no special ceremony such as had marked the opening of the new school at Yattendon. The log book announces prosaically 'Began work in the new school'. However there were some early visitors – first Sir Cameron and Lady Gull and later in the week the RevdG. Floyd and Miss Floyd 'who gave the children buns'.

two years and then left hurriedly in mid-term after a terrible report from Her Majesty's Inspector, coupled with a threat to remove the grant. Louise Stevens did much better, lasting five years, and by 1885, with Alice Browning in charge, the Inspector was able to declare the year's work 'of good merit'.

From the beginning, George Floyd and his wife were regular visitors. They had a duty as managers to check the registers, but the log book also records that they gave reading lessons, and the rector gave scripture lessons, both in the original school and in the later one built by Sir Cameron Gull and opened in 1900. One or two who were school children in those days remembered the rector as a gentle, kindly man, with a slight lisp which added a little whistle to his speech and gave pleasure to the more mischievous of his small listeners. Mrs Floyd was also kind, but larger and more awe-inspiring. She came regularly on Empire Day and talked about her ancestor, Sir Francis Drake.

Memories of the rector away from the school suggest that he was a conscientious parish visitor and that in the great religious divide of the nineteenth century he was on the Low Church or evangelical side. This would probably have put him in tune with most of his parishioners. He was on good terms with his Waterhouse neighbours with their strong Quaker connections and he was invited to preach when Yattendon Church was re-opened after the Waterhouse restoration. A note in Alfred Waterhouse's diary mentions an occasion when George Floyd

In all the early years of the school Mrs George Floyd was a very regular visitor. She is sometimes mentioned in the log book as having given a reading lesson or 'stayed to hear the arithmetic lesson'.

From this photograph in later life one would have said a formidable character but both an ex-pupil and a former housemaid spoke of her as 'kind'. The log book, however, does record one confrontation. It was in the new school and after a particularly long gap in her visits that she arrived one day to find one of the pupils reading and knitting and was very annoyed. 'She was a manager and would report the matter to HMI.' However, after what were clearly a stormy few weeks with frequent visits it seems peace was restored.

---

* He advised young Jack Wilkins 'Always shoot in front of your bird. That way you either miss or kill outright'.

joined a family party out shooting rabbits. Like his brother Tom he was an excellent shot.* Unlike him he does not appear to have hunted, nor did he farm though he kept a few Jersey cows in the rectory park. Another memory is of a family party from the Rectory walking regularly every Sunday afternoon to visit Thomas in Hermitage after his retirement. He was rector until his death in 1927 at the age of 93. For several years before that he had to be pushed to and from church in a bath chair, a forgetful old man but one, I am told, 'who had no enemies.' A window in the church commemorates his long incumbency of 58 years.

The enclosure of the Common

The manor house and the Old Rectory stand today as evidence of the changes the Floyds brought about. But to the villagers of their own time a far bigger change must have been the enclosure of the common in 1857. True it was no longer an essential part of the farming scene; the small farms had vanished and the two big farms had no need of it but, to many living on it, it was part of their way of life.

At the time of the enclosure its area is given as 184 acres. Without doubt it had once been larger for over the centuries, whenever land was scarce, commons were liable to be encroached upon and nibbled away. In one of the manor court

records for Frilsham which have survived, Henry Louch, Widow
Bluett and Richard Cornewell were presented to the court for
having encroached upon the common 'by taking in some part
thereof.' (This was in 1649 at the end of the Civil War). They
were ordered to lay it out again before the next Lady Day or
incur a fine. Was it ever laid out? We are not told.

This particular piece of land may have been small but large
areas could also vanish by sale or agreement. A 12 acre field on
Coombe Farm next to the wood is called Common Ground
which suggests its origins, and although in 1857 Frilsham marsh
on the far side of the river was still nominally part of the
common, to all intents and purposes it had been absorbed
into the manor farm lands.

Anyone wishing to picture those 184 acres at the time of the
enclosure must imagine a stretch of largely open countryside
reaching from the lower end of the Rectory Park to the field
at the bottom of Coach Hill, with no School Lane, but with
tracks leading to scattered cottages. (The map on page 11 shows
the area in terms of the village of today.) On the higher ground
the soil is a poor acid gravel on which, after centuries of
browsing and grazing by the village livestock, mainly heathland
plants would have survived: fine heath grasses, whortleberries,
gorse, heather, with some oak and birch. The most wooded
areas must have been the sides of Coach Hill but even these
would have been much more open than they are now. The best
grass would have grown on the lower and more fertile ground
to the south, east and west, in what is now the Potkiln field, the
field at the bottom of Coach Hill and the Rectory Park. On the
old map the Park is called Anthony's Mead so very likely it was
the hay meadow.

Common rights were, from early days, guarded as the preserve
of the local inhabitants, tenants of the manor. In most villages
they were restricted by manorial custom as to the number of
animals they could turn out, and probably this was true here too.
However, when the Abingdon estate sold Frilsham manor in 1760,
the sale deed simply stated that the pasturage on the common
belonged to the parishioners.

There are a few hints to be picked up as to how, in pre-
enclosure days, these parishioners were using it. There is the print
of Frilsham House on page 15 which shows cattle and sheep
grazing at the eastern end (by the motorway). There is the lease
of 1833 stating that a tenant who was giving up his holding and
moving to a cottage retained his grazing rights on the common
for '2 horses, 2 cows, geese, ducks and pigs,' and there is a
description of Ashampstead Common, just a few miles away, by a
commoner who remembered it as it was in 1900 when many of

the cottagers at the western end kept a goat or a cow, and a boot-maker and a hurdle maker each kept a pony and cart. He remembered the beehives, and in summer the rows of coops with hens and chicks out on the grass and, later, much competition for the bracken needed for bedding. Memories handed down suggest that things were not very different at Frilsham. If there were bee-keepers here they would have enjoyed a good autumn honey flow. When, not so long ago, part of the woodland east of the four cottages was cleared for replanting, the first crop to emerge was a sea of heather. Smothered out, decades ago, as the trees invaded, its seeds had remained dormant ever since.

The process of enclosing was not quite as complicated as it had once been, but it still took time. An Act of 1845 had set up 'Inclosure Commissioners' to whom any landowner wishing to enclose common land had to apply (*see* note 3). They had to visit the area and satisfy themselves that enclosure would not only benefit the landowner, but was desirable for the 'health, comfort and convenience' of the inhabitants. A provisional order could then be made, setting out which land, and how much, was to be allotted for recreation and 'field gardens'. This had been laid down in the Act as a suitable way of recompensing the landless for any loss they suffered from enclosure.

The next step was to obtain the consent of two-thirds of those entitled to the land. It might be thought, and probably the villagers did think, that this referred to the parishioners, whose grazing rights have been mentioned. This was not the legal view. In the eyes of the law the custom of the manor carried no weight. Common rights only belonged to those owning or farming land in the common fields and to some old freeholds. In Frilsham these amounted to thirteen persons* in all, most of whom could expect to benefit from the enclosure. When enough of them had consented, the Commissioners could certify that enclosure was expedient.

A valuer was then appointed to divide and set out the land as agreed. He had also to plot any new roads and indicate who was responsible for new fencing. Another meeting had then to be held in the parish, attended by the Commissioners, to hear the proposals, listen to objections and make amendments. A final award followed. One way and another the whole procedure could easily spread over a couple of years.

The result of these deliberations can be seen on the ground today. No doubt because of the scattered nature of the parish, two pieces of land (of three acres and two acres) were earmarked for allotments. The 'recreation area' (three acres) is the piece opposite the football field, now registered as a 'village green'. The landowner was made responsible for fencing it. Perhaps he

* It seems probable that two – possibly three – of these had recently bought a piece of land in Frilsham in order to qualify for an award.

did, but it seems more likely that he chose to mark it off with the low banks still visible today. (That it was clearly intended to serve as a playing field shows how much more open it must have been.)

To fit in with the new boundaries, two new roads had to be made. One, School Lane, replaced an earlier track (or tracks) which had led across the common from somewhere near Yew Tree (now Manderley) to Hatchets Gate. The other, called the Bucklebury New Road, runs from Frilsham Park Lodge to Magpie Farm. Formerly the road had gone straight on from the bottom of Coach Hill before turning left to Yattendon or carrying on to Stanford Dingley. This road was now blocked up.

How the rest of the land was allocated depended, as already explained, on 'common rights', and in the event awards were made to thirteen people. Robert Hayward Floyd, the major land owner, was allotted 100 acres. Thomas Floyd twenty acres (the field at the bottom of Coach Hill) and the Revd Flory Howard, the rector, 40 acres (now the Old Rectory park). Between them, these three accounted for 160 of the 184 acres. Of the ten other awards, the largest was to Henry Bunbury, the Squire of Marlston, who owned much land in the parish west of the Pang. He was awarded the Potkiln meadow (or as much of it as lies in Frilsham); Tom Barr, owner of the Potkiln and the brickworks, gained a small piece of land by Potkiln Lane, and Elijah Bew, keeper of Yattendon Stores and a staunch Methodist, was awarded the piece of land on which the old chapel was standing. Other freeholders had small additions to their holdings, among them Toms the shoemaker, (at what is now Appledown) and the two families of Werrells, one at Hatchets Gate and one at Holly Cottage. Whether any objections were raised at the final meeting, whether the villagers felt that their new allotments made up for the loss of most of their grazing land we do not know. With most of them in the employ of the landowner and living in his cottages, voicing disapproval would not have been easy. Enclosure could arouse bitter feelings, not least because so often there was nobody qualified or able to put the villagers case. At Cold Ash, the owners of the first house built on the common did not dare to move in for two years, for fear it should be burnt down over their heads. Resentment in Frilsham is unlikely to have been on that level, simply from the fact that the changes at first were far from wholesale. The central, most wooded, part of the common which had been awarded to Robert Hayward Floyd remained untouched. It could still provide some grazing together with fuel, bracken and other benefits, and in contrast to other villages there is nothing to suggest that anyone lost their home. In fact some housing was being improved. The row of the Four Cottages dates from 1856 and the two pairs of cottages near the well look to be of the same date. Was this done to make the enclosure less unpopular? It seems very possible. Few people enjoy being on bad terms with their neighbours and Mr Floyd was dealing with people whom he had known, and who had known him, since childhood. Whatever the motive, in the opinion of the day he could have done nothing more beneficial. The state of farm labourers' cottages in Berkshire had been deplored by the Board of Agriculture Inspector many years before, and by other influential voices since.

One way and another it can be argued, I think with justice, that Frilsham villagers suffered less from the enclosure than those in many other places. All the same the loss was real. Some families on the common must have had memories of fathers or grand-fathers who had farmed on their own account. Now they saw the door closing on any hopes they themselves had of attaining even partial independence; and for village society as a whole, the gulf between the landowning few and the landless many had become even deeper. The passage of time was to show that so radical a change was not easily accepted or forgiven. When some forty years later the then landowner set about fencing off the woodland, the posts put in each day disappeared each night until he gave up the attempt. And much later still, in the 1920s, Mrs Monger remembers her father being told by Mrs Maurice Marshall 'You put your old pony where you've a mind to, Oliver. They got no right to stop you.'

The enclosure here was only one of many. In the 32 years, between the passing of the General Enclosure Act in 1845 and 1877, it is reckoned that 600,000 acres of commons and wastes passed into private management. In this neighbourhood alone, Cold Ash Common was enclosed in 1851, Beedon and Stanmore Commons soon after. Bucklebury was only saved by the heroic efforts of John Morton, a small farmer and Congregationalist preacher. With a rapidly rising population – it trebled in the course of the century – and large scale food imports from over-seas still a good many years away, it was not hard for farmers and landowners to argue that increasing the area under cultivation was in the national interest, as well as their own. If they had needed any urging, it would have come from the Board of Agriculture Inspectors who almost universally condemned the commons as barren wastes, over stocked with half-starved animals.

No doubt some merited this description, but from the first there were men who saw a different scene and who would not accept that enclosure always increased the food supply. William Cobbett, that pugnacious champion of the underdog, was one of them. It was of a Dorset common of 150 acres that he wrote : 'The cottagers produced from their little bits, in food for themselves and in things to be sold at the market, more than any neighbouring farm of 200 acres. I learnt to hate a system that could lead English gentlemen to disregard matters like these! That could induce them to tear up "wastes" and sweep away occupiers like those I have described.' With the passage of time, the feeling spread that less than justice had indeed been done and, when the enclosures began to threaten the open spaces near large towns, the alarm bells really started to ring. The Commons and Open Spaces Preservation Society was founded in 1867 and made its name in the long battle to preserve Hampstead Heath from Sir Thomas Maryon Wilson, who wanted to sell it as building land. It was a battle which led to urban commons being given legal protection, and with the passing of the Commons Act of 1876, the conditions for the enclosing of rural commons were made a good deal more stringent. From then on, what had been a flood subsided to a trickle.

Today, both the benefit to the community and the equity of such a wholesale enclosure of the old commons have been increasingly questioned. 'Legalised land grabbing' is how it has been unkindly described by W. G. Hoskins, the foremost local historian of our time. Many like him will regret that the remains of an ancient way of life, one that had fostered many virtues, should have been done away with so abruptly and often, it appears, so uncomprehendingly. What cannot be denied, how-ever, is that its future could only be limited. The changes that the twentieth century was to bring were too great. Motor transport doesn't care for gates across roads; and cars and grazing animals make the worst companions. Nowadays for the most part the commons that have survived meet new needs. They are for the walker and rider, for nature lovers and wild life; valued perhaps above all for the sense of freedom they bring, something hard to find in our increasingly fenced-in landscape ... we could do with more of them.

A changing village

In the years following the enclosure of the common the Floyd brothers saw the coming of a second agricultural revolution. The seventeenth and eighteenth century pioneers had brought improved crops and livestock but work in the fields was still done mainly by hand as it had been since time immemorial. Now new machines – horse-hoes, drills, hay-turners, barn machinery – were competing for prizes at the agricultural shows. At the Great Exhibition of 1851 farm machinery stands were some of the largest. It was here that the McCormick reaper from America made its first appearance, and it was from then on that the scythe and the sickle began to give way to horse drawn hay mowers and corn reapers, though only very slowly. It is estimated that by 1870 just a quarter of the harvest was cut by machine.

In Frilsham in the 1880s there were still many men and boys working on farms but not so many as formerly – 49 out of a working male population of 75; and there were more men with other skills – wheelwrights, carpenters (five of these), smiths, millers and a plumber. By now too the requirements of the big houses had made their mark. Laundresses, grooms, domestic servants, cooks and gardeners and a governess add up to seventeen in all. There were other changes. Frilsham had a grocer's shop and a butcher and at the very end of the century the children moved into their new, larger school, built by Sir Cameron Gull on a corner of the old common given by the Floyds.

Most noteworthy of all was the appearance of a post office at the Yattendon end of the parish, a sign of the transport revolution which, in time, would transform the countryside at least as much as the coming of the motor car would do in the next century. The Great Western line to Reading was opened in 1840, to Newbury in 1841, the Newbury–Oxford line in 1882. Heavy farm equipment could travel from distant works, coal could be delivered to Hermitage station cheaper and more reliably than by canal, factory-made articles, from boots and shoes to hand tools would begin to replace the work of the local smith and shoemaker.

The slate roof at Frilsham Mill has been mentioned and in time other building materials, – machine-made bricks and imported timber – would prove cheaper than the local product.* It was perhaps in the early years of the next century that a wagon would fetch from Hampstead Norreys station the corrugated iron roofs for the cattle yards at the Manor Farm.† Like many other villages Frilsham was being drawn out of its centuries-old hand made world into the world of industrial England.

The railway also carried passengers at a fraction of the price of the mail coach, enabling workers to travel further afield in their search for jobs. It was to Hampstead Norreys station that Mrs Nell Wyatt's father came from his Oxfordshire village to apply for the post of cowman at Frilsham Home Farm. It was probably from Hermitage station that the newly founded *Newbury Weekly News* began to be widely distributed in this area and now there were more people able to read it. Many young villagers in the 80s and 90s must have felt they were growing up in a world of greater opportunities and a widening horizon but, at the same time, local household budgets suggest that farm workers were little better off than they had been fifty years previously (*see* note 4). The hoped for rise was very slow in coming.

It is not surprising to read that the population of many villages

* However some bricks were being fired at the Potkiln works up to the start of the Second World War.

† The carter (and my informant) was the late Mr Charlie Kent.

was falling as the more enterprising began to look elsewhere for betterment. By the turn of the century farmers in the south were complaining of the difficulty of finding young workers and there was talk of 'the drift from the land'. In Frilsham the ten year census figures from 1800 onwards had remained remarkably stable at between 180 and 200. In 1890 they do show a sudden drop to 159 but the dip was only temporary. Ten years later the numbers had gone up to 210.

Although George Floyd continued as rector till 1926, long before that the very many years in which the family had been the dominant figures in the village had come to an end. By the 1880s the Robert Hayward Floyds had left. Thomas and his wife followed in 1893. Perhaps the farming depression was not the only cause for their departure, but it must have played a large part. As the prices of corn, wool and meat continued to fall, and as it became apparent that no help would be forthcoming from Parliament, so the age in which gentlemen farmers could live busy, certainly, but comfortable lives on the profit of their acres was vanishing into the past. In this neighbourhood the new landowners were of a different kind – successful professional men like Alfred Waterhouse the architect and Sir Cameron Gull the lawyer, or manufacturers like George William Palmer, men who were not relying on their estates to provide them with a living. They would keep a home farm but most of the land would be let. The new country houses at Yattendon and Marlston would be built well away from bullock yards and pig sties. (With the new Frilsham House, Sir Cameron Gull took the other tack. Here it was the farm buildings that moved, down to the road where they are now.)

Of the Floyds only George had any surviving children and none of them remained in the neighbourhood although the one daughter, Mary, came back for a while to live in Frideswide after her husband retired. With her death the last remaining link with the family was broken.

Looking back on the Floyd era one can see that Robert Hayward was the key figure who laid the foundations. His will, which shows him owning property in London and large holdings of Bank of England stock, suggests that he was primarily a business man and that the faint rumour, which has somehow persisted, that he was a corn merchant could well be true. Why did he buy the manor? Was he attracted by the step upwards in social status associated with becoming Robert Hayward Esquire of Frilsham? If so, he was following a very well trodden path. Whatever his motives, it was his investment in land here and his endowment of the young Robert Floyd which enabled the latter to come through the difficult post-war years and hand over his inheritance to his children. They, in their turn, enjoyed the good years of the mid-century and probably, in those easier times, spent more lavishly than the previous generation had done. And then it all fell apart, the sudden drop in profits, a run of bad harvests, the absence of heirs, ill-health, all may have played a part.

Nowadays the family name is barely remembered though visitors to the church find it on a row of gravestones and in a stained glass window, and the farming community recognise it as a field name. But, as I hope this account has shown, it has better claims on our remembrance. Of all those who over the centuries were accounted owners of this corner of Berkshire, the Floyds were the ones most closely associated with it, some of them born here, all of them choosing to be buried here. By making it their home they helped to shape our surroundings and seem – at any rate to our backward look – to have given the village a greater sense of identity. They left as their legacy the handsome group of buildings by the church – manor, farm and mill, many fine trees, the Victorian Rectory, and the enclosure of the common which, whatever its rights and wrongs at the time, has led to the village of today.

To gather up the few surviving memories of the three brothers has therefore seemed a worthwhile exercise. The little instances that have stuck in people's minds – of Robert Hayward Floyd, the perfectionist, fussing round with his watering can, of the elderly Thomas wandering over his neighbour's rootfield and chatting with the carter, of the kindly, forgetful clergyman – all suggest that they were at any rate not remote figures, and one would dearly like to know what their fellow villagers thought of them. Was some loss of freedom compensated for by plentiful employment and no doubt a certain paternal care? Sadly there was no Flora Thompson living here to tell us. What is certain is that the family played a large part in the life of 19th century Frilsham. They deserve their place in its history.

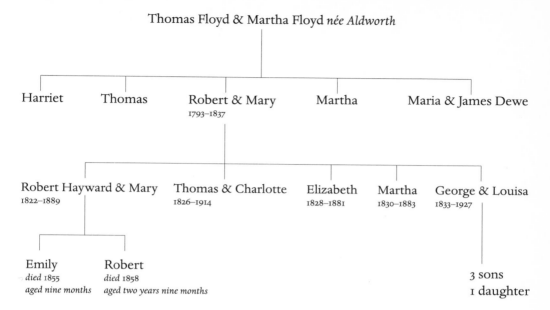

Thomas Floyd & Martha Floyd *née Aldworth*

| Harriet | Thomas | Robert & Mary
1793–1837 | Martha | Maria & James Dewe |

Robert Hayward & Mary · Thomas & Charlotte · Elizabeth · Martha · George & Louisa
1822–1889 · 1826–1914 · 1828–1881 · 1830–1883 · 1833–1927

Emily
died 1855
aged nine months

Robert
died 1858
aged two years nine months

3 sons
1 daughter

The Haywards, Aldworths and Floyds were all related. Robert Hayward's sister married William Aldworth. Their daughter, Martha, married Thomas Floyd.

Appendix: after the Floyds

Although Robert Hayward Floyd left Frilsham in the 1880s he, and later his widow, remained the owner of the manor and Frilsham continued to be virtually an estate village with all the land, and all but a few of the houses, owned by the Floyds.

The first steps towards the very different state of affairs today were taken through an unlikely figure. According to village memories (and that is all there is to go on) Mr Harry Weber had made a fortune in mines in the Transvaal. Probably some time in the 1890s he bought an old farmhouse at Bucklebury, close to the boundary with Frilsham and built the present Hawkridge House. When, in 1903, Frilsham manor was put up for sale he was the buyer and quite soon after he added to it a large part of Hampstead Norreys, including the manor farm there.

The stables, coach house and 'model farmery' at Hawkridge and the story that a German band used to be engaged to play at his tennis parties suggest a very comfortable life style. But it was to be a very brief venture – losses on the Stock Market the rumoured cause.

In 1907 his whole estate of over 1300 acres was up for sale. In the catalogue Hawkridge House was described as 'an exquisite and beautiful type of MODERN COUNTRY HOUSE, principally brick built, half timber and pebble dash standing high on sandy soil and enjoying charming views'. The farmery was mentioned and also Frilsham Mill, carrying on a corn gristing business and 'provided with three pairs of stones'. But the significant sentence was the one which ran that the property would be offered for sale 'in 46 convenient lots'. At the Septmber sale a successful lawyer Sir Cameron Gull, bought the manor and its land while of the 'convenient lots' in Frilsham a fair number were picked up by Tom Barr, the enterprising owner of the Pot Kiln, brick and tile works. Among his purchases were the Old Parsonage and the adjoining Ham Meadow, Parkside and Frideswide, the Forge cottages and the Four Cottages. He also bought the Limes (Little Orchard) and the Potkiln Meadow, which Harry Weber had bought a few years before. His brother-in-law George Wilson Toms bought Yew Tree Cottage.

It may not have been long afterwards that George Wilson Toms bought from Sir Cameron Gull a strip of the old common lying between School Lane and Beechfield Lane (an area which had been much used for gravel digging) and built on it a bungalow, The Beeches, for himself. After the last war his daughter, Mrs Spratt, was to sell off the rest of the land as building plots.

In the course of time much the same thing happened at the other end of the lane, on the land originally part of Potkiln Meadow. Here a younger member of the Barr family built his own bungalow, Byways, and also sold other plots for building. The properties Tom Barr had bought at the Weber sale also, in time, came on the market, several of them bought by their occupiers.

Before this and right at the other end of the parish in the 1890s Sir Cameron Gull built his large new country house on the site of Thomas Floyd's Georgian farmhouse. Once he and his family were established there they became, and would remain for the next thirty years, the leading figures in the village. The Frilsham House estate with its large indoor and outdoor staff must have resembled a little world. Mr Jack Wilkins, growing up on it, has left a memorable picture of it in a series of articles which he wrote for *The Broadsheet*.

Notes

1. It is not easy to identify these farms. The first, of eighty acres, bought in 1807, included some land in Stanford Dingley so was probably added to Cooke's Farm. The second, in 1812, was bought from William Matthews, yeoman of Yattendon and consisted of a house and hopkiln in Frilsham with various plots of arable and pasture and a house ('Hopkins') in Yattendon. The third buy was in 1818 from Gabriel Weston a cordwainer in East Ilsley and seems to have consisted of parcels of land in Frilsham which presumably were being farmed by a tenant of his.

2. It is a subject Cobbett returns to more than once: 4 September 1823 (in the Isle of Thanet) 'Invariably have I observed that the richer the soil and the more destitute of woods; that is to say, the more purely a corn country, the more miserable the labourer … In this beautiful island every inch of land is appropriated by the rich. No hedges, no ditches, no commons, no grassy lanes: a country divided into great farms, a few trees surround the great farm houses. All the rest is bare of trees and the wretched labourer has not a stick of wood and has no place for a pig or cow to graze or even to lie down upon. The rabbit countries are the countries for labouring men.'

3. Unexpectedly on the 1839 map it is the Revd J. F. Howard, rector of Yattendon and Frilsham, who is shown as owner of the common. Possibly it was he who applied for the enclosure, in any case the church authorites were involved in the proceedings from an early stage. There is a record of a meeting with the Bishop of Oxford at which it was decided that the Glebe lands, which were still scattered in small parcels throughout the parish, should be allotable. In the eventual award the church was awarded 40 acres of the common.

4. *Farm Labourers Weekly Budgets*
   From the report of the Royal Commission on Labour 1893–1894.
   Reprinted in *Village Life and Labour*, edited by Raphael Samuel:

   Aldworth
   Farm labourer, man, wife and five children, four under eleven years of age. Man's wages 10 shillings weekly, one boy earning 4s 6d weekly. Harvest money about 51 shillings. Michaelmas wage 21 shillings. (1 shilling = 5 new pence)

	s.	d.
Bread	6	5
Bacon	2	1
Wood and coal	2	0
Butter	1	8
Rent, house & garden	1	0
Sugar	1	8
Tea	0	5
Soap, soda etc	0	6
Oil and candles	0	3
Tobacco	1	0
Total expenditure	17	1

   Brightwalton
   Farm labourer, wife and seven children, wages 10s weekly; harvest about 81s; allotment 5s a year. In Compton Club.

	s.	d.
Bread	6	5
Cheese	0	8
Bacon	2	8
Sugar	0	11
Tea	0	11
Butter	1	7
Lard	0	8
Oil and candles	0	4
Soap, soda, starch & blue	0	6
Tobacco	0	7
Wood and coal	2	0
Club	0	5
Insurance	0	4
Rent: house, garden & allotment	1	1
Total expenditure	19	1

Sources

Abingdon Estate Papers, Berkshire Record Office

Archdeacons' Returns, Bodleian Library

Ashby, M. K., *Joseph Ashby of Tysoe* (1961)

Bourne G., *Change in the Village* (1912)

Bridges, Robert, *Poetical Works*

Census Returns Notebooks 1841, 1851, Public Record Office

Census Returns Notebooks 1881, Newbury Library

Cobbett, William, *Rural Rides*

Fox, Norman, *The Labourers' Revolt*, unpublished article Newbury Library

Frilsham Common Enclosure Award and map, Berkshire Record Office

Frilsham Manor Court Rolls, Bodleian Library

Frilsham School Log Books and Registers, Berkshire Record Office

Hoskins and Stamp *The Common Lands of England and Wales* (1963)

Iliffe papers, Berkshire Record Office

Newbury Weekly News

Orwin and Whetham *History of British Agriculture, 1846–1914* (1964)

Parfit, Canon J. T., *St Frideswide of Oxford*

Prothero, R. E., *English Farming Past and Present* (1912)

Samuel, Raphael, *Village Life and Labour* (1975)

Thompson, Flora, *Lark Rise*

Tithe Commutation Map for Frilsham Parish, Bodleian Library

Victoria County History (1839)

4 Elizabeth Waterhouse

Jill Greenaway

Elizabeth Waterhouse, who lived at Yattendon Court from 1881 until her death in 1918, is still remembered with affection and esteem in Yattendon village by those whose parents or grand-parents knew her. Her name figures prominently in all surviving records of village businesses and events at the time, both as patroness and participant. One of the 5454 items of beaten copper or brass, made by young men in the village under her supervision, is now in the collection of West Berkshire Museum, and books of her poetry and prose are in the British Library.

She was born on 16 July 1834, the second daughter and fourth child of John Hodgkin of Bruce Grove, Tottenham, and his wife Elizabeth (*née* Howard). Her mother died in January 1836, four days after the birth of her fifth child, when Elizabeth was eighteen months old. Elizabeth and her three surviving siblings were cared for by two successive stepmothers – Ann Backhouse and Eliza-beth Houghton. The family were Quakers and her upbringing in this belief seems to have endowed Elizabeth with the social conscience and desire to care for others which remained with her for the whole of her life. During her childhood she and her two brothers and sister, together with their half-siblings, cousins and friends, were encouraged to study and enjoy poetry, literature and art – although the family's Quaker beliefs forbade music and drama. This love of writing continued through to her old age. She and her sister Mariabella, to whom she was particularly close, wrote an 'Ode to Tobacco' as part of an essay club in 1849 when she was fifteen, whilst Elizabeth's last book, the second enlarged edition of her *Verses*, was published in 1912 – the year in which she became seventy-eight.

Elizabeth Waterhouse.
© Greenaway

Her brother Thomas attended the Quaker school at Grove
House, Tottenham, where Alfred Waterhouse, the eldest son of
another fairly affluent Quaker family, was also a pupil. In 1853,
after Alfred had completed his five-year apprenticeship and before
he started practising as an architect on his own, he and Thomas
went on an extended continental tour together. In 1859, Alfred
achieved what his mother described as 'the desire of his heart'
when he became engaged to Thomas's sister Elizabeth. John
Hodgkin was then living at Barcombe House near Lewes and
the marriage of Alfred and Bessie, as she was called by her family,
took place on 8 March 1860 at the Friends Meeting House at
Lewes.

Their first home was at Barcombe Cottage, Fallowfield,
Manchester, where their two oldest children, Paul and Mary
Monica, were born. In 1865 they moved to London to number 8,
and afterwards number 20, New Cavendish Street, Portland Place.
Edwin Waterhouse's memoirs record that Professor de Tivoli of
University College started classes at the house in 1865, teaching
Italian to Bessie and to Alfred and his brothers Theodore and
Edwin. In 1868 Alfred Waterhouse built Fox Hill, Whiteknights
Park, Reading, on land owned by his father who lived in the
nearby Whiteknights House. Alfred and Bessie and their five children lived at Fox Hill until they moved to Yattendon, although
they continued to spend some weeks each year at New Cavendish
Street. It was while living in Reading that the family became
members of the Church of England. Bessie, Alfred and their
oldest son Paul were baptised at Earley St Peter's Church on
24 February 1877, followed by the other four children, Monica,

Florence, Maurice and Amyas, a year later, on 23 February 1878. Bessie's niece, Lucy Violet Holdsworth, the daughter of Thomas Hodgkin, states that although Alfred and Bessie became loyal and devoted Anglicans, they never formally renounced membership of the Society of Friends. '"The ideal religion" she used to say, with a smile, in later life, "is to have been brought up a Friend and to have joined the Church of England".'

In March 1877 Alfred Waterhouse purchased the estate and manor of Yattendon from Mr T. A. Howard. During Whitsun that year he developed a 'rough idea' for the new house which his mother referred to as the 'House upon the Hill' when she saw the site where Alfred was beginning to build in August 1878. During the construction of the house there were delays due to bad weather and to the crumbling of the bricks which were being made on site. But by 16 March 1879 the house – the first Yattendon Court – was up to the transoms of the windows, and on 10 April 1881 the family moved to the new house – albeit without curtains or all the carpets and with the painters still finishing off. During the period of building the family spent a considerable amount of time in Yattendon, living at Yattendon Manor when they stayed in the village, and Elizabeth's involvement in the life of the local community dates from this time. Alfred was sinking the well in Yattendon Square to provide a safe water supply and covering it with the Well-house, and building the Reading Room to be a social meeting place in the village, as well as working on the construction of the Court. His diary records the opening of the Reading Room on 18 April 1879 when two hundred people came in the first two days. On 30 April 1879, a few days after the Reading Room opened and two years before the house on the hill was completed, he quotes a poem that Bessie had written in answer to a question in a game 'Would

The first Yattendon Court.
© Greenaway

you like to be the first man who buys a cup of coffee at the
Reading Room?' The first two verses of this poem show both her
humour and her knowledge and affection for the people in the
village that was to be her home for the rest of her life.

> Were I a rustic fatten'd on
> The famous loaves of Yattendon
> Or even an artificer at the house upon the hill
> How gaily had I hastened
> When the door was first unfastened
> To take the cosy corner by the eastern window sill.
>
> To entreat that rara avis
> The gentle Mrs Davies
> In her bib unwrought of needlework all swiftly to draw near
> And pour her first libation
> Which I with exultation
> Should drink with all good wishes to our Reading Room so dear.

Elizabeth was forty-six years old and her youngest child was
eight when she moved to live in Yattendon. The years between
then and her death at eighty-three in 1918 were filled with activity –
artistic, literary and social. At this stage of her life as her children
were growing older, perhaps she had more time to devote to
activities beyond the home and was in a position to use her considerable talents to benefit a wider circle. She played a full part
with her husband in the life of the community and they were
generous in their improvements in the village. The Reading
Room was built to provide a room where newspapers and
periodicals were available and where coffee and cake could be
purchased. Considerable refurbishment was undertaken in the
church which was closed for three months in 1881 during building
work that included adding the vestry and the south porch,
rehanging the bells on a new oak frame and providing a new
clock. A new organ was added in 1889. A new school and
teacher's house were built in 1885–6. They also seem to have had
a reputation for a warm and happy home life where guests were
always made welcome. Her niece's memoir of her aunt makes it
clear that Elizabeth played a pivotal part in the contentment of
their home life and the happiness of her children's upbringing.
She encouraged them not just in the art and literature which had
been part of her own childhood, but also in drama – writing little
plays for them – and in music. Her daughter Florence became a
talented musician and trained the Yattendon band which entered
competitions in Reading and gave concerts locally. Her niece
describes the upper parlour at the Court as being Elizabeth's
special sanctum where she read, wrote, drew, embroidered and
even carpentered with her young sons and grandsons, and acted
as Mother-Confessor to her children, friends, household and
many guests and neighbours.

> With each guest, as with each child and servant in her home
> and almost every cottager on her husband's estate, she at once
> initiated a special relationship. Varying degrees of intimacy there
> were, but with everyone she met there was a special 'you and
> me-ness' ready and waiting to be shared by all who had sympathy
> and imagination enough to respond.

At Yattendon, with her children growing up and, as her writing shows, feeling a delight in the country environment, Elizabeth's abilities led to activities which have left a tangible legacy. Most prominent of these are the products of the copper and brass industry which she organised, and her books of prose and poetry, all of which were published after she came to live in Yattendon.

She ran a night school for the young men of the village where she taught a variety of subjects including drawing and astronomy – the stars always fascinated her – and copper and brass working. The latter activity developed into a thriving and well-known village industry. This became affiliated to the Home Arts and Industries Association (HAIA) which was established in 1884 to promote and encourage the revival of rural craft industries which had declined partly due to the migration of the rural population to the towns. The association held an annual exhibition, normally, after 1888, in the Albert Hall, and Yattendon participated in a number of these exhibitions. In 1889 the Minute Book of the association records that the council passed a resolution of special commendation for the artistic quality of the work of three classes, including Yattendon. This resolution was to be written on parchment and sent to the classes.

The items produced in Yattendon were *repoussé* brass and copper. The designs were Elizabeth Waterhouse's own and she also taught her pupils how to beat the copper and brass. The classes took place once a week, at first in the laundry at the Court and later in a room in the basement. Florence Waterhouse records that many of the men continued working on their pieces on other evenings at home. Initially Elizabeth Waterhouse made up the finished items but eventually that aspect of the work was undertaken by Henry Smith, the blacksmith on Ashampstead Common, and his son Harry. A whole variety of items was produced, from simple pin trays, door plates and napkin rings, to candlesticks, lanterns, large fenders, plates, jugs and sconces. Perhaps the most unexpected product of this industry was the copper and brass ambone – a lectern and pulpit – which was made for the Church of the Ascension at Cala, South Africa.

The products of the industry were sold in a number of places. The record of the business between 1902 and 1914 indicates that Elizabeth Waterhouse was committed to the success of the enterprise as a business as well as an artistic and socially

Copper jug
© WBM

Yattendon Village
Industries shop.
© Greenaway

beneficial occupation. A Yattendon Village Industries shop was
opened in Yattendon Square and on the floor above this shop
Alfred Waterhouse had a studio with a north facing window to
get the benefit of a northern light. Many items were sold at the
annual exhibition and are recorded as sold at the Albert Hall or
at the HAIA. One of these appears to have been sold to Queen
Alexandra, who had herself organised a Home Arts and
Industries group at Sandringham. Other items were sold at
Liberty's in London and there seems to have been a sale or return
system in operation, because, although at least twenty-five items
were sold there, a number were returned unsold. Items are listed
as being sold as far afield as Somerset, Bournemouth, Newcastle
and Chester as well as at Oxford, Reading, Newbury and Cold
Ash. Many items were sold to or at the Court and Elizabeth and
her daughter Florence were closely involved in the marketing
as well as in the making.

Alongside the copper and brass industry a woodcarving class
also existed. It was under the overall direction of Elizabeth
Waterhouse but was actually taught by Mr Aldridge the estate
carpenter. It did not become as popular or as famous as the
metalworking but many of its products were exhibited at the
Home Arts and Industries annual exhibition.

As well as providing a skilled artistic pursuit, these classes, like
the Reading Room, were intended to provide a stimulating leisure
activity which was an alternative to the public house.

Elizabeth did not neglect the needs of the women. Her niece
records that 'her designs, when executed in embroidery, gave
employment for years to a number of poor ladies – her 'Tapestry
Club' – conducted by correspondence all over England'. She also
ran a fortnightly women's meeting on Ashampstead Common in

The House by the Cherry
Tree.

the House by the Cherry Tree. At each meeting there was a
reading and a short talk by Elizabeth. The two published volumes
of these readings and homilies – *With the Simple-Hearted*, first published in 1904 and *The House by the Cherry Tree* published in 1911 –
reveal much about Elizabeth as a person, her attitude to the
women around her, her love of the countryside and provide some
gems of information about life in the community at this time.

The homilies often draw inspiration from the countryside, the
seasons, the weather, or from Elizabeth's reading or memories.
They seem to have been intended to provide spiritual guidance
and support, but they reveal a warmth, respect and understanding
of the way of life and work of these ordinary country women
amongst whom Elizabeth lived. She seems to have enjoyed these
meetings – both the company and the house in which they took
place, which was a cottage very different in size and comfort
from the Court. This is very clear in her prefaces to the two
books. At the beginning of *With the Simple-Hearted* she describes
how the homilies were:

> guided sometimes in the course they took by the listening faces
> which seem so needful a part of any teaching that the written
> thought must always be poorer than the spoken.
>
> Poor, too, seem these lifeless pages without the sun-drawn

scent of the old box-hedges coming in through the open door in
summer, or the wood-smoke in winter from the great hearth-fire
where the oldest and youngest of our company gather in the
chimney corner.

Her preface to *The House by the Cherry Tree* clearly reveals her joy
in nature, her acceptance of old age and her indignation at the
slur on her group of women:

> They were spoken, as were those in "With the Simple-Hearted"
> to a small company of women in my own neighbourhood, who
> meet once a fortnight, summer and winter, in the House by the
> Cherry Tree. Of this tree, wild winds and heavy snows have now
> broken the main stem, but we still pass in to the house-door
> under great propped branches, full of blossom in spring and laden
> with fruit at the gathering time, and take comfort as we all grow
> older from this pleasurable parable.
>
> The first title of the Little Homilies has been discarded as it was
> found that "Simple-hearted" became "Simple-minded" to those of
> rather inaccurate memory. "Simple-minded" has now become a
> euphemism for a kind of gentle idiocy, and I should be very sorry
> if this mental condition were at all associated with the intelligent
> company who meet in the House by the Cherry Tree.

She was seventy-five when she wrote these words in 1910,
a widow, lady of the manor and running the estate. Age did
not make her inactive, narrow minded or socially exclusive.

All the homilies are of interest for Elizabeth's attitudes and
understanding – whether she is introducing her group to the
words of Julian of Norwich, a fourteenth-century anchoress;
urging her women to educate their children by example whether
they are babies or adults of thirty, forty or fifty; delighting in the
little child staying with her; explaining that Jesus only referred to
lilies because they grew where he lived and that had he lived here
he would have referred to the primroses, the wood anemones and
the daffodils instead; urging them to delight in the joys of nature
as a message from God. Two however are particularly delightful.
In the homily entitled 'Lavender and Lilies' occurs this particularly evocative passage of Yattendon in the past:

> All these thoughts have come to me because just now in our
> orchard a great deal of lavender is being gathered, and some
> women and children from the village are at work there. And
> when the children go home, their mothers say how sweetly they
> smell of the lavender; and when the women go to work in other
> houses, people tell them that they bring the pleasant scent with
> them; and all along the path through the coppice by which they
> come and go, one can smell it too, so fragrant and fresh and pure.

'The Outgoing of the Morning and the Evening' seems to contain
Elizabeth's philosophy of child rearing and would not be out of

place in a childcare manual today. She urges that children should go to school in the morning feeling loved and happy:

> I know that it may be sometimes rather a hurried time before the children go to school, especially when they have far to walk, but let them have a happy breakfast, and let them go with the feeling that their mother's kiss and blessing will not only cheer them till they see her again, but keep them from any naughty words or ways for her sake.

She also advocates that a mother should make sure that she is free for her children for an hour before their bedtime so that they can enjoy spending time together:

> She may help them to "make something out of nothing" – always a joy to children – a dolls' house out of an old box, or clothes for their dolls out of old scraps. She may read them a story while they are at work, or let one of them read to her if she is obliged to be sewing herself; or they can do a little gardening with her in the summer, or go with her into the woods for flowers or blackberries.

These seem to be the words of someone who had delighted in devising activities for her children and grandchildren.

Elizabeth Waterhouse was not reticent about expressing emotion. Her own writings and her collections of other people's prose, poetry and prayers address the full range of love and sorrow, life and death. Many of the works she wrote or selected delight in love and offer comfort in sadness. Her own grief and anguish after the death of her son Maurice in 1890, at the age of twenty-two, reverberates through her poem 'To M' in the first edition of her *Verses*, whilst her love for him is clearly expressed in the poem 'Grown Up' in *A Little Book of Life and Death*. Alongside this appreciation of people's emotional needs was a tolerance for their religious beliefs which is clearly expressed in *Thoughts of a Tertiary* and in her introduction to *Contemplatio Mortis et Eternitas*.

The forewords she wrote to her various books reveal her to have been widely read and well educated with a deep love of literature and philosophical writings. She lamented in her introduction to *A Little Book of Life and Death*:

> It has been a sorrow to me not even to touch that great storehouse of high thought, *The Divina Commedia*, but no translation seems in any way able to set forth its treasures worthily.

Her introduction to the seventeenth-century Manchester al Mondo *Contemplatio Mortis et Eternitas* shows that she was as familiar with the works of seventeenth century authors as with those of classical philosophers such as Plato, Cicero and Marcus Aurelius.

She was a remarkable woman: an artist who could paint delightful watercolours but could also hammer copper into shape; a writer and thinker who was also fascinated by science, particularly astronomy, and regarded the discovery of Röntgen rays as exhilarating; a scholar familiar with Latin who loved to see the wild flowers and to hear the birds singing; a businesswoman who could also enjoy the games of childhood; the lady of the manor who was also the loving centre of the home and a genuine friend to her tenants and servants.

Let us leave her with this evocative description by her niece:

> Her dresses in younger days were often of her favourite colour green, in later years, always black and grey. Above the straight lines of her gowns were the soft curves of her large caps which she always made herself, evolving them in her armchair in her own special corner of the hall, from a large neat basket of stored silks, satins, ribbons, and beautiful old lace. During her widowhood the caps became smaller and simpler, both in form and material, and her garb almost nun-like in its austerity: straight black gown, wide white collar and cuffs and then the rather severe lines of her plain white muslin coif, framing her face. The only ornaments she wore in those days were a pearl bar, fastening her collar, and at her watchchain a tiny cross of Saint Francis, brought for her from Assisi.

Publications by Elizabeth Waterhouse

The Brotherhood of Rest (date unknown)
A Book of Simple Prayers (1884); enlarged second edition (1893)
The Island of Anarchy (1887)
Verses (1897); enlarged second edition (1912)
A Little Book of Life and Death (1902)
With the Simple Hearted (1904)
Introduction to the seventeenth-century *Contemplatio Mortis et Eternitas* (1906)
Companions of the Way (1908)
Thoughts of a Tertiary (1909)
The House by the Cherry Tree (1911)

Sources

Holdsworth, L.V., 'The Centenary of Elizabeth Waterhouse 1834–1934', *Friends Quarterly Examiner* (July 1934)
Jones, Edgar (ed.), *The Memoirs of Edwin Waterhouse*
Smith-Masters, Revd J. E., *Yattendon and its Church* volumes 1 and 2
Waterhouse, Edwin (ed.), *Extracts from the Journals of Mary Waterhouse 1825–1880*
The reminiscences of many people in the village who have shared their family memories with me.

5 Sheep Markets & Fairs at East Ilsley

East Ilsley Local History Society

This essay has been produced by the East Ilsley Local History Society and is largely based on the research of the late Audrey Penn (*née* Groves-Jones) once headmistress of the East Ilsley primary school.

Between 1200 and 1400 AD, there were no fewer than 4800 charters granted for fairs and markets but, after that time, the numbers declined until, by the end of the fifteenth century, only about a hundred were granted annually. Even so, there were still about 1500 fairs in England each year. As so many were granted, a careful note had to be made of the date they should be held. Errors were made and all established fairs and markets were not always safeguarded, as happened on two occasions when charters were granted to lords of the manor of East Ilsley.

During the time of Henry III, Emeric de St Amand, the lord of the manor of East Ilsley, was granted a charter to hold a market for corn but this damaged the trade at the king's market at Wallingford. This weekly market at Ilsley flourished for several hundred years. Hundreds of carts brought wheat to the markets, travelling along the downland tracks and roads. After the markets ended the corn was taken to Streatley and then conveyed on the River Thames to London. One byway is still called the Wheat Road and links the East Ilsley windmill site to the Ridgeway at the top of Gore Hill.

A second charter was granted in 1620 by James I to Sir Francis Moore, the lord of this manor at that time. This also had an adverse effect on another market at Cuckhamsley-Hill. His Majesty therefore prohibited 'all persons from assembling at the aforesaid place called Cutchinloe to buy, sell, exchange or deliver corn etc,' ordering that they should transact their business 'at no other place but the town of East Ilsley'. This decree had the desired effect, and the market of Ilsley continued to prosper until, following the construction of the Kennet and

Taken from the Ordnance
Survey map of 1911.

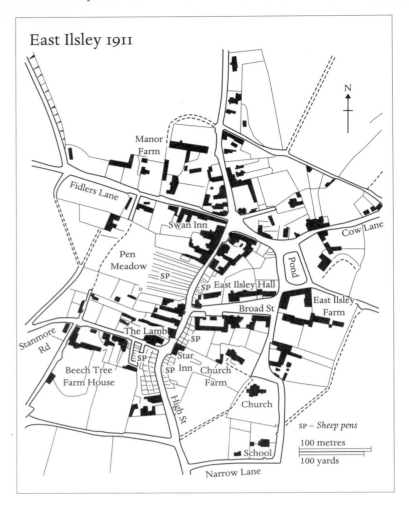

East Ilsley 1911

N

Manor
Farm

Fidlers Lane

Swan Inn

Cow Lane

Pen
Meadow

SP

Pond

SP East Ilsley Hall

East Ilsley
Farm

Broad St

Stanmore
Rd

The Lamb

SP

SP

Star
Inn

SP

Church
Farm

Beech Tree
Farm House

High St

Church

SP – Sheep pens

100 metres

School

100 yards

Narrow Lane

Avon canal in 1795, the East Ilsley corn market soon came to an
end.

The sheep markets and fairs continued to flourish and there is
probably no other village in Berkshire or for many miles around
which had so many fairs. The total number of fairs was about
fourteen, with fairs on the Wednesdays after Easter and Whitsun,
two in August, and three in the Autumn months. Markets were
held on alternate Wednesdays from February to July.

Sheep pens were erected in many places in the village, the
largest number being in the meadow on the west side of the
High Street (the meadow to this day being called Pen Meadow),
Broad Street, along the verges in the High Street, on both sides of
the road near the Star Inn and as far as the south side of Narrow
Lane. A small number of cattle were also auctioned and were
always placed on the south side of the footpath in Pen Meadow.
Thousands of sheep were driven into the village and their

Top
Pen Meadow on Fair Day.
© English Heritage
National Monuments
Record

Right
Cattle at the Fair.

numbers increased annually until the nineteenth century. The largest estimated number penned in one day was 80 000, of which number 55 000 were sold, and the annual average was around 400 000. These numbers show that the East Ilsley sheep markets were practically the largest in the whole country. The largest of the sheep fairs in the village was the Ram Lamb Sale held in August each year.

Sheep sold at these markets and fairs were driven across the countryside for many miles, from neighbouring counties and from those further afield, such as Kent, Surrey, Hertfordshire, Northampton and others to the south and east.

Only a few of the oldest inhabitants of the village remember the scenes of those busy days, when so many men and women

derived extra employment that provided a welcome addition to
the small wages from their normal work in the village. Every
'extra hand' was needed, not only at the actual markets, but also
at the inns, shops and in providing transport for the foreigners.
Carpenters and labourers were busy constructing hurdles for the
pens, old ones to be repaired, new ones supplied and erected for
the vast numbers of sheep, and larger and stronger hurdles for
the cattle. The dirt roads needed repairing, with young boys
helping their elders in last minute preparations.

Extra stocks of beer were brought to the public houses to
provide for the thirsty farmers, dealers, shepherds and drovers.
Additional stocks of food were needed for lunches and other
meals for those staying overnight. The blacksmith was busy
making sure that all the horses were shod properly, with the
wheelwrights overhauling the carts and traps for transporting
the 'visitors'.

The women in the village helped by preparing the rooms
at the inns for the overnight buyers and auctioneers. Each inn
played its own part in the scenes. The Swan made provision for
the farmers to stay overnight, the Lamb and the Star provided
accommodation for shepherds and drovers. The Lamb also providing nourishment in the way of meals throughout the day, vast
preparations being made to serve as many as possible, with sometimes a hundred hungry farmers being given a dinner at the cost
of two shillings and sixpence. The menu for the meal was as follows: boiled or roast leg of mutton, plum pudding or apple tart
and custard. These puddings were usually made in vast quantities
once a year by cooking in earthenware bread pans. A cheaper
meal could be provided, of meat vegetables and apple pie,
which cost one shilling. Women would be employed from early
morning to prepare the vegetables; the proprietor of the Lamb
would often employ 'an dozen pairs of extra hands'. The local
women would be paid a shilling for the day, being also given a
good meal and a glass of beer. Their day would be a long one,
not ending until all was cleared away and the washing up finished. Where visitors stayed the night, it would be a continual
round of meal preparation, serving meals and washing up.
Sometimes the inns had insufficient bedrooms and the families
had to vacate their own rooms; when sometimes there were far
too many drovers and shepherds and the Star and Lamb inns
were unable to accommodate them all. Many local cottages
rented sleeping space and shelter was also provided at Beech
Tree Farmhouse, many of the men occupying one large room,
although some preferred to remain with their flocks as they had
been doing on their way to East Ilsley. Many drovers had been
living and sleeping with their sheep, some for days and some for

Top
High Street at Pen
Meadow.
© English Heritage
National Monuments
Record

Bottom
Looking down High
Street.

weeks. They travelled through county after county, from one fair to another, driving flocks from one farmer to another. The flocks under their control might vary in size, a hundred or so sheep, perhaps even a thousand.

The village on fair and market days must have resounded with the bleating and crying of thousands of sheep, barking of dogs, shouts of men and boys, not forgetting the sound of sheep bells. The leader of each flock would wear a sheep bell around its neck and was known as a bellwether. On dry summer days, chalk dust in the roads and tracks would fill the air, and even as the sheep came over the tracks on the Downs, their cries would be heard long before they could be observed as the dust from the ground appeared like great clouds and enveloped them. The din of animals and shouts of the men would constantly interrupt the children's lessons at the school.

Dealers, drovers and shepherds would be easily recognised by their apparel. The drovers usually wore red knotted handkerchiefs around their necks; some carried a vast umbrella for use as shelter on the journey. Shepherds wore smocks, a soft hat, and carried a crook, wooden in olden times, later iron, made by the local black-smith. These crooks varied in size according to the size and breed of the sheep. Dealers often wore velveteen jackets; soft felt hats, and in later times a large white coat, which almost reached to the knees.

Many of these drovers were descendants of the drovers of olden days, when cattle and oxen were driven across the country-side. These men bore a great responsibility, as not only did they have to tend and care for any sick animal on these long journeys, but they also carried at times large sums of money for payment of sheep or cattle from one farmer to another. Each drover had to obtain a government licence before he could take on the task, and this could only be granted if he was at least thirty years of age, married and was a householder. Travellers would often request permission to join the drovers on their journeys and would 'work their passage' by helping to drive the great flocks and herds.

The auctioneer was also busy making preparations, seeing his stand was in position in Pen Meadow and his office in order. His wooden building was set up on the east side of the High Street, near the corner of Broad Street. When the fairs were discon-tinued, this office was purchased by the owner of Orchard Lea in The Old Stanmore Road and formed the sitting room of his home (now demolished).

Sheep were often sold over and over again, during the course of the day, each succeeding sale resulting in a higher price each time, perhaps as much as sixpence or even a shilling at each re-sale. As the day wore on, the price of the sheep would increase, particularly if news came through that there was a buyer from outside the district arriving on the scene.

When the railway station at Compton was opened, sheep and cattle could be transported so much more quickly that fewer drovers were required. The increase in traffic on the roads by the time of the First World War also greatly affected the passage of large flocks on the roads, and where possible, these men used the Green Roads across our countryside.

Early in the twentieth century, a ruling was made by the government that all sheep pens must be white-washed every time, before they were used again, to prevent any infection to the animals. This resulted in a great increase in the amount of work, and later became almost impossible because of labour difficulties.

By the 1920s, East Ilsley sheep markets were becoming less and less popular and almost run as private markets of the Wilson family who farmed large areas of land in Berkshire and Wiltshire. By the beginning of the Second World War, the markets had ceased. A plaque set on a sarcen stone, placed on the site of the pens in the High Street, provides a reminder of the importance of the fairs and markets to East Ilsley and a village event is held in most years to keep the memory alive.

6 The Ashampstead War Book
Portrait of a Parish at War June 1942

Dick Greenaway

September 1939 – Hitler sends his armies into Poland. Britain and
France declare war on Germany when he refuses to withdraw.

10 May 1940 – Hitler launches blitzkrieg on western Europe.

4 June 1940 – the British and Commonwealth armies and some
allies are evacuated from Dunkirk and on 16 June 1940 France
surrenders to the Germans.

2 July 1940 – Hitler orders Operation Sealion – the invasion of
Britain

August and September 1940 – The Battle of Britain and the London
Blitz

12 October 1940 – Operation Sealion cancelled. German forces turn
their attention to planning for the attack on Russia.

Step by cruel step these are the stages of the first part of the
Second World War. Britain had been expecting and planning
for aerial attack and possible invasion since before 1939. Military
experts, extrapolating from their experience of World War One
and studying the development of aircraft, both for bombing and
for transporting parachute troops, had forecast that a war would
involve massive aerial attacks on civilian targets. They considered
that these attacks could include gas attack and the landing of
invasion forces from the air. And so, to a limited extent, Britain
had started to prepare itself. The evacuation of the cities was
planned, gas masks were issued and air raid shelters were
constructed or designated in cellars, church crypts and underground railway stations. Information sheets and guidance notes
flooded onto the population. In 1937 the Ministry of Food had
been established to ensure the fair and equal rationing of food

Ashampstead Home
Guard.
© Greenaway Collection

and clothing should enemy submarines cause the same disruption
to imports as they had in the Great War.

In Berkshire the main north-south trunk road through
Newbury was recognised as a key strategic route and steps were
taken to keep it open. An emergency bridge was built over the
Kennet and Avon Canal between Victoria Park and the Wharf to
provide a reserve route should the main bridge be destroyed and
pill boxes were provided to protect it against ground assault. The
'black out' of all surface lighting after sunset was ordered and
enforced by the newly formed Air Raid Precautions patrols. In
May 1940 the Local Defence Volunteers were formed – later to
become the Home Guard. In an attempt to baffle and confuse
any enemy soldiers who succeeded in landing all signposts and
name boards were removed.

However, by June 1942 all of these precautions, and many
others, were in place and had become part of daily existence.
In June 1941 the Germans attacked Russia and in December 1941
the USA entered the war. The threat of imminent invasion had
receded – if not completely vanished – and at that moment the
government instructed Local Defence Committees to prepare a
War Book and provided a carefully printed form for its creation.

It seems strange that they had waited so long before preparing
such a plan. Waited, in fact, until it was unlikely that it would
ever be needed. Perhaps it was a way of drawing a line under the
many initiatives of the previous danger period without discarding
them and then allowing the population to focus its efforts outward
on the next phase of the war – the aggressive rather than defen-
sive phase. In October 1942 the Eighth Army defeated Rommel at

the Battle of El Alamein and the tide had started to turn.

War Books are remarkable documents that give a vivid picture of a community after three years of total war. They were classified as SECRET and contained defined sections describing the community and its resources and the needful activities should an attack happen. At the risk of tedium I have listed these headings to give an idea of the detail of the picture painted.

Composition of the Local Defence Committee.
Arrangements for the maintenance of services –
   electricity, water, sanitation etc.
Military units in the town or parish and details of
   the Home Guard strength.
Vulnerable points.
Collection of labour.
Conservation and distribution of food supplies including
   the situation of food depots and arrangements for
   communal feeding.
Location of Rest Centres and medical arrangements
   for dealing with casualties.
Arrangements for water supplies to include wells
   and water carts.
Arrangements for collecting transport. Lists of
   available vehicles.
A census of horses and farm vehicles.

To provide all this information a detailed house by house survey was carried out and it is the results of this survey that provide the detail and colour the picture.

Ashampstead is reported as being a parish of ninety households housing 301 permanent residents and a small number of part time residents. As with so many British activities a Local Defence Committee was formed to oversee the operation of the Plan. This consisted of a chairman and secretary, the senior military, ARP and police officers, a medical officer and two Authorised Food Organisers. Their names, addresses and telephone numbers are given.

Next come the arrangements for the maintenance of services. There was no gas in the parish (there still isn't) and electricity was supplied by the Wessex Electricity Company based in Mortimer. Piped water was supplied by three bodies – South Oxfordshire Water Company based at Goring on Thames, Lord Iliffe based at Yattendon and the Wessex Water Company based near Aldershot.

The Home Guard is shown as being organised in four Sections under the command of Captain Dunlop supported by Lieutenant Robertson-Glasgow. It had a total strength of forty men many of whom were Great War veterans.

The aerodrome between Ashampstead and Hampstead Norreys had opened in 1940 and this was considered to be the

Local Invasion Committee

A Local Invasion Committee has been set up in order to deal with invasion conditions.

DURING THE PRESENT PERIOD the Committee is engaged in making preparations to deal with the local problems which will arise in invasion such as :—

1. Organisation of civilian labour to assist the military in preparing defence works, digging trenches, clearing roads, etc.
2. Care of wounded.
3. Housing and sheltering the homeless.
4. Emergency cooking and feeding.
5. Emergency water supplies.
6. Messenger Service.

IF INVASION COMES the Committee will direct its action :

    (*a*) to meet the requirements of the military,
    (*b*) to attend to the needs of the civil population.

All civilians both men and women must be prepared to play their part.

Give in your name now to the Committee's Headquarters, or through your Warden or the W.V.S. Housewives' Service, for the work for which you are best fitted. The Committee will see that you are allotted a task, and if necessary trained to carry it out.

OFFER YOUR SERVICES NOW.

If Invasion comes the Committee instructs everyone

    NOT to spread rumours,
    NOT to block roads by becoming a refugee,
       but
    To follow the orders of the Police, A.R.P., Military and Home Guard,
       TO STAND FIRM.

The composition of the Committee and its Headquarters are :—

HEADQUARTERS:— LEYFIELDS.

CHAIRMAN - W.V.S		
Mrs E. Bootle-Wilbraham	Pyt House	Yattendon 240
VICE CHAIRMAN - FOOD OFFICER		
E. Bootle-Wilbraham Esqr.	Pyt House	Yattendon 240
DEPUTY FOOD OFFICER - W.V.S		
Lady Gray	Leyfields	Yattendon 241
O/C HOME GUARD		
L. Dunlop Esqr.	De la Bèche Manor	Compton 62
CHIEF A.R.P. WARDEN		
Rev. E. Hester	The Vicarage	Yattendon 272
RED CROSS REPRESENTATIVE		
Miss R. Montgomery	Quick's Green	Upper Basildon 287
CHAIRMAN of PARISH COUNCIL		
Councillor W. Wooders	Pinfold Lane	
POLICE		
P.C. W. Hedges	Bottom Lodge	Pangourne 307

Local invasion committee poster.
© Ashampstead Parish Council

A typical kitchen/
dining room scene.
© Greenaway Collection

most vulnerable point in the area and the most likely object of
any attack.

Due to the demands of conscription, the Home Guard and
the ARP the survey found that it was unlikely that any additional
labour would be available other than elderly people. This gives
a clear idea of the way the whole population of the parish was
mobilised behind the war effort. Simply to provide forty men
for the Home Guard out of a total resident population of 301
stripped the parish of the able bodied.

Food depots were to be established in the British Legion
Hut, the Vicarage cellar, the village shop, the village bakery and
'The British Ratin Co.' (This was a London company specialising
in pest control which had moved its headquarters and staff out
to a large house in the village. After the war it became Rentokil.)
It was decided that the scattered population made it undesirable
to organise communal feeding but the cooking facilities of
each house were listed. Emergency water supplies were considered. There was a village well and twenty houses, out of ninety,

had their own wells and the farms could supply three water carts.

Arrangements for dealing with casualties were detailed. There was to be a First Aid Point in one of the larger houses and the vicar would provide a mortuary in the vicarage.

The parish transport resources came to twenty-two cars, two lorries, one van and five trailers. The farms could supply three tractors. Many of the cars were probably 'laid up' for the duration of the war and would have been of little use in an emergency. Horse drawn transport was still important and the parish could muster eleven draught horses, three draught ponies (used for pulling small carts and lawn mowers) and four riding horses. Carts were listed, the three main farms having nineteen between them but there were also three milk carts.

In the event of an invasion the parish was instructed 'NOT to spread rumours, NOT to block the roads by becoming a refugee, to follow the orders of the police, ARP, military and Home Guard and TO STAND FIRM'.

The survey which provided the data for the plan survived with the Parish copy and gives a vivid picture of a community just emerging from the traditional locally focussed society where most items of daily life were provided locally into a more out-ward looking culture with links to the wider world. For example, the village still had a shop and a school. Bread baked in the parish bakery was delivered by the baker and milk produced by the parish cows was delivered by the families that milked them. Seventy-five out of ninety houses still relied on solid fuel ranges heated by coal for their cooking and heating. But this was supple-mented by logs from the local woods and coppices. However, eighty had bought oil fired 'broilers'. These were small cooking stoves with three or four rings and sometimes an oven, heated by burning wicks fed from a tank of paraffin. Sixteen households had invested in electric stoves or hobs. Sixty-nine houses had a piped water supply but sixteen still only had access to a well.

Almost all houses were making good use of their gardens, eighty-nine households reported that they were well supplied for vegetables, and thirty-nine were keeping chickens. Only one household admitted to having a pig. It seems strange that this figure was not higher. The previous generation had considered the cottage pig as an important part of the family diet and it seems strange that this resource had not been exploited. Possibly the shortage of suitable feed for both chickens and pigs limited their adoption. Nevertheless, one goat and seven cows were kept to supply milk.

The survey also looked at people's grocery arrangements. Most people claimed a week's supply 'in hand' – probably obtained from the village shop – but still required a regular supply of milk and bread. These were supplied locally as can be seen from the 'three milk carts' and the designation of the bakery as a Food Depot.

Thirty years – or one generation – on and the village shop, school and bakery had closed and the 'week's supply in hand' came from a supermarket in Pangbourne or Reading to be stored in an electrically powered freezer. Every house was supplied with piped water and almost all the wells had been filled in after an horrendous accident in Yattendon. The era of the 'fitted kitchen' had arrived.

Ten further years and the cars had multiplied ten fold. By 1991 the expanded village of 141 households housing 361 residents had the use of 233 cars and all draught horses and carts had vanished from the farms in favour of ever larger tractors, but the population of riding ponies had dramatically increased.

War Books must have been produced for all parishes and copies must still exist in parish archives or the local Record Office. Ashampstead's copy was found among the papers of a contemporary parish councillor. The copies rendered to the authorities may survive in the Public Record Office.

However, they should be used with care! Following up the anomaly of the single pig revealed that the survey was by no means as complete as it appeared! Firstly, if chickens and pigs were 'officially' kept this resulted in a reduction in the household's egg and bacon ration. One officially 'pig-less' resident clearly remembered the succession of family pigs named 'George I, George II, George III etc…'! The nearby village of Bradfield even had a Pig Club.

Digging a little deeper revealed an atmosphere of social resentment. The investigators were seen as part of the parish Establishment – as 'THEM' – and you were justified in not revealing to 'Them' any more of your personal affairs than was strictly necessary. This attitude may have been reinforced by a feeling that the survey was unnecessarily intrusive at a time when the war had clearly moved past the stage where invasion was likely. If one was to be more charitable, it could be that the investigators felt little obligation to pry too deeply into their neighbours affairs for the same reason.

Nevertheless, I strongly recommend a search for the local War Book to anyone interested in their local history or in the changes to society over a crucial period in the country's history.

7   Evacuation – a Reception Area in Berkshire

Miriam Ward

I found the following account after my mother's death. It was pencilled into a penny notebook. I don't believe it ever went further. It was undated but clearly contemporaneous, and may belong to the 'phoney war' period in 1939.

I have 'modernised' the spelling, but I have not edited the language or the attitudes, believing them to be representative of the class-conscious reaction of country people to the poverty and distress emerging from London sixty years ago, when the bombing was still only anticipated – a mixture of planning and chaos, good will and misunderstanding leading to exasperation!

Dorcas Ward

When the billeting officer sent in the report of his census of accommodation available in this parish of Bradfield in Berkshire, our RDC (Rural District Council) told us that we must be prepared to receive 300 evacuees, and that they would arrive in two consignments on the third and fourth day of the evacuation. About three weeks before the outbreak of war they sent more details. We should have approximately 270 school children and thirty teachers and helpers. Blankets and mattresses would be available. The whole parish was re-canvassed, and a fine response was made by those prepared to take in children up to this number.

They were to arrive at the nearest station, Theale, at 5.30 pm from which place they would arrive in busloads to the local men's clubroom for distribution to their billets.

The local representative of the WVS (Women's Voluntary Service) had formed a committee to distribute mattresses and blankets, help receive and sort the children and to provide transport to the billets of this scattered parish.

On 1 September the blow was [illegible] that there were no blankets or mattresses. However everything else was ready. The billeting officer had every household's voucher ready filled in with details as to numbers of children and money due, only the names of the children remaining to be added, so that we reckoned the whole 300 could be disposed of in about one hour. This being so we decided that it would not be necessary to provide refreshments other than water (which had to be fetched from a farm near by) and that the present sanitary arrangements would be sufficient.

On the evening of Saturday 2 September a telegram was received that the children would not arrive till Monday – a day

later than originally expected. At 11am on Monday another
telegram arrived, 'expect children this afternoon'. At 3pm a third
telegram, 'arrangements cancelled'. The billeting officer disperses
the helpers and goes out. At 5.30 a fourth telegram, 'children
arriving 6pm'. Billeting officer's small daughter cycles frantically
round parish searching for her father. WVS committee hastily
reassemble. 6.30 billeting officer found. Large numbers of club
members and children arrive on spot. 7.30 buses arrive. They
unload their contents – thirty-five school children, 220 mothers
and infants!

They straggle into the clubroom laden with babies, toddlers,
parcels and gas masks. The overcrowding, confusion, noise and
squalor is unbelievable. Some cannot speak English. Many have
lost their parcels or toddlers. Ventilation is inadequate because
of the darkened windows. We sort out unaccompanied children,
and without undue delay despatch them to their new homes.

Now for these mothers. Next billet has room for mother and
one child. 'You mother and young baby come this way please.'
'Oh I can't go without my friend here, I'd rather spend the night
where I am.' 'Well you there with the little girl then.' 'Oh these
other five belong to me.' Hasty search through books for accommodation for six.

So it goes slowly on. The first carloads come back with such
messages as, 'Mrs Hodge says she can't possibly take the mother
and four because her sister has just arrived from Manchester with
six', or 'Mrs Brown wouldn't let us in because she said she had
asked for two little girls and she wouldn't take a Polish family
instead'.

Meanwhile the countryside has grown dark. The mothers and
babies in the hut are tireder and less reasonable than ever. An
Irishwoman stands up and declaims in eloquent language against
all of us and all our race and all our ancestors. Some eight or nine
women refuse to part from each other and we agree to bed them
down for the night in the clubroom. Our transport drivers report
that householders have gone to bed and billets can be found for
no more. We bed up the residue as comfortably as we can on
sacks of straw, and retire to our respective homes for the night.

I lie awake wondering how these dregs from Limehouse,
Poplar and Stepney are to fit into our prosperous country homes.
The poorer of our inhabitants to whom they might not be quite
so foreign are already living in houses which are too small and
crowded to take in more. These women – Jewish, Irish, Poles and
Chinese – have been placed with our artisans, postmen, farmers
and gentry. What wonder that the following morning should
bring a ceaseless flow of householders who declare that they
cannot and will not keep such women in their houses? Some

refuse to make use of the usual sanitary arrangements.

For the last two days we have laboured unceasingly to fix up the worse cases of hardship. The LCC (London County Council) helpers, both men and women, have been unfailingly tactful, hardworking and efficient. We appeal to the RDC for help. They tell us we must keep them all in the parish somehow, but can offer no helpful advice. We have fixed up a few empty cottages and sheds for some families. The school children and the sprinkling of respectable families are happily housed. But there is a residue so uncivilised as to completely defeat our efforts at solution. Some refuse to believe that they must buy their own food and do their own work, saying 'when you take rooms for a holiday you don't expect to do your own work'. This attitude is not uncommon. Accusive [sic] Jewish fathers have now begun to appear to add to our troubles. Some twenty or so mothers refused to be reasoned with and insisted on returning to London forthwith.

The RDC has succeeded in requisitioning a large house for the district, and we locally have taken over an empty rectory. If the LCC can find us supervisors for these, much genuine misery and discontent will be saved. If you will help us with the real undesirables we will do all we can to look after your decent folk for you.

8   Yattendon 1939–45

Ruth Mott

Two things have remained from those years – queuing and bartering! I think it was early in 1939 when we went to the Village Hall to collect our identity cards and ration books. My parents thought that ration books were a good thing as they well remembered the 1914–18 war when rationing did not take place until 1917. To enhance the family diet then my sister cycled to Newbury on Saturdays to see what she could find.

Our ration book for 1939 entitled everyone to equal amounts and this was very hard for households of only one or two people. You registered at the shop of your choice for tea, butter, sugar, cheese, lard, bacon, meat and eggs. You could hand over a ration page to someone who kept pigs and chickens in return for all your kitchen scraps. He then kept you supplied with bacon and eggs. This arrangement very often worked out better than using the shop!

Milk was rationed at some stage. The Estate had a good herd of Channel Island cattle so our milk had a high fat content. We took off the cream and when we had a nice jar full we shook it about until butter formed. This gave us about four ounces (about 100grams) of butter and the remaining milk still had a reasonable fat content.

Offal was un-rationed and was sold using a system based on family name. Surnames between A and D one week, E to H the next and so on so that everyone had a fair share. We took the bus to Reading to queue for fish, saccharine sweetener tablets and cigarettes. Often we joined a queue just to find out what was on offer and sometimes the door was closed just as you reached the head of the queue!

Now to the bartering! One soon found out who had a surplus
of something and then you would arrange a swop. Clothing
coupons could be sold for two shillings each. Although this is
only ten pence in modern money it was a substantial sum in 1939
when a good wage was only £3 a week. We bought army blankets
from surplus supplies and made coats. Soap was in short supply
and we bought 'off the ration' powder called 'ROO' – I suppose
it was Australian with a name like that! It almost took the skin
from your hands! The local Women's Institute kept busy at the
Village Hall. They hired a canning plant from Reading and
everyone took their fruit to the hall and had a big day filling their
store cupboards. We collected rose hips which were sent away to
be made into a syrup rich in vitamin C to replace the vitamins
obtained from oranges in peace time. Mrs Palmer who lived at
the Grange in Yattendon arranged most of these things and this
was the time when her two daughters – Susan and Felicity –
became interested in farming; an interest which remained with
them all their lives.

After the harvest had been cut villagers were allowed to walk
the fields to glean fallen corn for home use. This could be used
to feed chickens as well as being ground for meal.

Potatoes were grown in some of the fields and after all the edible ones had been picked up – a back breaking task – one could collect the remainder for pigs and hens.

The day the pig was killed was a big day. If you were lucky and no one wanted the intestines you carried them off home in your old galvanised wash tub. Cleaning them was not the friendliest of tasks as this had to be completed while they were still warm. You ran them through with water to get the worst of the muck out and then you soaked them in salt water for three days alternately pulling them inside out until they were clean. After plaiting and boiling they made a lovely breakfast or supper dish and also provided a basin of lard. Perhaps you did not care too much about the 'innards' but the lard was a real reward!

The Village Hall was used a lot then. Whist drives and dances were run to make money for the Welcome Home fund. It does not sound much by present day standards, but we managed to raise £10 for our local men. We made our own entertainment with concerts of local talent. There was no television to compete with!

I feel sad when walking and riding around our lovely countryside today, thinking of all the lovely fields of grain in the past. So many of them are in 'set aside'. I wonder what would happen if…?

9 Two Berkshire Villages in the Twentieth Century – a view through the obituaries

Dorcas Ward

One of the glories of Yattendon and Frilsham is *The Broadsheet* – an outstanding monthly parish (not church) magazine which has been published continuously since 1956 – and one of the glories of *The Broadsheet* is the quality of the obituaries. Felicity Palmer's father was one of the three founders of *The Broadsheet*, and she herself was an editor for a large part of its life. She also wrote many of the most perceptive and informative obituaries, giving vivid pictures of the characters and lives of people who had been an integral part of the two villages over more than a century.

It therefore occurred to me that here might be a rich vein of local history. As archaeologists deduce so much about the life and times of ancient civilisations from graves and tombstones, so might we about more recent times from this modern necrology of local obituaries, some of which are summarized in the margin.

There were 373 obituaries in forty-four years, averaging eight or nine a year throughout the period. They vary from brief nods of respect and sympathy, to loving tributes, comprehensive pen portraits, and mini-biographies, and are probably the only written record of much oral and family history. They appear to represent a complete, though perhaps not balanced, cross section of the population, as indicated by the range of recorded occupations from a major general to a mole catcher, a colonial governor to cowmen, newspaper magnates to milkmen, an MP to parish councillors.

However, it is clearly a biased record. Obituaries do not normally record the quarrelsome or dishonest side of people's characters, and an unnaturally idyllic picture of village life may result. *The Broadsheet* was largely the organ of the educated and

1986. **Archie Clarke** was an orphan in Bradfield Workhouse, brought to be fostered in Burnt Hill, and always kept up with the Methodist chapel there. Worked for Suttons Seeds in Reading for 51 years.

articulate, so the choice of people to write about is probably biased towards the land owning and professional inhabitants and those who worked for them – as well as those who were marked 'characters' or 'good village men' contributing to the community. It may under-represent those who lived private lives and commuted to work outside the area. It certainly includes a lot of people who retired to the villages, having lived their working lives elsewhere, as well as some who had moved away by the time of their death.

For the purposes of this exercise the following information was extracted – as far as possible – from all the 373 obituaries:

Date of obituary
Name
Dates of birth and death
No. years in Yattendon and / or Frilsham
Main occupation(s)
Connection with the Estate?
War experience
Family (spouses and offspring)
Community contribution
Main hobbies or pastimes.

It was then summarised by the decade of death. These summaries are attached as appendices 1–3. It would probably have been easier to trace periodic changes and trends if the information had been grouped by date of birth rather than death, but this was not practicable in my manual system.

In most decades more men were recorded than women but the balance tipped the other way in the 1990s. Where marital status was reported, ninety-two per cent of the men were married, some more than once, but only eighty-three per cent of the women. Perhaps this resulted from the awful casualties of two world wars: the village war memorials record the deaths of thirty-five (young) men in the first – seven families lost two men – and seven in the second.

No attempt was made to trace kinship patterns, but the distribution of surnames does indicate some local dynasties – for instance, there were more than five Barrs, Pococks, Waterhouses and Wyatts and five Loaders. Other names which appear at least four times were Butler, Caesar, Iliffe, James, Print, Palmer, Pilkington, Pizzey, Taylor, Toms and Wakefield. Strangely all but one of these seem to be families who escaped losses in the wars.

Those recorded had spent anything from one to ninety two years in the villages by the time they died, but the average was thirty-six years. Rather surprisingly this increased to forty-three in the last decade – this, like the repeating names, suggesting considerable stability of population. If I had had detailed local maps, showing the changing names of roads and houses, I could have also traced the movements of many families around the villages, because their homes were so often recorded.

As might be expected in this deeply rural and wooded part of Berkshire the main occupations were agriculture and forestry. Seventy of the men (thirty-five per cent), as well as twenty-five of the women's husbands, had worked on farms – farmers and general or specialised farm-workers –, or in the woods – woodmen and gamekeepers. However, twenty-six had left agriculture during their working lives.

The other most common areas of work for men were gardening (twenty-eight), building (twenty-five), and public – usually local – service (nineteen). There is some evidence of a move out of gardening as well as agriculture into these other areas of work. Sixteen followed other 'trades' – engineers, blacksmiths, saddler/cobblers, a hurdle-maker, a chimney sweep, a carrier, a butcher, a fitter, a clock repairer. Thirteen were in business. Eleven were drivers (HGV, coach and taxi drivers, and chauffeurs, one having started as a coachman) and another eleven had been in the armed services – some very distinguished indeed. Ten worked in factories and eight in shops, mostly locally, including the Yattendon post office. Seven had been publicans in one of the four local pubs, the George and Dragon, the Axe and Compass (later the Nut and Bolt), the Pot Kiln, and the more upmarket Royal Oak. The first two seemed to attract retired gamekeepers, the last a gentleman from the film industry.

Other professions were followed by fewer, but often distinguished, men: five schoolmasters, four clergymen, seven an architect or lawyer, five in the arts – writers, artist, actors – , four in the colonial service, including a governor of Hong Kong, and two local doctors.

Thirteen men could have been described as 'in service' – including grooms and chauffeurs as well as a valet and a butler, but for women this was the biggest single occupation. Thirty-six of the 105 women whose occupations are recorded either starting life 'in service', not only in the big houses but also in more modest households, such as farms and rectories, or continued to work as cooks and housekeepers or valued 'helps' right through the century. Forty-four per cent of women (only nine per cent of men) are not recorded as having any paid occupation at all, many being known only as 'wife of'. In addition to those doing housework for others or being 'in service', eight worked in shops, eight as nurses, seven in agriculture, and seven as teachers. Six had been in business or done secretarial work. Four had been in the arts and four in public service.

1986. **'Shepherd' Marlow** shepherded on arable at Frilsham Manor Farm, later on grassland for the Estate. Gardening was his chief recreation.

1998. **'Jack' Kieldsen** born and raised in Frilsham ... helped parents and grand-parents on their farms ... electrician ... wireless operator ..., Teneplas ... driver ... Organised many coach trips ... driving the love of his life ...'.

1988. **Judge Peregrine Blomefield** was appointed to the new Crown Court at Reading.

1995. **Nora Hamblin** 'went into service at Marlston Farm ... married ... both did a lot of work looking after animals on Parsonage Farm ... [She was a] gifted gardener and flower arranger ...'.

1980. **Mrs Panting** married 'a member of a well known local family and gardener at Yattendon Court ... [She] served in Yattendon Stores and later ... supervised meals at Yattendon School'.

Overall the range is very wide for such a small rural community. And even these classifications have varieties within them, such as horse and dog breeders, school matrons, dressmakers and lady's maids, stonemasons and brick-makers, nannies and foster mothers, land girls and missionaries, publishers and newspaper magnates. This partly reflects the area's attraction as a rural retreat within fairly easy reach of London, and partly the circle which gathered at the beginning of the century round the Waterhouse architectural dynasty in Yattendon Court, with their energetic, artistic womenfolk, one of whom was married to the poet laureate, Robert Bridges.

There was also much more village self-sufficiency in the first half of the century. We had 'our' doctor and 'our' district nurses, 'our' blacksmith and 'our' saddler and cobbler, as well as 'our' postman/woman. There was a shop in Frilsham as well as those in Yattendon, and each village had its own village school with long serving school-mistresses playing an important part in village life.

To an outsider arriving in the 1980s Yattendon, especially, seemed to be a community still dominated by 'the [Yattendon] Estate' to an unusual extent. That is why I noted which of the obituaries recorded some connection with the Estate (including all those who had worked for either the Waterhouse or Iliffe families elsewhere). It is a considerable proportion – twenty-eight per cent overall, thirty-five per cent of the men – and apparently it remained fairly constant during the century – despite the general decline in agricultural and 'personal' employment. I think this is because in the first part of the century there were a number of local establishments employing men and women in farm, woodland and house. There was Sir Cameron Gull's estate based on Frilsham House (later a prep school, then demolished with the coming of the M4) with its Home Farm, and there were manor houses and manor farms in both Yattendon and Frilsham. Others are recorded as working for farmers on Birch Farm, Magpie and Coombe Farms, Parsonage Farm and the Barr's Farm in Frilsham, Everington and Calvesleys Farms in Yattendon.

National events were catalysts for change, especially the two world wars. They also had a big impact on many individual lives, and wartime experiences are separately recorded in more than half the obituaries – including one man in the Boer War. Thirty-five men and four women had First World War experiences recorded. Eleven men were gassed or wounded in the First World War, but only one was a prisoner of war. The Royal Berks Regiment was the natural route into the army though fifteen joined other parts of the army and other services, including the navy, and one the veterinary corps and another as a farrier. Eleven

1965. '**Amy Winkett** aged 89 ... [had] spent half a century here ... in the service of Miss F. E. Waterhouse ... organiser, disciplinarian, protector of her mistress ... her splendid alto voice carried the choir ... viola player in the orchestra which Miss Waterhouse formed ...'.

1972. **Cicely Maggs**. Head teacher of Frilsham School 1938–61. 'Played her part in village affairs with particular enthusiasm and selflessness'.

1960. **1st Baron Iliffe of Yattendon**, newspaper magnate, but also 'to many of us he was employer, to most of us he was our landlord, to all of us he was our friend'.

1996. **2nd Lord Iliffe** 'most generous in helping the village...it was sometimes said that Yattendon lived in a time warp, but this was never Lord Iliffe's idea.'

1960. **Frank Wheatcroft** [aged 99] 'In 1902 came to Frilsham and took [a] small holding...later worked on Sir Cameron Gull's estate.

1962. **Bill Burnham** 'our saddler and (rather reluctant) cobbler for sixty-one years ... During the First Word War he served in the Sappers and must have been a useful member even of that versatile corps.'

are specifically recorded as going abroad, mostly to the killing fields of France and Flanders. One woman worked in a munitions factory and one in the Red Cross, and two were widowed.

1997. **Mrs Cool** 'did voluntary work ... during the war when Frilsham House became a convalescent home ... mending clothes for the soldiers.' [She had first come there in 1926 with her gardener husband].

Local women played a bigger part in the Second World War. Twenty were involved in the 'Home Front', some at Bletchley Park and in other intelligence work, some in munitions factories and as land girls, while others either took in evacuees or were themselves 'evacuees'. Eight were nursing (VAD, Red Cross etc) and two were in the Forces.

1969. **General Sir Miles Dempsey** ... gassed and wounded in WWI ... Commander of 2nd Army on D Day (WWII) ... then C in C Middle East. But 'walked so quietly along our lanes ... as if anxious not to incommode so much as a dandelion'.

The Second World War also involved many more of the men in these obituaries (66), at every level from Commander in Chief Middle East to handyman to the Red Cross and petrol pump attendant for the US forces. Thirty-one were in the armed forces, twenty-four went abroad, not only to Europe but also to North Africa and the Far East. Seven were taken prisoners of war, though none was wounded. (Seven had been killed.) Twenty-five worked on the 'Home Front' on ammunitions dumps and factories, and the local aerodromes, or served in the Home Guard and Air Raid Precautions Service (ARP).

Ten men were involved in both world wars.

The lives of these men and women was by no means only work and war service. Naturally parish magazine obituaries celebrate contributions to village life, but even so, nothing at all is recorded of over half (52%) of them, sometimes specifically reporting that he/she was 'not a joiner', 'a very private person'. They contrast with at least two described as 'a very good village man'.

1964. **Vincent Taylor** was Frilsham churchwarden for 24 years. 'Nothing deterred him from the worship of his creator Sunday by Sunday.'

Eighty people (twenty-one per cent) were involved in the religious life – the majority with the two parish churches. Of the rest fourteen attended the (Primitive) Methodist chapel, and two were Quakers, two Roman Catholics and one a Christian Scientist. Activities and responsibilities round the parish churches involved twenty-one in the Mothers' Union, eleven in practical work such as maintaining the churchyards, eleven as church-warden, ten as bell ringers, and eight in the choir. Tribute was often paid to faith, devotion and practical Christianity.

1960. **Frank Stephenson**. Electrician, 'chorister and bellringer, cricketer and tennis player, Special Constable, secretary, treasurer, committee man ... active, eager ... charm ...'

The next largest group of community activities was the local clubs. Their rise and fall could be traced through their reports in *The Broadsheet*. Membership, and often office, was recorded in the obituaries as follows:

Friendship Club (for the elderly)	20
Women's Institute	19
British Legion	13
Men's Club	7
Drama groups	7

1997. **Reg Wheeler** [with his wife] 'ran the Youth Club for 20 years … [He] was a first class sportsman', especially football – manager of Frilsham Sunday Side.

Social Club	3
Youth Club (in leadership roles)	3

Participation in the villages' sporting life tended to be in the distant past of those who had obituaries, but contributions to the clubs were recorded:

Cricket	7
Football	4
Badminton	1

1996. **Katherine Blandford** was a district councillor, also Women's Institute, and she ran fortnightly working parties, largely to raise money for the Frilsham Clubroom. She took 'great pleasure in the domestic arts'.

Others contributed more as citizens. Twelve were parish, district or county councillors, and five school managers. Five were involved in political parties or trades unions (agricultural workers). One was a JP and two were special constables.

Typical local contributions were to the maintenance of the Village Hall and Club Room (eleven), *The Broadsheet* (eleven), the Fete and Management Committees (nine) and National Savings, the allotments and 'Dig for Victory'.

2000. **Sir Peter Hudson**, Secretary General to the Order of St John, Deputy Lieutenant of Berkshire, Lieutenant of the Tower of London etc.

Others played their part on a wider stage, in the Royal Institute of British Architects, Royal College of Music, Royal Watercolour Society, Lawn Tennis Association, Shakespeare Museum, Sea Scouts, Lifeboats etc., and as Deputy Lord Lieutenant or High Sheriff of Berkshire.

On a more modest, but probably no less costly or valuable, scale, a high proportion of the obituaries pay tribute to the support of neighbours in illness and old age.

1996. **George Ralph**, head cowman, then charge hand at Harwell AERE. 'His favourite pursuit, gardening': his garden 'gave pleasure to countless passers by'.

Finally: play. A great variety of hobbies and pastimes were recorded in more than half the tributes, dominated by gardening. Eighty men and women – over one in five of the total sample – were reported to have loved their gardens, sometimes as specialists and prize-winners.

1976. **Arthur Hancock**, aged 92 – cowman, carrier, smallholder devoted to Burnt Hill Chapel and Common, 'a man of the common'.

The next most popular pastimes were needlework (thirty-one) animals and birds (twenty-nine) and music (twenty-nine). What a peaceful rural idyll – reinforced by the many tributes to 'a true countryman/woman' alongside the 'good village men'. They are followed by cricketers (twenty-one) and footballers (fourteen), drama (thirteen) and racing (nine) enthusiasts, book readers (twelve) and walkers (nine), bridge and whist players (ten), craftsmen in iron and wood (nine). Smaller numbers were involved in painting, tennis, wild life, cooking, flower arranging, dancing, parties, snooker and darts, hunting and shooting, cars and history.

Population

The census figures show that Yattendon remained small throughout the century, but was overtaken by Frilsham after the Second World War when the council houses were built there, creating a centre of population independent of the Estate. A number of obituaries record the establishment of local young families in these new houses.

	Yattendon	Frilsham	Total
1921	283	233	516
1961	265	288	553
1991	288	317	605

After 100 years the individual census records will be available, with detailed snapshots of the families and occupations of those living in the two villages – confirming or modifying the picture from the obituaries. But only the latter tell of their life histories, their community and leisure activities.

It is striking how varied were their lives and interests. Wars and cars (by 1991 eighty-five per cent of households had a car) brought huge changes, but strong strands of continuity also persisted. Throughout the century those who had been successful elsewhere were attracted to this village life, while many others continued to live and work within the community with which they already had strong ties. Farms and woods always provided the context within which hard work and solitary enthusiasms flourished alongside family life, neighbourliness and the waxing and waning of a wide variety of community activities.

1976. **'Albert ('Rowley')
Barr** ... was born at the
Pot Kiln ... worked for his
uncle Tom at the brick kiln
... the War ... lorry driver
on local airfields ... [then]
Harwell [Atomic Energy
Research Establishment]
until he retired ... All this
time living at the Pot Kiln
... helping ... in the pub
as necessary but happier in
the garden.... A natural
games player ... football ...
billiards ... darts'.

Appendix 1: Analysis of Broadsheet obituaries 1956–2000

	1956–1960	1961–1970	1971–1980	1981–1990	1991–2000	total or overall average
number of obituaries	39	80	81	84	89	373
average per year	8.7	8	8.1	8.4	9	8.4
men	25	42	42	47	43	199
married men	4	23 (3 twice)	27 (1 twice)	16 (1 twice)	29 (1 twice)	99
single men		2	4	1	1	8
women	14	38	39	37	46	174
married women	7	27	26 (1 twice)	21	25	106
single women	1	8	6	3	5	23
average no. of years spent in Yattendon/Frilsham*	34	32	36	33	43	36
people connected to the Estate						
men	9	15	14	17	14	69
as %	36%	36%	33%	36%	33%	35%
women	2	5	10	4	14	35
as %	14%	13%	26%	11%	30%	20%
estate connections as % for time period	28%	25%	30%	25%	31%	28%

*ranges from 1 to 92 years

Kinship
219 surnames were recorded
131 only once
56 twice
16 three times
11 four times (Butler, Caesar, Iliffe, James, Print, Palmer, Pilkington, Pizzey, Taylor, Toms, Wakefield)
1 five times (Loader)
4 six or more times (Wyatt, Waterhouse, Pocock, Barr)

Appendix 2: Analysis of Broadsheet obituaries by occupation

	1956–1960			1961–1970			1971–1980			1981–1990			1991–2000			total		
	m	w	s	m	w	s	m	w	s	m	w	s	m	w	s	m	w	s
no occupation recorded	6	6		4	11		2	3		3	8		2	5		17	33	
agriculture *farmers, farmwork, forestry, gamekeepers*	9	1		15	3	7	16	2	8	13		4	17	1	6	70	7	25
left agriculture	1			5			6			4			10			26		
moved to agriculture	1			2			4									7		
in service *cooks, housekeepers, cleaners, grooms, chauffeurs*	1	1		4	5	1	5	6	1	1	9		2	15		13	36	2
gardeners	3		1	8		3	8		1	6		1	3		2	28		8
building trade	2			3			8		1	6			6			25		1
public services *local and national*				2			6	3		4	1		7		1	19	4	1
tradesmen*	1			4		1	4	1		2	1		6			17	2	1
shopkeeping *including post office*	1				1			1	1	2	4	1	5	2		8	8	2
business *including 3 people in the newspaper industry*	2			1			3		1	4		1	3	3	3	13	3	5
factory work	2			1	1		3			1	1		3			10	2	
teaching				1	1		2	4	1	2	1			1		5	7	1
drivers *HGV, chauffeurs, taximan, coaches, etc. (1 started as a coachman)*				5		1	1			2			3	1		11	1	1
armed services *including Indian army*	3			2		1	2			3		1	1		1	11		3
arts *writers, artists, actors, film industry*				1	2	1	1			2	1	1	1	1		5	4	2
medical *doctors, nurses*	1	1		1	1	1		1			1			4		2	8	1
publicans	1	2		1			3			1			1	1		7	3	
other professions *legal, architects, etc.*			1				2			3			2			7		1
accountancy/clerical					1		1	2		3	1					4	4	
colonial service	1			1			1		1			1	1			4		2
clergy							1		1	2			1		1	4		2
total occupations recorded	28	5	4	51	16	14	68	27	16	62	25	10	64	32	17	313	122	58

*tradesmen

3 engineers, 1 telephone engineer, 1 lift engineer, 3 blacksmiths, 2 cobblers, 1 hurdlemaker, chimney sweep, carrier, butcher, fitter/turner, clock repairer, 2 dressmakers

abbreviations

m *men*
w *women*
s *spouses*

spouses

spouses were counted to 'place' women who had no occupation of their own – there is some duplication with the other men

Appendix 3: Analysis of Broadsheet obituaries by recorded war experience

	1956–1960			1961–1970			1971–1980			1981–1990			1991–2000			total		
	m	w	s	m	w	s	m	w	s	m	w	s	m	w	s	m	w	s
Boer War				1												1		
First World War	3	2		12	1		15			3	1		2	1		35	5	
prisoners of war							1									1		
gassed/wounded				3			5									8		
abroad (including forces)	1			4			5			1			2			13		
Royal Berkshire Regiment				2			4						1			7		
navy/marines	3						1									4		
other armed forces including Vet corps				4			4			2			1			11		
widowed					1									1			2	
munitions factory																	1	
Red Cross																		1 (not specified)
Second World War	6			13	3		11	8		21	9	1	21	14		72	36	1
prisoners of war							1	1		2		1	2			7		
abroad (including forces)	2			3			1			7	1		11			24	1	
armed forces	4			4			5			8			11	2		32	2	
'Home front' including Bletchley Park and 5 land girls	1			5	1		5	5		8	5		7	8		26	19	
nursing/Red Cross					2			2			3			4			11	
in both world wars	1			2			4			2			1			10		

abbreviations
m *men*
w *women*
s *spouses*

spouses
spouses were counted to 'place' women who had no occupation of their own – there is some duplication with the other men

The Place

10 How the Land was Formed: The Geomorphology of the Pang Valley

John Downes

The River Pang and its tributaries drain a catchment area of some 136 square kilometres of the Berkshire Downs and adjacent lowlands. The catchment is illustrated on the map.

One branch of the river rises near to the village of East Ilsley and a second branch rises to the north of Compton. The branches unite in Compton and then flow south across the dip slope of the chalk downs through Hampstead Norreys and Frilsham. The sources are explored in more detail in Linnet McMahon's essay *The Sources of the River*.

The *dip slope* is so called because it mirrors the slope of the underlying chalk strata which dips gently to the south. The chalk is a permeable rock since it allows water to percolate down to the underlying water table. Where the water table reaches the surface, a *spring line* develops. In Anglo Saxon times, the site of scarp foot and dip slope springs attracted agricultural settlements such as Blewbury at the base of the steep chalk escarpment and Compton on the dip slope. This is more easily understood from the diagram.

The landscape is typically undulating open country reaching a height of 186 metres on Lowbury Hill three kilometres northwest of Compton. Hereabouts the plateau surface is much dissected by small *dry valleys* which are tributary to the River Pang. In winter some of these valleys will carry surface water and are called 'winterbournes', but for much of the year the water table is below the surface and the valleys are dry. However, it is clear from the general shape of these valleys that they have been cut by flowing water. One theory postulates a *periglacial* origin. The Pleistocene Period is the most recent geological period and

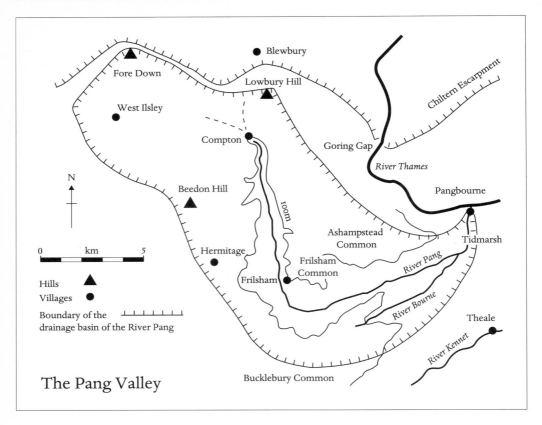

The Pang Valley

N

0   km   5

Hills ▲
Villages ●
Boundary of the
drainage basin of the River Pang

Blewbury
Fore Down
Lowbury Hill
West Ilsley
Compton
Goring Gap
River Thames
Chiltern Escarpment
Pangbourne
Beedon Hill
100m
Ashampstead
Common
Tidmarsh
Hermitage
Frilsham
Common
River Pang
Frilsham
River Bourne
Theale
River Kennet
Bucklebury Common

Based upon the Ordnance
Survey Map with the
permission of Her
Majesty's Stationery
Office.
© Crown Copyright
MC100036335

started about 1.8 million years ago. It has had a history of Ice
Ages interspersed with warmer periods. At the onset of these
interglacials the ice cover dispersed but left the ground frozen to
a considerable depth. These permafrost conditions exist today in
places such as Alaska and Greenland. In these conditions meltwater would have been unable to infiltrate through the chalk. As
a result, streams would flow across the surface and cut their valleys into the chalk. As the climate subsequently became warmer
the chalk became defrosted and water began to seep through the
rock and the water table was lowered leaving most of the upper
valleys dry. Another idea relating to the origin of dry valleys is
based on the concept of *scarp recession*. The chalk scarp would
have previously been at a higher level to the north of its present
position – this is again illustrated in the diagram – but as erosion
gradually cut back the scarp, the water table was lowered and
the surface water disappeared.

The main valley of the River Pang can be outlined by the
hundred metre contour as shown on the map. At the head of the
valley there is a shallow *col* or low area in the crest of the scarp
and this was formerly used by the Newbury–Didcot railway to
reduce the gradients to the north of Compton.

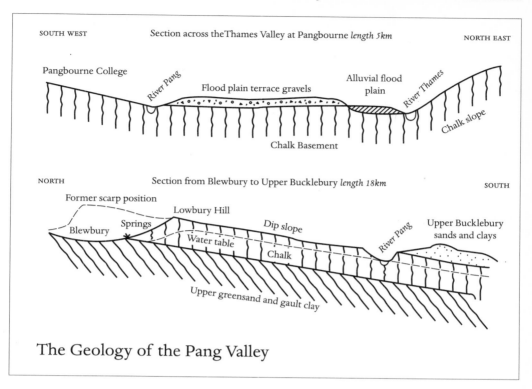

SOUTH WEST Section across the Thames Valley at Pangbourne *length 5km* **NORTH EAST**

Pangbourne College

River Pang

Flood plain terrace gravels

Alluvial flood plain

River Thames

Chalk slope

Chalk Basement

NORTH Section from Blewbury to Upper Bucklebury *length 18km* **SOUTH**

Former scarp position

Lowbury Hill

Springs

Blewbury

Dip slope

Water table

Chalk

River Pang

Upper Bucklebury sands and clays

Upper greensand and gault clay

The Geology of the Pang Valley

The higher land is formed of the Upper Chalk which contains layers of *flint nodules*. The origin of these flints contrasts markedly with that of the chalk. The chalk was formed of calcium carbonate deposited in the Upper Cretaceous period 100–70 million years ago by the deposition of microscopic coccoliths from suspension in relatively deep seas beyond the continental shelf. Coccoliths are the minute skeletal plates of tiny marine algae which accumulated as a carbonate rich mud on the sea floor and were converted to chalk by being buried under thick layers of deposits and subjected to massive pressures over immense lengths of time.

On the other hand, the flints are formed from silica rich water percolating through the chalk along the bedding planes after the chalk had compacted and depositing silica on the inside of hollows left by decayed organic matter. This is why so many flint nodules take the form of plants, *echinoids*, shark's teeth etc. The silica in the water was derived largely from sponge spicules (skeletons) or from sandy beds *overlying* the chalk.

There are also patches of *clay with flints* on the chalk surface. This material is a residual superficial deposit resulting from the chemical weathering of the chalk which leaves insoluble clay minerals and flints forming an impermeable covering to the chalk. This deposit is usually very acid in stark contrast to the alkaline chalk below it and has caused problems for farmers throughout history. The problem was solved by digging pits through the clay and spreading and mixing the alkaline chalk with the acid clay to reduce its acidity and thus produce a fertile soil. This is the origin of the pits common in most woods and fields in the area. On the lower slopes of some of the dry valleys *solifluction* deposits can be seen. These are accumulations of calcareous (chalky) mud which slid down the steeper slopes at the end of the Ice Age when meltwater lubricated the surface material and caused it to slide over the still frozen sub soil.

South of the M4 motorway the valley widens out as the river turns eastwards across its developing floodplain. Here the geology and the landscape change considerably as clays and sands of the *Reading Beds* form the low hills on either side of the alluvial flood plain. Woodland and heathland cover an arc of high ground extending from Hermitage through Upper Bucklebury around to Chapel Row and Bradfield Southend on the south side of the river; and to the north, similar wooded hills occur on Frilsham Common, Burnt Hill and Ashampstead Common. Ancient woods and heaths usually survive where the land was considered as unfit for anything else and these soils are usually less than fertile.

The Reading Beds were deposited during the Palaeocene 65–58 million years ago. They overlie the chalk and are therefore younger and appear to have been deposited by rivers meandering across marshy mudflats producing a wide variety of clays and sands.

About three kilometres downstream from Bradfield there is a sharp right angle bend in the river which then flows north through Tidmarsh to join the Thames at Pangbourne. Interestingly this part of the river may formerly have flowed south to join the Kennet at Theale since the low ground now followed by the M4 embankment may well indicate an earlier outlet. However the more powerful Thames has clearly cut a deeper channel than the Kennet and subsequently diverted the Pang into its own catchment. The valley below Tidmarsh is floored with the *flood plain terrace gravels* which extend along the Thames valley on either side of the present flood plain. These river terraces gravels were formed during the warmer interglacial period which followed the Anglian glaciation (400 000 years ago). During this time the proto Thames had been forced to cut a more southerly course, approximating to the present route, by ice sheets from the north extending down to the edge of the Chilterns. It is significant that with the increase in flow during interglaicial times, the rivers were able to cut down relatively rapidly, as for example in the Goring Gap where the Thames breaches the Chiltern barrier and cuts a deep gorge. With increased downcutting the old flood plain of the Thames has been left as river terraces above the present river level and such terraces extend into tributary valleys like the Pang. This is illustrated on the diagram.

This complex pattern of rocks and soils has had a marked effect not only on the wildlife of the valley but also on the patterns of settlement and industry. For example, until recent times settlement was sparser at the head of the valley on the chalk because of the shortage of water, but the chalky soils have proved ideal for the production of cereals as long as they can be well fertilised. The clays and sands have decided the location of the brick and pottery industries and the wider wetter alluvial floodplains have provided grazing for cattle. The less fertile edges of the valley were left to woods and heaths which produced the woodland products so necessary to pre-industrial farming. These aspects will be explored in greater detail in other essays, but the underlying geology essentially controls the soils, vegetation and land use!

11 The Sources of the Pang in and around the Parish of Compton

Linnet McMahon

Pang valley above Hampstead Norreys

This essay has been adapted with updating from *The Story of Compton: a Berkshire Downland Village*, by Linnet McMahon, with David Mankin, published by Compton Parish Council, 2000. Some of this material first appeared in Compton's parish magazine *Compilations*.

The River Pang rises in the parishes of East and West Ilsley, Blewbury and Compton, in the chalk country of the Berkshire Downs, which rise to 186 metres or so. The two separate streams meet in Compton, after which the Pang flows south down a wide valley towards Hampstead Norreys and on to Bucklebury. There it bends sharply east, through Stanford Dingley and Bradfield, and then north to meet the Thames at Pangbourne. This broad valley, which runs into Pangbourne from Calcot and Tidmarsh, now has an even smaller stream than the Pang but it may once have contained the River Kennet before it was 'captured' lower down the Thames. The Pang is probably named from Panga(n)burnan, the clear stream of Panga's people (Gelling 1976).

Like many chalk downland villages, Compton and the Ilsleys are situated on the spring line, the point at which the underground natural aquifers of the chalk reach the surface. In its upper reaches the Pang is a 'winterbourne' stream. This means that the springs run only when the water table rises to a certain level, which happens in the course of a wet winter. In 1844 Hewett wrote in his book *The History and Antiquities of the Hundred of Compton, Berks* 'it is only about once in six years that the springs burst forth from the chalk hills, and never till the Thames has been thrice flooded'. This observation is supported by well records of the past century which indicate that the ground water levels were high once every six to eight years. For some years the streams flowed for two or three months, if at all. However, the winter of 2000–01 was exceptionally wet and the streams ran from before Christmas until the following June.

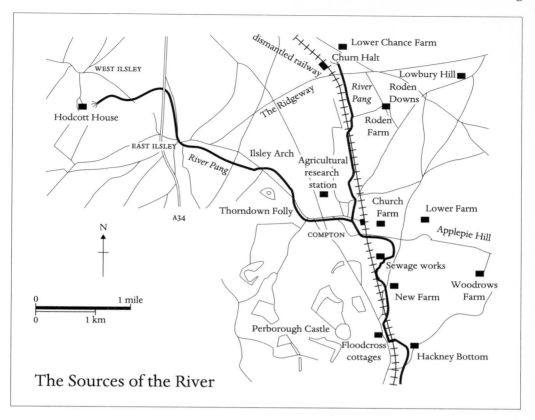

West Ilsley · Hodcott House · East Ilsley · River Pang · A34 · N · 0 1 mile · 0 1 km · The Ridgeway · Ilsley Arch · Thorndown Folly · dismantled railway · Lower Chance Farm · Churn Halt · River Pang · Lowbury Hill · Roden Downs · Roden Farm · Agricultural research station · Church Farm · Lower Farm · Applepie Hill · COMPTON · Sewage works · New Farm · Woodrows Farm · Perborough Castle · Floodcross cottages · Hackney Bottom

The Sources of the River

How the landscape was formed

This is covered in more detail in the essay on the geology of the valley, but for the sake of convenience a brief account is included here. The chalk of the Berkshire Downlands was laid down under the sea 100 million years ago in the Cretaceous period, and tilted up out of the sea by earth movements. The sea returned in the Paleocene-Eocene, sixty million years ago, to lay sand and clay sediments over the chalk. These sediments were later worn away, leaving only a few patches of clay, for example towards Aldworth (providing clay for the for Woodrows Roman pottery kilns), and sandstone 'sarsens', those brown stones often seen in fields, some of them large boulders like The Stones in the centre of Compton. In the Miocene period fifteen million years ago, the chalk was pushed up and folded by the ripples spreading outwards from the formation of the Alps. Over the ages some of the more exposed parts of the chalk weathered into clay with flints; for example the hilltops of Thorn Down, Perborough and Cheseridge. These were less easily worked and so often remained as hilltop woods.

The ice sheets of the last Ice Age, in the Pleistocene period a million years ago, did not get as far south as the Berkshire

Downland villages, but the melting water washed rocky material over the whole area. The wide Pang valley with its present tiny winterbourne stream may have been formed by a great river flowing out from higher ground in Oxfordshire (or even from a huge lake in the Vale of the While Horse) before the Thames cut through the Goring Gap. That there was a great river then is supported by the high level river terraces on either side of the valley, particularly clear just below the hill fort of Perborough Castle. The two arms of the upper Pang Valley now contain alluvial soil and gravel. Flint tools from the Middle Stone Age found in the extensive alluvial gravels at Churn, where the Pang now rises, are the earliest evidence of people living locally. The climate has varied considerably over the ages, with some warm dry periods (the Roman and early medieval centuries) and some very wet ones (late medieval times), and we again seem to be experiencing climatic change.

The western source of the Pang: from Hodcott to Compton

One source of the Pang is in West Ilsley at Hodcott, where springs rise when the water table reaches that level. Hodcott is the site of the medieval manorial village of Hodcott. Later the magnificent Hodcott House was built, it is said by Inigo Jones. The springs were said to rise under Hodcott House itself, perhaps one reason why it was demolished.

From Hodcott the stream flows east, crossing the road between the Ilsleys at the bottom of Windmill Hill, going under the A34 and coming into East Ilsley from the north. It flows where huge ponds sometimes appear in the fields by the slip road from the A34 (the old Abingdon road) – despite attempts to fill them in. The water continues underground, rising in wells, cellars and the village pond as the water table rises. East Ilsley was prone to flooding and piles for staging were put in so that people could continue about their business. From East Ilsley pond the Pang stream flows out through a clearly defined river bed (walk up Haydon's Lane from the pond to see this) and then disappears in the fields. It has reappeared from time to time as pools. For years we could only occasionally see the course of the stream, and it seemed hard to believe that anyone could canoe from the Ilsleys to Compton, as Mr Chapman of Woodrows Farm is reputed to have done many years ago. In the winter of 2000–01 the stream was continuous, flowing below Thorndown into a lake in an area which long ago had been a gravel pit. Waterfowl appeared; moorhens, coots and mallards raised large families, and shelduck and other rare species arrived. Mr Chapman's exploit became comprehensible, although the fences between fields prevented a similar journey.

The Pang flowing strongly west of Compton during the wet winter of 2000–01. © Greenaway

The Pang stream passes under the Ilsley – Compton road at the parish boundary, known as Ilsley Arch, or more simply Halfway. Compton Downs, the hillside above the stream, has a vast area of ancient fields as well as the site of the four Bronze Age Compton Cross Barrows. Again in the winter of 2000–01 there was another large pool here. The water flows through or under the fields to the Compton pumping station, the site of the former village gravel pit. When the gravel ceased to be worked the pit filled up with water. Ernest Golby, who kept the Compton post office, shop and bakery, remembered going there as a young-ster with his friend farmer Eric Stone. It was said that children used to swim there, but he said there was far too much duck-weed. The nearest to a swim Eric had was when his hat landed in the water and he went in to retrieve it!

Pumping on a large scale began at the end of 1965 when Thames Water, licensed to extract up to 13.6 million litres per day, began operations in Compton, supplying water as far as Wallingford and Didcot. This lowered the groundwater level and thus the flow of the Pang. A voluntary 'environmental' limit to abstraction of five million litres per day was agreed in 1991 when pumping at Gatehampton in Goring started to take over. Water from Compton now supplies Compton and East Ilsley villages and, via the Applepie Hill booster station, Aldworth (David Pike in *Compilations* 1994).

Compton flooding near
the church, 1915.

The western Pang stream in Compton village

Before entering Compton village the Pang crosses under the
road again and then runs beside it to the south, and then across
Mayfield. In 2000–01 the water formed lakes in the fields. It was
so deep in Mayfield that children could not get to school until
a pontoon bridge was erected; and then there was an accident
when a horse fell when crossing the bridge. It is said there was
always a pond with ducks in the Fair Field, entirely believable in
2000–01 as I watched the water flowing into and out of a huge
pond and across the road into the 'ditch'.

The stream goes behind some cottages and reappears by
Pilgrim Cottage, named for its link with the famous Compton
Pilgrims – one of the first and most successful rural friendly
societies; this cottage also held the earliest known school in the
village. At the foot of Newbury Lane the road is still liable to
flooding. A photograph taken before the war shows floods right

Photo taken by Mr Golby
of Compton floods in the
1930s near the Church.

across the road here by the Compton Gun, a trophy from the
First World War. In the village, the stream collects more water
from nearby springs, as well as some run-off from the Institute
of Animal Health. Some springs rise around Compton House and
the Dovecote, and run through old brick underground culverts to
the main stream. In Cheap Street, across from the Swan, was the
village Green and a stream-fed pond, the watering place for livestock until Enclosure in 1814.

The northern source of the Pang: from Churn to Compton village

Another branch of the Pang stream joins the stream from East
Ilsley at the ditch opposite Yew Tree House and Stables in
Compton. This stream has a source which lies in Churn Basin
in Blewbury parish some miles to the north near the Ridgeway.
Churn Basin, with its many tumuli or barrows, is not far from
Lowbury Hill and its Saxon barrow and Roman temple site.
When the springs are rising they can be seen literally bubbling
up into the field east of old Churn Halt railway station. In Anglo-
Saxon times the boundaries between big estates were described
in charters. The northern boundary of Compton is still the same

as it was when it was detailed in the Blewbury Charter in 944 AD (Gelling, 1976: 758–60). At the Ridgeway at Churn, south of Lower Chance Farm, lay 'the water channel at swine path's slough at the junction of ways' (flodan aet swin weges slo), a broad hollow, wet and muddy, as it often is still. In the winter of 2000–01 there were large pools north of the Ridgeway and a fast flowing stream crossed The Ridgeway itself.

Springs rising around Churn feed into the ditch or stream (flode) flowing south, parallel to the course of the old Southampton to Didcot branch of the Great Western Railway. The stream may have been a reason for the 'extensive, but ill-understood, Romano-British settlement' in the broad Slad valley (Fulford *et al.* 1994: 200), with its Roman cemetery (and skeletons in lead and wood coffins) on Roden Down above. There was almost certainly a Roman farm or villa in the area but the site has never been found, although there are finds which hint at its existence. The Pang flows eventually into Stocks Meadow, and into a pool which now appears only in the wettest years but may once have been more significant. Hewett in 1844 said 'when the old mere banks were levelled at the time of the enclosure of this manor, about thirty years ago, an immense number of Roman antiquities were discovered.' It is not clear, however, whether the 'mere' refers to the pool or to field boundaries.

Village springs, streams and the Great Pond in Compton.

The stream runs along ditches to the old Wallingford road, sometimes flowing across it so that people had to cross on duckboards. The Great Pond, now usually dry, in front of Roden House (medieval Stokes manor). was fed by springs which then ran to join the Pang stream in Rookery Meadow. In the 1940s 'the pond was reed-fringed and surrounded by pollarded willows where a nightingale sang throughout a spring night… A local basket maker used withies from this site' (P. D. M. in *Newbury Weekly News* 1989). 'Ralph at the Mill' probably lived near here in medieval times, with the water from the stream or the numerous springs driving a water mill. One of the eight Richard Smiths who were landowners in Compton in the sixteenth century lived 'at the Weyer' or weir. Hewett mentions a Weir Cottage still there in 1844 but the site is now under Meadow Crescent and Orchard House. When the springs are 'up', water bubbles up in the road and in the garden of Chestnut View, as well as in the pond, a sure sign to villagers to empty their cellars before they flood.

Memories of floods

Just before the northern stream joins the western Pang stream from East Ilsley there was a small pond at Yew Tree Stables, where Bessie Brown and the other children put studs in their shoes to slide better on the ice in winter.

The stream follows the road through East Compton. Children used to try and jump it, sometimes fell in, and then got caned at school. A villager remembers dipping her boot into the water in the ditch so that her mother thought the road was flooded and she could miss school. There was frogspawn every spring, and ducks where the stream bed widens in front of Church Farm Cottages. A 'duck frost' was cold and wet! The road here was regularly flooded. Along School Road the floods were sometimes so deep that children could not get to school. The flooding would go under the railway bridge and all the way along the road past the church and a little thatched cottage, towards the foot of Applepie Hill. The floods could last six or seven weeks and people used to go over Compton station footbridge, cross Church Meadow (a deserted medieval village), and cut through the churchyard to avoid them. Duckboards were put up, and the bus had to be re-routed. For many years the floods disappeared but, after some years of low levels, the water table rose again in the 1990s. It is hard to know how much difference the abstraction of water at the pumping station, more limited in recent years, has made, and how much is due to climate change.

The floods of the winter of 2000–01

However, in the winter of 2000–01 the floods returned. Water flowed fast down the Ilsley road, ripping up sections of road and pavement. For a while even the middle of the village, opposite Compton Manor, was flooded despite the deep ditch here. One low-lying house was inundated and many people were anxiously watching the water rising high in their cellars.

School Road was deep in running water and a little bridge was constructed so that children could reach the primary school. Aldworth Road up to and beyond the church was closed to traffic all winter because the water was so deep, in places well over the tops of your wellies! There was subsidence in the churchyard and some of the graves became unsafe. After the water went down in June, the rest of 2001 saw extensive deepening of ditches and clearing and enlarging culverts throughout the village. Owners of river bank properties were reminded of their responsibilites for maintenance, an echo of 1654 when 'tenants were presented for failure to scour the ditches in Great Meade and Bartons Close' (Brooks, 1982: 57).

The Pang from Compton village to Flood Cross Cottage

At Chaubury Cottage the stream turns sharply south. The soil here is rich alluvial which may have been why the field was once the Hop Garden. Further down are flat meadows once known as Upper and Lower Bowling Alley where the stream meanders gently. Nowadays the stream bed goes to the sewage works, with the remains of a bridge where the footpath crosses the stream. In 2000–01 the meadows were inundated and quite impassable.

Below the sewage works the water flows all year round, going first into the lovely wild garden at Apple Tree Cottage and then through Pond Meadow by New Farm, where the public footpath allows you to walk by the stream. Where the river meandered close by her cottage 'Granny H as a girl gathered watercress for her Sunday tea' (P. D. M. in *Newbury Weekly News* 1989). Brooklime and forget-me-nots grow here, and so does celery-leaved crowfoot, but the watercress has gone. The pond here reappeared in 2000 and 2001, with moorhens dabbling and house martins swooping over it.

The Pang flows on south, joined by streams and springs below Perborough Castle. The valley is very broad here and a sharp turn of slope quite high up reveals the old river terrace. Perborough is a fine Iron Age hill fort, with ancient field systems still clearly visible on Cow Down. From Perborough you can look east across the Pang Valley to the site of the Roman pottery above New Farm. Below Perborough more springs rise in wet years and join the main stream. The Pang reaches the parish boundary at the well-named Flood Cross Cottage, and flows on into Hampstead Norreys.

References

Brooks, J., 'The Deserted Medieval Villages of Northwest Berkshire', PhD thesis, University of Reading (1982)

Fulford, M. *et al*, 'Lowbury Hill, Oxon: a reassessment of the probable Romano-Celtic temple and the Anglo-Saxon barrow'. *Archaeological Journal* 151: 158–211 (1994)

Gelling M., *The Place Names of Berkshire parts 1–3*. The English Place Name Society (1973–76)

Hewett, William, *The History and Antiquities of the Hundred of Compton, Berks*. Reading: John Snare (1844)

PDM, *Newbury Weekly News* (1989)

12 Watermills on the River Pang

Dorcas Ward

Recent experience of flood waters racing down the straighter and narrower stretches of the Pang reminds us that for a thousand years it was an important source of power for the villages in the valley.

By the eleventh century – in 1086 – the *Domesday Book* already recorded nine water mills, some of which may have been ancient even then:

In Yattendon 'a mill worth 5 shillings'
  (probably near Everington barn)
In Frilsham 'a mill worth 4 shillings'
In Bucklebury 'a mill worth 4 shillings'
In Stanford Dingley 'a mill worth 12 shillings'
In Bradfield 'three mills worth 53 shillings'
  (probably one mill with three sets of millstones)
In Pangbourne 'a mill worth 10 shillings' and 'a mill worth
  20 shillings' (though one or even both of these may
  have been powered by the Thames)

There is also some evidence of a watermill even further upstream at Compton in medieval times.

The mill at Tidmarsh (between Bradfield and Pangbourne) is also later. It was established in 1329 for Reading Abbey and was worth 30 shillings.

It is noticeable that the mills became more valuable further downstream. Their main purpose was to grind corn, probably wheat and rye (for bread) and malted barley (for ale). In the west of England, Wales and Scotland, in places where it was too wet to grow wheat, local mills were primarily for oats for porridge and oat cakes.

In the early middle ages, when transport was very limited
and populations rising, village water mills were crucial to local
peasants and farmers for getting their corn ground. Where water-
power was not available corn had to be ground by hand on stone
querns until windmills were introduced. It is thought that this
technology was brought to Britain by soldiers returning from the
Crusades who would have seen windmills in action in the eastern
Mediterranean. Windmills were common on the heights above
the valley and examples are recorded at East Ilsley and Compton
on the Downs and at Yattendon.

The water mill was a considerable capital investment,
requiring civil engineering to divert and control the water, as well
as the wooden waterwheels and stone grindstones, and the racks
and pinions which linked them. Mills were monopolies, a fruitful
source of income to their owners who had the right of 'sokage'
and could insist that their tenants used their mill – an unpopular
power, usually attached to the lord of the manor, who might, as
in Tidmarsh, be the abbot of a monastery. The miller seems to
have been a salaried servant (certainly for monasteries). He held
back a proportion of all the flour or meal he ground, and was
traditionally unpopular as a kind of tax collector. There are many
scurrilous folk tales and rhymes about dishonest millers.

After the decimation of the rural population by repeated
waves of the Black Death in the fourteenth century, many of the
smaller mills fell into disuse, but they revived under the Tudors
and Stuarts (sixteenth and seventeenth centuries), and the miller
rose in social status, as evidenced by the 'substantial and attractive' mill houses built from then on. The decline re-commenced
in the nineteenth century when harder, imported, wheat from
the 'New World' was ground in big industrial mills near the sea-
ports through which it was imported. Nineteenth century millers
must have resisted the Repeal of the Corn Laws as urgently as
the farmers and landowners, and were driven to attempt
'diversification'. Diversification sometimes had strange results.
New equipment was installed in Tidmarsh mill in an attempt to
boost output. When it was started up for the first time all the
first floor windows fell out of the mill building! Most water
mills ended their days as 'grist mills' grinding cereals for animal
fodder.

There are signs of all these trends affecting the Pang water
mills, although they were small and insignificant outside their
immediate localities – for instance in the 1830 *Commercial Directory
of Berkshire* none are mentioned, and in 1840 only the millers at
Tidmarsh and Pangbourne.

Today the remains of eight mills, usually the water wheel, but
also in many cases the mill race or pond, can be seen at Frilsham,

Frilsham Mill.
© Greenaway Collection

Bucklebury (three), Stanford Dingley, Bradfield, Tidmarsh and
Pangbourne. Except for the River Barn mill (Bucklebury) it can
be assumed that they are all on ancient sites, being within 250
metres of the village church. Both were central to medieval
village life.

In Frilsham, a water mill supplemented by a steam engine
operated well into the twentieth century. The last miller was
Miller Sparkes, who came to Frilsham in 1874, and died in 1915.
His grave is close to the mill. His daughter remained in the village till her death in 1956. The big grey brick nineteenth century
mill, part of the great re-building of the manor house and farm
from the 1850s, may have been just built when he came. There is
no miller mentioned in the 1841 and 1851 censuses, so the old mill
may have fallen into disuse, perhaps during a period of low water
in the Pang. In 1907 when it was offered for sale with the rest of
the Manor properties it had 'three pairs of stones'.

The 'new' mill has now been converted into flats, and the
gear removed, but the millpond, often graced by swans, can
still be clearly seen from the churchyard, and the sound of water
diverted over the weir still charms the ear when the stream is
high. Frilsham mill appears to have always been a corn mill,
and as late as the 1880s families from Frilsham Common were
taking their annual gleanings there to be ground into meal.

Between Frilsham and Bucklebury village the remains of a
water wheel made in Bucklebury Foundry in 1884 can still be
glimpsed through the high beech hedge at River Barn. This was a
small farm mill, and the wheel drove a chaff cutter, saw etc. until
about 1960. In 1963 it was one of a handful of Berkshire water
mills recommended for preservation.

In Bucklebury village a gaunt weed draped waterwheel still
adjoins the houses converted out of the old ironworks or foundry,

in which it was cast in 1875. It powered ventilation, such as forge
bellows and furnace fans, and other machinery until the foundry
closed in the 1950s.

A hundred yards downstream there are the substantial remains
of another small farm water mill, in an old wooden shed previously attached to a big black barn, often known as the Tithe
Barn, burnt down in 1998. The wide, iron, undershot, water
wheel is still connected to other wheels, including the main pit
wheel with wooden cogs driving the teeth of the 'stone nut'
attached to the shaft of the upper (runner) stone, still in place on
top of the fixed bedstone. The means of transferring power from
the vertically turning waterwheel to the horizontally turning mill-
stone is clear to the most un-mechanically minded. It had barely
changed since described by Vetruvius 2000 years earlier.

At Stanford Dingley the Pang still flows under and through
what is now Mill Cottage. The sound can be heard from the
wooden footbridge at the back, overlooking the mill race. This
must have been a prosperous mill long after Domesday, because
the nineteenth century Mill House just upstream is large and
imposing as well as gloomy!

Another industry at Stanford Dingley depending on the Pang
was the tannery which thrived in the middle of the nineteenth
century. The oak bark used in the process was probably crushed
in the mill. From 1841 to 1854 the Tan Yard was run by Sparke
Evans who presented a pair of benches for the green outside the
Bull. The fancy iron frames, in the form of branches, were probably wrought or cast at Bucklebury. The wooden seats have been
renewed several times since then.

Below the Kimberhead Springs (Blue Pool) the Pang is a more
substantial stream, which never runs dry. The mill remains at

Stanford Dingley Mill
in 2002.
© Greenaway Collection

The Mill at Bradfield.
© Rural History Centre
The University of Reading

The Mill Bradfield

Bradfield reflect this. The three storey brick mill in the centre of
the old village is preceded by a weir and handsome Victorian iron
sluice gate controlling the mill race, and water rushes through
the two exits from the mill. The mill, which 'was rebuilt in the
nineteenth century when it was enlarged from being a corn mill
to incorporate water pumping [from the nearby St Andrew's
Well, for the whole village] and a laundry', abuts a charming
eighteenth century mill house, with a lean-to extension for what
was a general store and post office in the 1940s. Was this the
home of 'R. Giles, baker, grocer and sub-postmaster, The Mill'
listed in the 1854 *Billings Directory*? Perhaps, because soon afterwards the squire built another mill manager's house behind the
mill in the same brick and flint style as the college buildings, with
a St Andrew's cross incorporated in the façade.

In the middle of the twentieth century the mill still housed
machinery owned by the Wessex Water Company connected with

pumping the water from the artesian wells nearby into the main water system, but it is now used as a store for Bradfield College.

In the 1870s Thomas Stevens, the then rector and squire, was already trying out additional uses for the water power. He used a nearby spring and perhaps the power of the Pang to manufacture soda water, which was 'clean and pure ... with ... plenty of prickle'. But it was not, apparently, a commercial success, though in 1895 a Herbert Jupiter 'mineral water manufacturer' lived close by in Tutts Clump, and 'I. C. E. Berg and Sons, mineral water manufacturers' were based in Stanford Dingley for several years after that.

Even more ambitious, but even less successful, was an 1874 project to form a new limited company – British and Foreign Frozen Meat Co. – to be directed by the indefatigable rector, though he couldn't legally be shareholder – to use the Pang to power a refrigerating plant. Four tons of machinery were installed in the old mill, and the rector's son wrote that even though 'the chemicals have not come ... there's the most tremendous draught, and the fan goes round 5000 times a minute and makes a row like a thrashing machine. There's a good deal of leakage of air along the pipe at present... that has to be remedied ... if that old thermometer will only go down it will be settled.' But it didn't. After six months, the rector noted sadly that 'the machine has not produced good results as yet and I am not pressing on with more tinkering'.

There was once a mill on the Maidenhatch Brook, just above its junction with the Pang, a mile downstream from Bradfield, but it has long since vanished without trace.

The mill at Tidmarsh, was closed in 1937, a mere six hundred years after it was built, but the wheel and mill gear were restored as an internal feature in the attractive old, but much extended, Mill House (which was the home of Maynard Keynes and Dora Carrington for a few years in the 1920s). Old millstones lean against the wall by the bridge.

For a short time around 1600 the mill was used for the dirty process of 'fulling' woollen cloth – washing out the excessive oil from the wool with fuller's earth and hammering the cloth with water driven hammers to felt and strengthen it.

In the Post Office Directory of 1847 J. Hammond (seven years earlier it was William Child) is listed as the miller, whereas no miller, only a 'baker and flour dealer' was listed in Pangbourne. But in 1888 the Tidmarsh mill was taken over by the successful Pangbourne miller Robert Stone.

The water mill at Pangbourne no longer exists, only the attractive wisteria covered Mill House behind the Cross Keys, and the mill cottage, and some buildings taken over by the Reading Waterworks in 1929 as a pumping station. They demolished the

Tidmarsh Mill.
© Rural History Centre
The University of Reading

Tidmarsh Mill 2001.
© Greenaway Collection

old three storied mill, and most of the other buildings – 'a granary, cart shed, stabling, coachhouse, loading room, wheat room and fowl house'. Thames Water now own the site and there is a training room in the 'new' building over the mill stream, which meets the main course of the Pang just below Somerfield's car park. Corn milling in a new, steam then electric, mill by the railway was continued by Percy Stone up to 1971, mostly for animal feed.

It was Percy Stone's grandfather Robert who took over the tenancy of the mill at Pangbourne in January 1871. It had to be in the name of his father, a chair manufacturer, because he was still only 19. But he had almost completed his four year apprenticeship at one of the two mills in High Wycombe. Extracts from his diary of this period have been published and are full of fascinating social and technical detail.

His mill was 'a trading mill with two waterwheels and four pairs of millstones' – separately for wheat and barley. At first he bought his grain from the miller at Mapledurham, who had it shipped from London in barges, and later from the Reading and London Corn Exchanges. No longer did the local farmers provide the wheat for good bread making flour, and he does not record grinding the gleanings of local families like the miller at Frilsham. But he 'had to find his outlets among the [local] bakers', which was slow going to begin with, but by October of the first year he was selling about twenty sacks of flour a week, and 50 of grist (meal for animals). Sometimes he had to 'hunt for his money' and walked miles to do so!

He spent a great deal of time mending and maintaining his mill and its machinery. Not only did the barley and wheat millstones themselves require regular 'dressing', which often took all day, and periodic 'furrowing', to maintain the grinding surface, but the wooden framework was also in poor condition when he took over, so carpentry work was also required, and a new 'gate' for the waterwheel. Sometimes millwrights were required for more specialist work, such as installing an extra pair of wheat stones. One day 'whilst flour dressing in the mill an old post gave way causing the crown wheel to strip all her cogs, 100 in number' and on another a 'nutt' got in the dressing machine and bursted it…damage £5', so he had to get twenty sacks of flour dressed at Tidmarsh Mill.

Although this energetic young miller must have represented competition with other local millers there seems to have been considerable co-operation as well. One June evening in 1871, after working in the mill from 8 a.m. till 6 p.m. he 'went to Mr Lintott at Tidmarsh Mill, then [across the Thames] to Mr Shelton's Whitchurch Mill and afterwards to Mr Wooster at Mapledurham. [And] walked back to Pangbourne at 11 o'clock'. In those early days Mr Wooster at Mapledurham was a real friend and mentor.

Soon Robert became more established and ambitious. He made improvements and additions to the mill, as well as building a henhouse and pigsty. In October 1873 he married to his boyhood sweetheart and they began planning improvements to the mill house into which they finally moved in 1877. His staff, which fluctuated according to the workload and seasons, included a miller, a carter, and an apprentice. At busy times the mill was often worked at night as well as by day. Sales increased to fifty-four sacks of flour some weeks, which became an average by 1879.

Over the years, despite the agricultural depression of the late 1870s and 1880s he built up a business to support his large family, and expanded to include the lease of Tidmarsh Mill. In 1894 he bought Pangbourne mill and finally died in 1918. He became a

great local character – the people's champion against high handed
authority, such as the rector who locked the graveyard, or the
authorities who closed a local toll road. Then he led direct action
with appropriate tools. Another story told of him concerns a
group of labourers mowing hay in the meadow alongside
Tidmarsh Mill while the mill staff were unloading the massive
two hundredweight (approximately 100 kilos) grain sacks from
a wagon into the mill. The usual chaffering was taking place
between the groups as to who had the hardest job. The smallest
of the mowers was challenged to carry one of the sacks and
agreed provided that if he could carry it home he could keep it.
Home was in Tilehurst several miles away up a very steep hill.
The challenge was accepted and he carried it home and kept it!
In Pangbourne at least the miller was no longer the bullying
profiteer portrayed in Chaucer and medieval folktales.

Sources (*most quoted)

* Kenward, Jean, *Percy Stone Ltd – a century of milling 1871–1971*
  Luckhurst, D., *Monastic Water Mills*
* Major, J. Kenneth, Watermills of Berkshire – *Berks Archaelogical Journal* (1963–4)
  Palmer, Felicity, *Frilsham and the Floyds, 1800–1900 – a century of change*, (1997)
  Philips, Daphne, *Berkshire, A County History*
* *Robert Stone – Miller of Pangbourne* – Diary, edited by J. Kenneth Major for
  The International Molinogical Society (1980)
  Sims, John, *Walking down the Pang* (1990)
* Unpublished Stevens family papers, see pp.64–5 of *Thomas Stevens* (1984)
* *Victoria County History of Berkshire* – translation of the Domesday records (1906)
  Vince, John, *Discovering Watermills* (1993)
  Vince, John, *Watermills and how they work* (1993)
  Wailes, Rex, *Windmills and Watermills – a source book* (1979)
  Warren, Peter, *Watermills* (Gazetteer only mentions 4 in Berks
    – none on Pang) (1989)
  Watts, Martin, *Corn Milling* (1983)

Directories

1830 and 1840 Commercial Directories of Berkshire
1847 Post Office Directory
1854 Billings Directory
1895, 1899 and 1915 Kelly's Directory

13 The Blue Pool

Dick Greenaway

The Blue Pool is a deep pond fed by the Kimberhead Springs.
It lies in the Pang flood plain just over half a kilometre downstream from Stanford Dingley and beside the bridleway which
runs alongside the river from Stanford Dingley to Bradfield. It
was once a place of pilgrimage and picnics with trimmed hedges
and mown grass. The owner made a small charge for entrance to
the area and many people made it the destination of their walks.
A plan has been proposed by the present owner to re-route the
footpath which passes through the farm so that it runs along the
western edge of the site and touches on the western pool. The
bank edge will be left open so that walkers can see the springs
and have views across the pool.

The pool gets its name from the startlingly blue colour of the
clear water. This is derived from the suspension of fine particles
of clay minerals in the groundwater. These cause light to be
defracted at the blue end of the spectrum. Algae growth adds
a blue-green tinge to the colour.

The springs are caused by the local geology of chalk with
overlying clay, and this can best be understood from the diagram.
Basically, chalk acts like a sponge. If you take a slab of sponge
and soak it with water the surface of water in the sponge will be
horizontal and will stay horizontal as the water drains from the
sponge. This surface is the water table. If you raise the edges of
the slab the water table will curve upwards and water will puddle
in the hollow. This is the mechanism which causes the springs to
flow at Kimberhead. The effect is enhanced by a layer of clay in
the valley bottom which concentrates the upward flow of water
at a break in the layer.

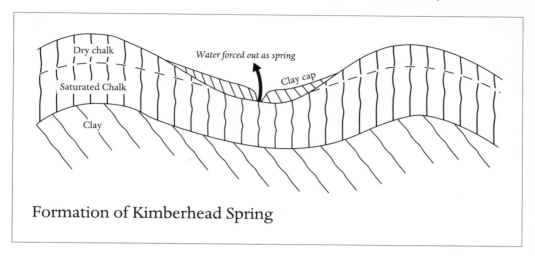

Dry chalk

Water forced out as spring

Saturated Chalk

Clay cap

Clay

Formation of Kimberhead Spring

The springs are the perennial head of the Pang. During the 1980s, and at other recorded times in history, the river dried up completely from Stanford Dingley upstream, but the springs at Kimberhead continued to flow and maintained a reduced flow down to the Thames. Even in normal times the springs contribute over fifty per cent of the flow of the river, supplying a steady 0.2 cubic metres per second. The lowest recorded flow was 0.086 cubic metres per second in July 1976 during one of the severest drought periods on record.

It seems strange that such a remarkable natural phenomenon should not have attracted attention in the past. One would have expected it to have attracted a settlement of some sort and perhaps a temple complex, but I have been unable to find any early references to either the springs or the pool. The Ordnance Survey notes the finding of 'Roman Remains' two hundred metres away in 1875 but the two earliest maps – Rocque's Survey of Berkshire (1761) and Pride's Survey of Berkshire (1791) – ignore the site altogether.

The Ordnance Survey first surveyed the area in 1831, but at a scale of 6 inches to the mile (1:10560) which does not allow much fine detail. However, it shows a short channel joining the Pang. The first really detailed survey of the area is the Tithe Award Map of 1847. These superb maps were drawn to allow the church's tithe, or one tenth of the increase of the land, to be changed from a payment in kind to cash payments; from every tenth lamb, or every tenth sheaf to its equivalent in money. They are, therefore, very detailed. The map for Bradfield Parish shows a small pool with a channel of the same width as the Pang flowing down past a farm complex. There is no sign of the watercress beds.

Thereafter the maps become larger scaled and more detailed.

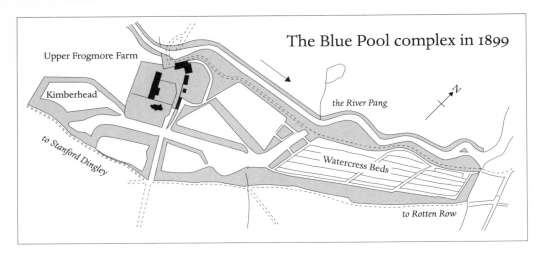

Upper Frogmore Farm

Kimberhead

to Stanford Dingley

The Blue Pool complex in 1899

the River Pang

Watercress Beds

to Rotten Row

With acknowledgement to
the Ordanance Survey.

By 1887 the farm is called 'Upper Frogmore Farm' and is
surrounded on two sides by large and elaborate ponds. It was
probably the excavation of these that uncovered the Roman
Remains. By 1899 the map shows the ponds extending downstream to the confluence with the Pang and labelled 'watercress
beds'. This seems to have been the culmination of the exploita-
tion of the site. The diagram shows how complex the site had
become.

To help increase the flow five or six narrow diameter boreholes
about eighteen feet deep were driven into the bed and these provide a strong additional flow to supplement the powerful natural
spring at the western end of the pool. There is a local tradition
that the narrow banks between the beds were reinforced with
animal bones and skulls from the abattoir at Bradfield! A watercress seller is mentioned in *Kelly's Directory* for Bradfield.

In the 1980s the owner of the site recognised that the water
in the pool became turbid after periods of heavy rain. He also
recognised that there was a delay of about sixteen hours between
the rainfall and the appearance of the turbidity. This was examined by hydro-geologists from Thames Water in 1988 and traced
to two natural swallow holes at Holly Lane and Tylers Lane
Bucklebury. These swallow holes are some five and a half kilometres to the west of the pool. Swallow holes are fissures in chalk
caused by rain water dissolving and enlarging small joints and
faults. Chalk is almost insoluble in pure water, but rain water
contains a small amount of dissolved carbon dioxide from the
air and is a weak carbonic acid. Over very long periods this acid
water percolating through small fissures in the chalk enlarges
them and may cause the surface to collapse into the hollow
forming a cone shaped depression which then concentrates
and increases the flow of water. In the case of the two polluting

swallow holes, one had filled with debris washed in during storms
and the other received water from Tylers Lane. The identity of
these swallow holes as the source of the turbidity was confirmed
by adding harmless flourescein dye to each. The dye was
observed in the Blue Pool some sixteen and a half hours later.
Attempts were made to divert flows away from the two swallow
hole complexes, but it is probable that other swallow holes are
also providing surface water to the pool. Another interesting
feature of the site are the algae which grow in the water. These
are *melosira varians* a type of algae that actually prefer cold water
and therefore flourish in the constantly cool water flowing from
the chalk which stays at 10 degrees Celsius regardless of the
weather.

Sadly, in 1987 Newbury District Council Environmental Health
Department pronounced the spring water unfit for watercress
growing as bacteria indicating faecal contamination had been
found in the pool at levels higher than EEC Drinking Water
Standards allowed. Since that date commercial watercress
production has stopped.

Attempts were made to trace the causes of the contamination.
It was thought that the sewer pipe which passes near the pool
might be leaking, but this was tested and found to be sound. A
wider study was carried out and the source of the pollution was
traced to the many farms and domestic septic tanks scattered
around the valley. Dairy farms and pig units were thought to be
the main culprits since the accepted practice for the disposal of
slurry was to dig a hole into the chalk and to pipe the waste into
the hole where it would soak away.

The National Rivers Authority and their successors The
Environment Agency worked closely with the farmers in the
valley to change this practice with considerable success.

E coli counts dropped from 7600 to 140 between 1989 and
1996 but this was still too high for commercial watercress
growing to restart. More recently, research by the present owner
of the site indicates that this low level is not constant. Regular
testing of the water at short intervals has shown that the count
can vary from almost negligible to extremely high over very short
periods. Research is being carried out to identify the causes of
this pollution.

Although the pool and watercress beds no longer have an
economic agricultural value they still have a very definite
environmental, historical and emotional value. The owners have
put forward plans to the Planning Authority for managing the
whole site and some of the neighbouring fields for the benefit
of wildlife. The plans include a considerable amount of work
intended to enhance the wildlife value of the site – particularly

the wetland aspects. Historically the Blue Pool has always been private land but it has been the custom of successive landowners and tenants to permit interested members of the public to visit the site. It is intended that this custom will be continued on a managed basis so that the Blue Pool does not disappear into folk memory but remains a loved and valued part of the valley's heritage.

Sources

Berkshire Record Office: Early maps

Hydrogeological Report on the Role of Swallow Holes in Feeding the Blue Pool, Stanford Dingley, Berks, Thames Water (1988)

Jessop, R., Kimberhead Springs & the Blue Pool, Stanford Dingley, Pang Valley Studies Bulletin No 6. (1979)

Johnson, John, and Moore, *Survey of the Plants and of the Abiotic Environment of the Blue Pool: a spring fed pool in the Pang Valley, Stanford Dingley, Berkshire,* British Museum (Natural History) London (1987)

Ower, J.S., *Pollution Prevention – a Study of Farming Practices in the Pang Valley,* National Rivers Authority (undated)

The Blue Pool – a personal postscript   by Dorcas Ward

In the nineteenth century the Blue Pool and surrounding land belonged to the Connop family at Bradfield Hall. An eccentric member of that family built the quaint *cottage ornée*, now known as Kimberhead or Upper Frogmore Farm, as a rustic retreat where – it is said – the water gave the illusion of being beside the sea.

However in the 1890s the Cannops began to sell their land and in 1892 my grandfather Thomas Stevens bought 'Frogmoor Farm' which was tenanted by a pessimistic farmer who had to make 'extra efforts ... to make the Frogmoor Farm Watercress Bed answer'. Nearly every year he complained about the poor market for watercress – so it may never have been a thriving project, despite the care taken to keep the clear water from the Blue Pool running evenly over clean gravel beds.

In 1898 the rest of the Bradfield Hall estate was sold, and Thomas Stevens bought land which included the Kimberhead Springs and the Blue Pool. He and his family sunk extra artesian pipes from which water bubbled to increase the supply of water to the cress beds. It remained in their ownership until the 1950s. In 1908 the tenancy was taken by Jim Emm, a watercress specialist from Wiltshire and Jim's son Edgar bought the land from the Stevens family. During the 1940s and '50s the watercress business appeared to flourish. There must be many local people who remember walking down in winter to watch Edgar in his waders cut and bundle up fat sixpenny bunches of watercress for market or for sale on the spot. Edgar Emm was succeeded by his son Jim who had to abandon cultivation of watercress, but who did not finally sell the farm, including the Blue Pool, until he retired in 2000.

Throughout this time the Blue Pool was an important 'tourist attraction', open to any member of the public who paid a nominal fee to the Emms, who maintained its banks, and sought to keep the surface weed at bay. The 1951 *Berkshire Book* waxed lyrical over the 'deep pool where the chalk below and the overhanging trees above combine to reflect in its translucent depths, hues of the deepest peacock blue to the palest azure, while the sand at the bottom is ceaselessly stirred by the springing waters.' A later edition speaks of 'the sandy bottom fuming with miniature volcanoes.' Year by year we have brought our friends and relations to admire and contemplate this scientific and poetic phenomenon, debating whether the apparently dimmer blue of recent years was due more to pollution or nostalgia. My last visit was with the widow of Thomas Stevens' grandson, also Thomas, to scatter his ashes into his beloved Blue Pool, a few weeks before Jim Emm left. History goes full cycle. The black and white 'cottage', the Blue Pool, and the farm is once again a part of Bradfield Hall.

14 Perborough Castle Cow Down, Compton

Andrew Payne

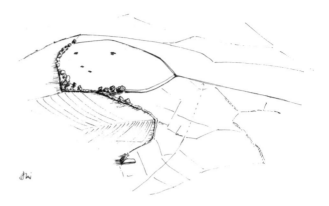

Andrew Payne is an archaelogist with English Heritage and has carried out many surveys of hill forts and other important sites.

Introduction

Perborough Castle in the parish of Compton is an oval hillfort defended by a simple bank and ditch enclosing an area of approximately six hectares. The site occupies the shoulder of a spur overlooking the wide valley of the upper Pang to the east at National Grid Reference SU 520780. The local geology consists of Cretaceous upper chalk overlain by shallow well-drained calcareous silty soils within which striped soil patterns occur. Around most of the circuit of the enclosure the earthwork defences now consist of a simple scarp sloping down from the interior. The defences are more pronounced or survive better along the northern side of the site where they cross the more level neck of the promontory on which the fort is situated. Here they consist of a bank, ditch and counterscarp (or secondary outer bank). The defences around the southern and western sides of the site have been largely ploughed out. There is an entrance on the northern side of the fort in the form of a simple gap in the banks and a causeway across the ditch. This gives access to the most level approach to the site and an adjacent well preserved system of ancient fields, trackways and linear boundary earthworks on Cow Down. Other entrances may not be recognisable because of the destruction of two thirds of the perimeter earthworks by ploughing. The interior of the earthwork was deep ploughed in the Second World War and has been cultivated fairly continuously since then (Wood and Hardy 1962).

Perborough Castle and
Cow Down from the Air.
© English Heritage

A geophysical survey of the hillfort interior was carried out in July 1996 as part of the Wessex Hillforts Survey – an extensive programme of non-intrusive survey of hillfort sites in central southern England undertaken by English Heritage and the Institute of Archaeology at Oxford (Payne *et al* 2002 forthcoming). The project was initiated in 1996 to answer a need for more wide-ranging data on hillfort interiors for the purposes of placing their future management on a sounder footing and enhancing knowledge of the internal character of the various forms of hillfort represented in Wessex. It was hoped that the combined results of the project would considerably extend academic understanding of the socio-economic role of hillforts in southern England during the first millennium BC thereby allowing a greater level of interpretation to be offered to visitors at those sites with public access. The primary methodology employed by the project was magnetometer survey (one of a range of geophysical techniques used in archaeology) supplemented by examination of aerial photographic evidence, documentary research and selective digital modelling of site micro-topography. The examination of each hillfort was to be as comprehensive as possible without resorting to more costly and unnecessarily destructive intrusive techniques.

Perborough Castle is the most easterly of the hillforts examined by the project and is an outlier of the grouping of hillforts linked by the Ridgeway running along the top of the northern escarpment of the extensive block of chalk upland between the Kennet and Thames river valleys. Beyond the limit of the study area, the line of hillforts is continued northwards across the Thames onto the chalk upland of the Chiltern Hills by two more sites at Blewburton Hill (Harding 1976) and Castle Hill, Little Wittenham (Payne 2002). In common with the majority of the forts in the Ridgeway group, Perborough Castle occupies a down-edge location. The neighbouring hillfort at Blewburton Hill was partially excavated between 1947 and 1953 by A. E. P. and F. J. Collins (for Reading Museum) and further limited excavation took place in 1967 sponsored by Reading Museum in collaboration with the University of Durham Department of Archaeology (Collins 1947; 1952; Collins and Collins 1959; Harding 1976). Our current knowledge of hillfort development on the Berkshire chalk still draws heavily on the results of these excavations as there has been little excavation on hillfort sites elsewhere in the county (Cotton 1962).

Chronology

Knowledge of the dating and phasing of Perborough Castle is largely based on surface finds of pottery from the hillfort interior and cross referencing of this material with similar more closely dated material from excavated sites elsewhere (particularly Blewburton Hill). Around thirty sherds of Early Iron Age pottery have previously been recovered from Perborough Castle and smaller amounts of Middle Iron Age and Roman pottery are also reported to have been found. On this basis Perborough was thought to be comparable with Blewburton phase II A (the box-rampart or earliest hillfort phase at Blewburton; Wood and Hardy 1962). This would place the construction of Perborough Castle in the early Iron Age sometime during the sixth to fifth centuries BC (Harding 1976).

Environs

Adjacent to the site on Cow Down is a system of celtic fields surviving partially as earthworks and as soilmarks visible on aerial photographs (see for example National Monuments Record, NMR 4229/17 : SU5278/9, photographed 1988). The field system consists of regular lynchets running with the contours and cross-contour banks. The fragmentary outlines of about 40 fields each about an acre (0.4 hectares) in extent and short-oblong in shape are apparent. It is not possible to determine from the existing evidence if the fort was superimposed on this field system or if the fort was already in existence at the time when the field system was laid out. The line of the western defences follows a similar alignment to one of the major field boundaries and may therefore have been laid out using a pre-existing boundary of the field system. Vague traces of possible banks within the hillfort marked on a survey plan by Wood and Hardy (1962), suggest that the hillfort interior was either divided into fields at a date after its construction or that it overlies an earlier field system of prehistoric origin. A Romano-British settlement is also known to be present in the area of Cow Down 400m to the north of Perborough Castle based on a concentration of third- to fourth-century Roman pottery and a third-century coin hoard (discovered in 1852).

It is worth noting some parallels between Perborough Castle and Woolbury hillfort near Stockbridge in Hampshire. Both possess very simple entrances – nothing more than gaps in the defences. These are sited to give access to adjacent chalk downland divided up into blocks of fields constrained by major linear boundary earthworks (see Wood and Hardy 1962, figure 2 and Cunliffe 2000, figure 4.14). Recent excavation by the Danebury Environs Project has shown that the boundary bank, which formed the north-western limit to the Stockbridge Down field-system at Woolbury, was of two phases, one apparently pre-dating the adjacent hillfort, the other developing after the fort ditch had been dug (Cunliffe 2000). It appears therefore that the hillfort at Woolbury was integrated into a pre-existing field system (linked

to major spinal linear boundary earthworks) which then continued in use after the hillfort was established. On present evidence (Cunliffe 2000) it is believed that the laying out of the fields
and boundaries on Stockbridge Down is best placed in the Middle
or Late Bronze Age. The relationship between Woolbury and its
adjacent field-system may also be informative for understanding
how Perborough Castle articulated with the surviving archaeological landscape within which it is set.

Present condition and surface features

Although the hillfort sits in a partially well preserved archaeological landscape, the monument itself is in a very poor condition,
the defences having been erased by ploughing around much
of the circuit of the enclosure. Hewett wrote in 1844 that the
stone foundations of houses could be augered everywhere in
Perborough Castle, and talked of elevated ridges and depressions
which might disclose the sides of the original habitations
(William Hewett: *History and Antiquities of the Hundred of Compton,
Berks*, Reading 1844, p. 71; quoted in Wood and Hardy 1962). Since
Hewett went on to say that these features occurred all over Cow
Down as well as within the earthwork, it is probable that he was
referring at least in part to the 'celtic' field boundaries which,
well preserved outside the rampart, may well have once been
visible as low banks and scarps in the interior. It was not possible
at the time of the 1996 geophysical survey to confirm whether
these minor earthwork features are still extant within the fort
because of the long grass then covering the site. It is possible that
they might remain visible in more favourable ground conditions.
Five large circular hollows visible on the ground inside the hillfort
are probably marl pits. Similar hollows occur elsewhere in the
locality and therefore they are unlikely to be directly associated
with the original use of the hillfort.

The 1996 magnetometer survey

Objectives

Perborough Castle would appear to represent an example of a
simple medium sized univallate hillfort of a type commonly constructed in Wessex during the Early Iron Age. The purpose of the
magnetometer survey was to attempt to characterise the nature
of any internal activity, test for characteristics in common with
other neighbouring hillforts in the Ridgeway group of hillforts
and identify any recurring patterns of internal spatial organisation associated with such univallate forts. Furthermore there
were strong arguments for including the site in the Wessex

Top (opposite)
Figure 1. Greyscale plot
of magnetometer data in
relation to the plan of
the hillfort.

Bottom (opposite)
Figure 2. Interpretation
of the magnetometer data
from Perborough Castle
related to the plan of
the hillfort.

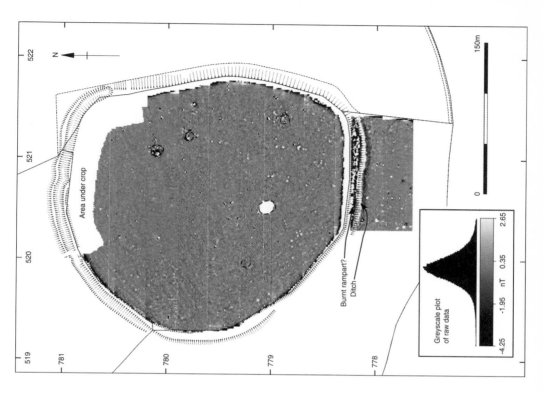

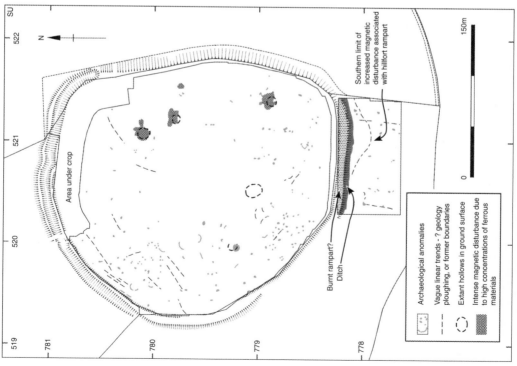

Hillforts Survey programme on management grounds because of the long history of ploughing which has contributed to the current degraded state of the monument.

Methods

Magnetometer survey involves the measurement of local magnetic field strength at close intervals (1.0m or less) across the ground surface. The magnetometer (usually a fluxgate gradiometer) responds to changes in the vertical gradient of the Earth's magnetic field caused by localised concentrations of soil, magnetically enhanced as a by-product of human occupation, that infill buried archaeological features such as pits, ditches, gullies and large post-holes. The technique also detects the remanent magnetisation of hearths and industrial features such as ovens, kilns and furnaces. The archaeological features present are revealed as patterns of magnetic anomalies visible in computer generated plots of the areas surveyed.

The survey results

Across large areas of the site, the magnetic signal is subdued and undisturbed suggesting an absence of archaeological features, but some possible archaeological activity in the form of loose clusters of pit-type features has been detected with a particular concentration around the western to southern periphery of the enclosed area. The central part of the site is distinguished by a relative absence of magnetic anomalies. This may be an indication that a greater amount of agricultural erosion of archaeological layers has taken place in the central area compared to around the extremities of the site but could also be a genuine reflection of the original pattern of occupation. The activity at Perborough is defined by around 100 localised positive magnetic anomalies most of which are likely to represent pits and short lengths of ditch or gully. Some of the pits are clustered tightly together in groups with intervening larger gaps between other pit groups. The density and clustering of the pits is quite similar to the patterning seen at other hillforts where occupation was largely restricted to the early Iron Age, such as Uffington Castle, Oxfordshire (Cromarty *et al* forthcoming) 23 kilometres to the west and Woolbury hillfort in Hampshire (Cunliffe and Poole 2000). A further similarity with Uffington is the possible presence of some four-poster type structures (rectangular settings of pits that retained large upright timber posts) at several locations inside Perborough. Traditionally these have been interpreted by archaeologists as the remains of granary structures, hay-ricks or fodder racks. Other examples of such structures inside Perborough Castle may have been truncated by ploughing resulting in a low

detection rate. The tendency for the pits at Perborough to concentrate towards the periphery of the enclosure is reminiscent of
the magnetometer survey results obtained from Norsebury Ring
in Hampshire (Payne *et al* forthcomimg 2002), where the central
area of the hillfort was likewise largely left free of pits. There is
no geophysical evidence for the presence of a ditched enclosure
in the south-east corner of Perborough Castle as suggested by
Wood and Hardy (1962), although there is a concentration of
anomalous magnetic activity within this area.

The northernmost part of the hillfort interior had to be
excluded from the magnetometer survey due to the presence of
crop cover. The omission of this area inside the hillfort enabled
some additional magnetometer survey to be carried out immediately outside the hillfort to the south in order to test for the presence of external features (suggested by the aerial photographic
evidence; for example NMR Film No. 7093, Frame No. 929) and to
examine a section of the degraded defences. The magnetic signal
from the bank and ditch of the hillfort is much higher than would
be expected from a chalk or earth built rampart suggesting the
presence of considerable quantities of burnt material in the make
up of the bank and the fill of the ditch. The positive magnetic
signal from the bank ranges from 25–50 nanotesla (the unit of
magnetic flux density) bracketed by a negative trough of up to
minus 15 nanotesla (nT). The positive component of the anomaly
is generally double-peaked suggestive of discrete parallel structures within the rampart. The anomaly from the adjacent ditch
averages at about a 16 nT positive deviation from background
readings, again unusually pronounced for a chalk cut ditch with
a typical in-fill of weathered material. A possible interpretation
of these results is that the defences of the hillfort may have been
fired and subjected to intense heating at some time in the past –
perhaps in antiquity. The extremely pronounced and variable
response over the rampart certainly suggests an element of
thermo-remanent magnetisation acquired during an episode
of intense heating. An area of generalised magnetic disturbance
extends for a distance of up to 20 metres south from the hillfort
ditch suggesting the incorporation of re-deposited burnt material
from the rampart and ditch into the topsoil in the field beyond
the rampart by ploughing. The presence of a possible burnt rampart has also recently been recognised at the hillfort of Cissbury
Ring in West Sussex, also based on evidence provided by a
magnetometer survey (Payne 2001).

In the sample of the field to the south of the hillfort defences,
a number of localised positive magnetic anomalies are present.
Those to the west form an alignment suggesting a response
to a former field boundary but overall there is not any coherent

pattern. The majority of the anomalies could indicate further pits cut into the subsoil but could equally represent natural pockets of clay within a more chalky matrix. The density of the anomalies in the area outside the hillfort defences is not significantly lower than inside the hillfort and if they do represent archaeological activity might indicate a spread of occupation not constrained to the hillfort and possibly pre-dating the construction of the hillfort defences. Pre-hillfort phases of unenclosed occupation activity have already been recognised at St Catherine's Hill (Hawkes 1976) and to a lesser extent at Danebury (Cunliffe 1986).

Conclusions

The magnetometer survey has produced clear evidence of occupation within the fort, although judging from the density of the features mapped this does not appear to have been particularly intense or prolonged. This would fit in with the pottery evidence which suggests that the main episode of occupation was limited to the early Iron Age with perhaps more sporadic use in later periods. This interpretation is supported by the smaller quantities of later Iron Age and Roman material recovered from the site and the probable presence of Romano-British settlement on the adjacent area of Cow Down to the north of the hillfort.

Acknowledgements

The author gratefully acknowledges the help of Emma Bray and Peter Cottrell in carrying out the magnetometer survey.

Sources

Collins, A.E.P., 1947, Excavations on Blewburton Hill, 1947, *Berks. Arch. J.*, 50, pp. 4–29

Collins, A.E.P., 1952, Excavations on Blewburton Hill, 1948–9, *Berks. Arch. J.*, 53, pp. 21–64

Collins, A.E.P. & F.J., 1959, Excavations on Blewburton Hill, 1953, *Berks. Arch. J.*, 57, pp. 52–73

Cotton, M.A., 1962, Berkshire Hillforts, *Berks. Arch. J.*, 60, pp. 30–52

Cunliffe, B., 1986, *Danebury – Anatomy of an Iron Age Hillfort*. B.T. Batsford, London (paperback edition)

Cunliffe, B., 1962, *The Danebury Environs Programme – The Prehistory of a Wessex Landscape, Volume 1, Introduction*. English Heritage / Oxford Uuniversity Committee for Archaeology Monograph No. 49 (Part 1)

Cunliffe, B. and Poole, C., 2000, *The Danebury Environs Programme – The Prehistory of a Wessex Landscape, Vol. 2, Part 1. Woolbury, Stockbridge, Hants, 1989*. English Heritage / Oxford University Committee for Archaeology Monograph No. 49, (Part 1)

Harding, D.W., 1976, Blewburton Hill, Berkshire: Re-excavation and reappraisal in D.W. Harding (ed) *Hillforts – Later Prehistoric Earthworks in Britain and Ireland*. Academic Press (London).

Hewitt, William, 1844, *History and Antiquities of the Hundred of Compton, Berks*, Reading.

Hawkes, C.F.C., 1976, St Catharine's Hill, Winchester: The Report of 1930 Reassessed, in D.W. Hardind (ed.), *Hillforts – Later Prehistoric Earthworks in Britain and Ireland*. Academic Press, London.

Lock, G., Gosden, C., Miles, D., and Palmer. S. in press, Uffington White Horse Hill and its Landscape: investigations at White Horse Hill, Uffington, 1989–95 and Tower Hill, Ashbury, 1993–4, Oxforshire. Thames Valley Landscapes Monograph. Oxford University Committee for Archaeology.

Payne, A. *Castle Hill or Sinodun Hill Camp, Little Wittenham, Oxford*. Report on geophysical survey June 2002. Centre on Archaeology Reports 70/2002. English Heritage (Unpublished report).

Payne, A., 2001, *Cissbury Ring, Worthing, West Sussex. Report on geophysical survey, April 2000*. Centre for Archaeology Reports Series. 91/2001. English Heritage.

Payne, A., Comey, M. and Cunliffe, B., 2002 (in press). *The Wessex Hillfort Project – An Extensive Survey of Hillfort Interiors in Central Southern England*. English Heritage Archaeological Reports Series monograph.

Wood, P. and Hardy, J.R., 1962, Perborough Castle and its field system, *The Berkshire Archaeological Journal*, Vol. 60, (1962), pp. 53–60.

15 Industry in the Pang Valley

Dick Greenaway

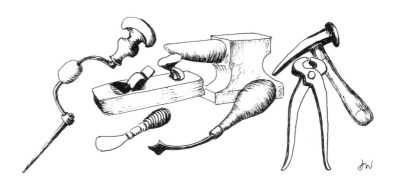

Moving through the Pang Valley one could be excused for thinking that the area had never been touched by industry. The fields and woods roll to the horizon with never a sign of smoking chimneys and the only roar of machinery comes from the cars and trucks on the motorway. However, one would be wrong in thinking so. Although the valley has been predominantly agricultural for the past four or five thousand years there is plenty of evidence of industry, but until very recently it has been small scale industry producing goods for the community immediately around it.

There is little direct evidence for anything that could be called 'industry' for the distant past. There have been finds of Mesolithic and Neolithic flint implements at various places and a hoard of broken bronze tools and weapons was found on the site of Yattendon Court. These may have been intended for melting and recasting by a bronze smith or they may have been a ritual deposit. Nevertheless, someone made them originally and it may have been locally. The blacksmith working in iron must have been a familiar part of every community from well before the Roman Conquest. He made not only the swords and spear heads for a war-like society but also the ordinary domestic and agricultural items such as kitchen knives, nails and ploughs. These are found on every archaeological excavation but as yet no early iron working sites have been found in the valley. My earliest documentary reference to a blacksmith is to 'Eustache – once smith of Yatyngedon' in 1315–16 but the chain must lead back unbroken to the Early Iron Age and forward to the present day.

Pottery survives from the earliest periods, but this may have been made by individual households rather than by specialists.

However, when we come to the Roman Period we find an organised pottery industry producing high quality pots and bowls of many patterns at Woodrows Farm on the valley side near Compton. There were other Roman kilns at Maidenhatch near Bradfield and probably at many other – as yet undiscovered – sites in the area.

The Lailey Bowl Turners of Bucklebury. George William Lailey and his father, William Lailey. © Rural History Centre The University of Reading

The Saxons were not great users of pottery. They appear to have preferred wood and many of the bowls, buckets and other wooden items found in waterlogged sites from this period show that they were highly skilled and artistically gifted craftsmen. Contemporary documents and surviving fragments show that this expertise extended to their houses and other constructions which were often richly and expertly carved. We can therefore expect there to have been a thriving local woodworking industry providing everything from platters and bowls through ploughs and carts to timber houses and churches.

Potting came back to the area soon after the Norman Conquest. In the twelfth and thirteenth centuries potters were working on the western edge of Ashampstead Common producing good quality domestic wares which they traded to surrounding towns and villages. Fragments have been found in Newbury, Reading, Wallingford and Oxford. This could certainly be classed as industrial scale production.

Closely allied to potting is, of course, brick and tile making and these were made at several sites throughout the valley. John Pocock is named as a brickmaker at Frilsham in 1664 and in 1703 Isaac Jeram worked at Burnt Hill. By 1785 Robert States was advertising in the *Reading Mercury* that he had 'taken over' Yattendon Kiln, so it must have started considerably earlier. The Kiln was near the site of the present Yattendon estate office on the eastern side of the village and the surrounding land has been visibly lowered by a long period of digging for brick making material.

Many of the early houses in the valley must contain bricks and tiles made in these kilns. Many small brick making sites probably went unrecorded. There was brick making on Burnt Hill Common and at Ashampstead at some time in the eighteenth or nineteenth centuries and many large building projects burned their bricks on site. In February 1878 Alfred Waterhouse advertised for a brick maker to make bricks on site for his new Yattendon Court and the bricks for the 19th century 'brick and flint' buildings for Bradfield College were almost certainly made close to the College. The most likely site is Kiln Copse on the southern side of the hill above the College.

The Barr family at Frilsham were probably the last brick makers in the valley. Local tradition has it that the kilns were closed down in the Second World War because the light they generated during firing would have contravened the Black Out Regulations and attracted the attentions of German bombers.

From the sixteenth century onwards references to local manufactures become increasingly common. Wills and Inventories detail the possessions of craftspeople from the Tudors to the eighteenth century and in the nineteenth century the great Trade Directories – notably *Kelly's Directory* – provide increasingly detailed information for every town and village. I have analysed the directories from 1840 to 1920 when centralised production in large factories had taken over supplying most of society's needs from the small local producer. I have concentrated on the major villages in the upper Pang Valley between Bradfield and East Ilsley. These are Bradfield, Bucklebury, Stanford Dingley, Frilsham, Yattendon, Hampstead Norreys, Ashampstead,

The 'Pot Kiln' brickyard at Frilsham. Unfired bricks stacked to dry before being fired.
© Greenaway Collection

The Scotch Kiln – beyond
the building on the left.
© Mr and Mrs Gent's
collection

The 'Pot Kiln' brickyard
on the edge of Frilsham
Common.
© Mr and Mrs Gent's
collection

Compton and East Ilsley. During this period Hermitage was
considered a hamlet of Hampstead Norreys and the entries
in the directories are combined.

The information has to be accepted with care. It is not clear
how rigorously the information about each village was checked
before a new directory was published, but, allowing for this the
lists do give us a fascinating picture of village life.

The first thing one notices is the range of services available
in every village. Villages which now lack even a post office had
several shops, more than one boot and shoe maker, blacksmiths
and frequently wheelwrights and tailors. As time went on new
trades creep in and old ones drop out. The Ilsleys lost their wind

Above left
Bricks on a brick barrow.
© Mr and Mrs Gent's
collection

Above right
A village cobbler.
© Rural History Centre,
The University of Reading

miller about 1887 but Compton acquired a chemical manure manufacturer in the same year.

The effects of the growing mass production of clothing and other daily items and the growing ease with which they could be distributed can be seen as the village industries struggled to compete. Hampstead Norreys' boot and shoe maker advertised shoe repairing and their watch and clock maker diversified into bee farming. Frilsham's brick maker emphasised that he also produced pottery and dealt in underwood products. These would have been the surplus poles and brushwood left over from his coppicing for fuel for the kilns. In the Ilsleys two blacksmiths amalgamated and in Bucklebury the foundry advertised that it also carried out motor repairs.

The upheaval of the First World War and the increasing availability of motor transport finally killed most of the rural industries. Village people could get to Reading or Newbury and back quickly and cheaply. A shopping expedition no longer demanded a dawn to dark day in a carrier's cart and the greater variety of goods on offer in the towns was more attractive than the limited products of the local craftsman or woman.

Mechanisation of farming removed the main market of the saddler and harness maker and of the blacksmith and farrier. Some firms managed to hang on until the increase in horse riding for leisure arrived in the 1960s and 1970s and demand for their

Mr Burnham's shop in
Yattendon Square.
© Rural History Centre,
The University of Reading

Mr H. J. Pearce, saddler,
of East Ilsley.
© Rural History Centre,
The University of Reading

The Foundry
at Bucklebury.
© Mrs Sue Hopson's
collection

Saddler's workbench and
tools.
© Rural History Centre
The University of Reading

A wheelwright's shop.
© Rural History Centre
The University of Reading

products grew again. The blacksmith frequently turned his hand to motor repairs and the forge became the local garage.

The future for rural industry looks better now in 2001 than it has for many years. Many factors are influencing this. There is a growing demand for homes in the country and traffic congestion in towns has made the new villagers anxious to avoid the morning and evening rush hours and to find somewhere closer to home to work. As will be seen from the essay on Yattendon Estate, where there is a demand someone will rise to the challenge of filling it, and redundant farm buildings are increasingly being converted into industrial units for many purposes. The cowshed becomes a motor repair workshop, the barn becomes the office for a company supplying the wherewithall for children's parties and the stable block becomes a veterinary laboratory. All this can only be a good thing, bringing life back to villages which had largely become dormitories. There will be people in the streets again, the village shop and post office will stay open and there will be children for the village school. Working together in small units should build friendships which hopefully will develop into a sense of community.

On the environmental side the reduction in the use of motor vehicles and a decreased demand for ever newer, wider and faster roads will improve the quality of life for the wildlife as well as for the humans, and if the new communities can be influenced to take an interest in the heritage and environment of their area the benefits to the wildlife will be even greater.

Top
Wyatt and Sons
Wheelwright yard,
Yattendon c.1900.
© Greenaway Collection

Opposite
Models of the types of
wagons produced by
Messrs Wyatt made by
Robert Wyatt.
© Greenaway Collection

Bottom
Stanford Dingley Tannery.
© Rural History Centre
The University of Reading

Industry in the Valley 1840–1920

A dash '–' means
no industry is mentioned.

Ashampstead	1840	1843	1844	1864	1887	1903	1911	1920
boot & shoe makers	–	–	1	1	1	1	1	
blacksmith	–	–	1	1	2	1	1	1
wheelwright	–	–	1	1				

Bradfield	1840	1843	1847	1864	1887	1903	1911	1920
boot & shoe makers	–	–	2	1		2	2	1
brickmaker	–	–	1		1		1	
mineral water manufacturer	–	–			1			
blacksmith	–	–	2	1	2	2	2	2
miller	–	–	1					
tanner	–	–			1			
gas works	–	–					1	

Bucklebury	1840	1843	1847	1864	1887	1903	1911	1920
boot & shoe makers	–	–	3		2	1	1	
potter	–	–	1					
brickmaker	–	–			1	1	1	1
iron founder & blacksmith	–	–	1	1	1	1	1	1
blacksmith	–	–	1	1				
bowl turner	–	–	1		1	2	1	1
wheelwright	–	–	1	1				
artist	–	–				1	1	

Compton	1840	1843	1841	1864	1887	1903	1911	1920
boot & shoe makers	–	–	1	2				
iron founder, millwright	–	–	1	1			1	1
blacksmith	–	–	1	1	1	1	1	1
wheelwright	–	–	2	1	1			
chemical manure manufacturer	–	–			1	1		
miller (windmill)	–	–	1					

East & West Ilsley	1840	1843	1844	1864	1887	1903	1911	1920
boot & shoe makers	–	–	5	3	2			
dressmaker	–	–					1	
saddler	–	–	1	1	1	1	1	1
whiting manufacturer	–	–	1	1	1			
blacksmith	–	–	3	2	1	1	2	2
wheelwright	–	–	1					
tailor	–	–		1	2			
miller (windmill)	–	–		1	1			

Industry in the Valley 1840–1920 continued

A dash '–' means
no industry is mentioned.

Frilsham	1840	1843	1844	1864	1887	1903	1911	1920
boot & shoe makers	–	–	–	1				
brickmaker	–	–	–	1		1	1	1
miller (steam & water)	–	–	–		1			

Hampstead Norreys	1840	1843	1847	1864	1887	1903	1911	1920
boot & shoes	–	–	3	2	1	1		
harness maker	–	–	1					
watch & clock maker (& bee farmer)	–	–	1				1	1
blacksmith	–	–	3	2	2	1	1	
wheelwright	–	–	1	1	1	1		
hurdle maker	–	–	1	1	1	1	1	1
surgeon	–	–		1	1			
whiting manufacturer	–	–			1	1		

Stanford Dingley	1840	1843	1847	1864	1887	1903	1911	1920
boot & shoe makers	–	–			1	1		
tanner	–	–	1	1	1			
mineral water manufacturer	–	–				1		
blacksmith	–	–	1	1	1			

Yattendon	1840	1843	1847	1864	1887	1903	1911	1920
boot & shoe makers	–	–	1	1				
saddler	–	–	1					
harness maker	–	–			1	1	1	1
blacksmith	–	–	1	1	1		1	1
wheelwright	–	–	1	2	1			
farrier	–	–		1				

16 Sixty years of farming in the Pang Valley, 1940–2000

Tim Culley

This story is partly woven around Felicity Palmer who came to live in Yattendon in 1940, and who farmed in Frilsham at Coombe Farm in the 40s, 50s and 60s, keeping up her interest in farming right to her death. She regularly rang me up over thirty years to ask 'what is happening on the farm?' Although she was a 'natural farmer', never using fertilisers or weed killers, she never chided me for our modern methods of intensive farming.

Between Marlston Farm in the south and Hampstead Norreys in the north (see map), a distance of two and a half miles, there were ten working farms, farmed by nine farmers, during the 1939–45 war. Seven of these farms had dairy cows ranging from shorthorns and red polls to Guernseys. There were also small holders who produced butter, kept cattle, goats and hens and had other jobs to eke out a living.

There were two large farms: Eling Farm at Hampstead Norreys and Manor Farm at Frilsham, each with a handsome set of Victorian brick buildings. Eling was farmed by Sir William Cook from Wyld Court, and Manor Farm by Mr Saunders who built Shockendon House for £1 000. He was a livestock dealer who exhibited and won prizes at various agricultural shows, including the annual Smithfield Fat Stock Show in London. He also had a small abattoir in Yattendon, and the water mill at Frilsham was used to grind corn for the livestock.

Farming, like life, seems to go in circles. In 1900 Imperial Preference saw cheap grain from Canada and Australia, cheap butter and lamb from New Zealand, and depression in all UK agriculture. Today, with the World Trade Organisation removing tariffs from many foodstuffs, we are again seeing the prices of

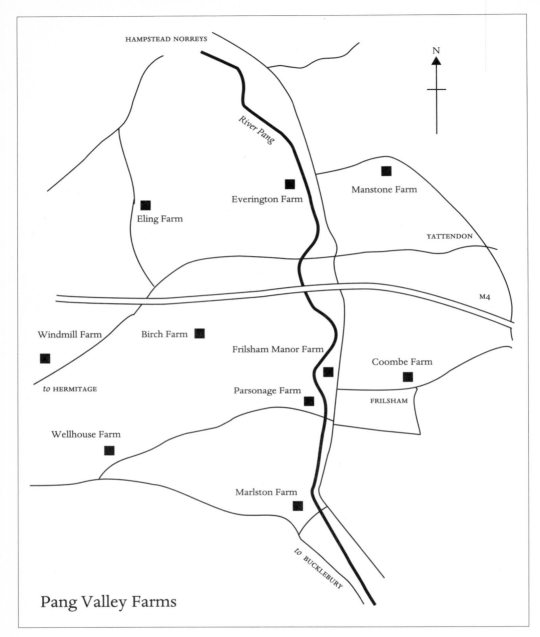

Pang Valley Farms

most foods falling below the cost of UK production, and our farmers are changing production methods to reduce cost yet further, or are looking for 'niche markets' to get premiums for their products.

Organic farming has also come full circle. In 1900 inorganic fertilisers were just beginning and crop sprays had hardly been invented. In the 1940s fertilisers were essential to boost food production to make up for losses due to German submarines, and

Mr Fred Cannons
ploughing the headlands at
Ashampstead with Smiler
and Ginger.
© Greenaway Collection

so began sixty years of development of intensive farming to
increase crop and stock yields to produce cheap food for the
industrial world. Today we are seeing some farms going back to
organic production to meet a niche market for the five per cent
of the population who are prepared to pay extra for organic
food which they see as 'healthier food'.

Farm staffing has not gone in a circle. One hundred years
ago all work was done by hand or with horses. By the 1940s some
farms had gone over entirely to tractors and milking was done
by simple machines in existing cowsheds. The numbers of staff
on our ten working farms was probably about forty-six in all,
including family labour. Today the number working this farmland
is down to five, and this will reduce further.

During the 1939–45 war when many men were called to the
colours, there were four ways to make up the shortfall: mechanisation, land girls, prisoners of war, and contractors, and our
farms used them all. Land girls worked on various farms in the
locality. Mr Goodenough had two POWs (prisoners of war) – a
Germans and an Italian – who shared a cottage and looked after
themselves.

In winter, when work was slack and meat short, everybody
would be issued with a shotgun and told to go out and shoot
rabbits, which were desirable and numerous in the days before
myxomatosis.

Mr Goodenough also had a land girl who came from London
with her mother. It was her job to deliver milk in the area which

Top
Harvesting wheat at
Childs Court Farm
Ashampstead about 1940.
© Greenaway Collection

Bottom
Pedigree Ayrshires at
Jewell's farm, Stanford
Dingley, 1937.
© Rural History Centre,
The University of Reading

she did from a succession of vans. On the day the war ended
in Europe the land girl and her mother went back to London.

Felicity Palmer worked as a land girl on several local farms
during the war. In October 1948 she took the tenancy of Coombe
Farm, Frilsham, which belonged to the Yattendon Estate. The
rent was fixed at £30 a year for the 35 acres of the farm. At this
stage she still lived in Yattendon. In 1950 she moved into the farmhouse and the rent went up to £102. This meant the rent on the
farmhouse was £5 12s 0d (£5.60) a month. Today it would be
£900 a month.

In 1955 she asked the Estate if part of the barn could be
converted for milk production. A four stall abreast parlour was
installed (and is still there today) and Felicity milked between

Top: Women's Land Army
harvesting wheat 1939.
© Rural History Centre,
The University of Reading

Bottom: Fordson Tractor
at Jewell's Farm, Stanford
Dingley 1937
© Rural History Centre,
The University of Reading

twelve and fifteen cows herself. The milk was sold to, and
collected by, the Milk Marketing Board.

As the farm was small only Ann Blandford helped regularly,
but others came to help for hay making and corn harvesting.
There was a T20 Ferguson tractor on the farm – very modern, the
first in the world to have 'hydraulics' for attaching implements, and
a 'power take off' for driving a mower or hay making machine.

The tractor is still in Hampstead Norreys at Fir Tree Farm, her sister Sue's old farm.

Felicity farmed in a simple way, producing milk, rearing some store cattle and keeping hens for egg production. There were many small farms and smallholdings of this type, seldom producing enough to live on. But they enabled the owner to do other work during the day and to follow a way of life that suited them.

Felicity retired from farming Coombe Farm in 1962, but bought the farmhouse and lived there for another thirty eight years. The farm land was let again, and used for young cattle and cows not in milk by a farming business in Upper Basildon.

Mr Saunders gave up Frilsham Manor Farm in 1945 when it became part of Yattendon Estate. A keen young tractor driver, Cecil Pearman, married and went to live in one of the cottages there. He had lived with his parents and worked on several local farms. He found his bride amongst the land girls. She came from Bradford in Yorkshire – a far cry from rural Berkshire, but I expect people had got used to strange accents from the RAF and Army personnel in the area.

Cecil Pearman's early tractors were Internationals or Fords. The International 10/20s came over from the USA. They had to be started on petrol and once warm could be changed over to TVO (tractor vaporising oil), a forerunner of the kerosene now used in our central heating systems. They were 30–40 horsepower and could pull a two or three furrow plough, had hard metal seats and no cabs – you had to be hardy and frequently got wet.

Frilsham Manor Farm had beef cattle, sheep that were hurdled on roots (swedes and turnips) for most of the year, fattening pigs in the buildings and cereals that were still cut with a binder and made into large 'ricks' or stacks in the rickyard near the farm. At sometime during the winter a travelling threshing machine would have come to the farm, and 'all hands', up to twelve people, would have had a week's dusty, sweaty, hard physical work, at the end of which all the corn would have been in hessian sacks – wheat 2 cwt (hundred weight), barley 2 cwt, and oats only 1 cwt because they were so bulky that was all you could get into the sack. A hundredweight equalled about 55 kilos and everything was manhandled – no Manual Handling Directive from Brussels in those days!

Has the landscape in this valley changed much in sixty years? It seems surprisingly little. The two great changes occurred together in the late 1960s, one man made, the other a disease.

The first was the M4 which came across the valley thirty feet high, all raw earth and huge machinery, and we all thought it would never be the same again. But now, thirty years on, with grass, bushes and trees and rabbits burrowing into its banks,

Mr Sid Hannington and
Mr George Herbert
building a rick at Childs
Court Farm Ashampstead.
© Greenaway Collection

kestrels hovering above the verge looking for mice and shrews,
and trout swimming up the Pang underneath the motorway, it all
seems quite natural. Perhaps the greatest intrusion is the noise,
particularly on summer Sunday evenings.

The second was Dutch elm disease which took away all the
huge elm trees in the valley – and there were many. Some hedges
had lots of forty foot high trees that measured three to four feet
across at ground level. Their loss seemed to have a bigger impact
on the landscape than the M4.

Christmas trees for the Yattendon Estates are increasingly produced on the lighter soils of Frilsham Manor Farm. The light soils
suit the trees and make the extraction in November and December
easier in a wet autumn. At first only Norway spruce were grown,
but they drop their needles in centrally heated houses. They were
followed by noble fir, which held their needles but were tempera-
mental in growth. The favoured variety now is nordmannia
which has come to dominate the Christmas tree market.

Field boundaries and hedges in the valley have changed little.
The river meadows have stayed the same, with hedges dividing
the drier arable land from the wet meadows. The arable fields
were already large, from twenty to fifty acres. Some fields were
the successors of the medieval village open fields, so few hedges
have been taken out, although a few were moved or replanted

Rick building.
© Greenaway Collection

after the building of the motorway. During our period barbed wire was used to keep stock in fields, so hedges were less important. With the coming of tractor mounted trimmers hedges have become narrower and shorter – neater, but not so favourable to wild life. Few hedges in the valley show any evidence of having been 'laid' to make a stock proof barrier, a practice now being encouraged by the Countryside Agency's 'Countryside Stewardship Scheme'.

In 1973 Great Britain joined the Common Market and this had a great effect on farming. Before 1973 the government fixed farm prices according to the needs of the country, so if the production went above government targets prices went down and vice versa. After 1973 there was no upper limit on production, so farmers expanded production, leading to the lakes and mountains of wine, cereals, beef and butter. This Common Agricultural Policy lead to an expansion of cereal production in our valley and a shrinking of grass and livestock, which has continued to the present. During the 1980s Brussels started to limit production by applying 'quotas' to milk, beef and sheep production and reducing the support for cereal production. This policy, together with the strong pound and the influence of the World Trade Organisation has seen the collapse of all farm prices, taking us back to the depression of 1900–10.

Output and quality have both increased enormously since the 1940s. Milk yields have doubled then trebled, and the quality is the best in the world. Better breeding, feeding and milking equipment have all contributed to this. Cereals have seen similar increases. One ton per acre was a good yield in the 1940s. In the 1960s we got up to 1 or 2 tons. Now yields are between 3 and 4 tons per acre due to new varieties, better understanding of the soil, and improved weed killers and fungicides.

The detrimental effect on wildlife of fertilisers, herbicides, fungicides and anthelmintics was not appreciated or understood thirty years ago. But new methods of farming are being developed that will produce safe crops with the minimum use of chemicals, and these chemicals are constantly being improved to minimise their harmful side effects. Genetically modified crops will play their part in crop production when they are better understood. They offer benefits to the consumer, the environment and the farmer, but they must gain public confidence.

The alternative way forward brings us round full circle. The Goodenough family, who came to Birch Farm in the 1930s, now farm six of our ten farms, and are converting to organic farming. They are moving away from cereals and hoping to expand their dairy herd to 300–400, which will be more than all the cows in the valley on those ten farms in 1940.

The Ten Farms	*Parish*
1 Marlston Farm	Bucklebury
2 Parsonage Farm	Frilsham
3 Coombe Farm	Frilsham
4 Frilsham Manor Farm	Frilsham
5 Birch Farm	Frilsham
6 Wellhouse Farm	Frilsham and Hermitage
7 Windmill Farm	Hermitage
8 Everington Farm	Yattendon
9 Manstone Farm	Yattendon
10 Eling Farm	Yattendon and Hampstead Norreys

17 Yattendon Estate: a modern country business

Nigel Petter

The Background

Yattendon Estate in its present form is the result of the amalgamation of several smaller estates acquired by the first Lord Iliffe between 1925 and 1940. The company is chaired by his grandson the present Lord Iliffe who, together with his wife, lives on the Estate – as do their son, daughter in law and grandchildren.

The Estate comprises 8 968 acres and fills a large part of the landscape between the Ridgeway to the north, the M4 motorway to the south, the River Pang to the west and the Thames to the east. Of this holding 3 863 acres are farmed directly by the company under the management of a Farms Director assisted by specialist managers for arable and dairies. Another 1 983 acres are let to tenant farmers and 536 acres are used for growing Christmas trees. The estate is well wooded with some 2 181 acres of mixed woodlands and plantations. In 2001 twenty-one staff were employed on the estate and twelve on the farms. In addition twenty-seven pensioners are looked after.

The Farms

After the Second World War the Estate had several dairy herds of pedigree dairy Shorthorns and pedigree Jerseys which supplied a large retailer milk round. There was also a pedigree Hereford herd, a ewe flock and an increasing arable acreage. In the early 1960s the dairy units were shut down and the Herefords and sheep disposed of. In 1963 an outdoor pig herd was introduced which was built up to 350 sows. Between 1972 and 1982 three indoor Camborough Pig Units were built. The first Unit was built for 220 sows, the second was built in 1976 for 240 sows and the outdoor herd was phased out. The third Unit was built in 1982. Following the devastating slump in pig prices in the late 1990s it was decided to close down the Units. Fortunately, tenants were found to take on the buildings to use them for fattening pigs. The breeding herd was sold to one of the tenants for outdoor breeding.

Today the main farming enterprises are:

– Two Friesian dairy units of 130 cows each. The first was built at Frilsham Home Farm in 1969 and the second at Ashampstead in 1974. Heifer replacements are reared and the milk is sold to Milk Marque. A new – state of the art – dairy is due to come on stream in the autumn of 2002.

– The arable and grass leys acreage amounts to 3800 acres and the crops grown are wheat, barley, oats, grass seed, oil seed rape, peas, beans and linseed.

The milking parlour at Frilsham Home Farm. © Greenaway Collection

British White Cattle at Frilsham Home Farm. © Greenaway Collection

Ploughing near Aldworth
2002.
© Greenaway Collection

- A small herd of British white cattle was introduced in 1996 consisting of five heifers in calf. The herd has now grown to seven cows, eight heifers and one bull and was started to help maintain this rare breed.
- The Estate has recently launched a range of 'ready to bake' products produced from wheat grown on the farms. The newly developed products are made by qualified local craftsmen and women with the same care and attention as is applied to producing the flour from which they are baked.

Countryside Stewardship

The whole in-hand farm has been entered into the Countryside Stewardship Scheme. This involved a survey of the farms to record the state of the hedges and fields. From this a Management Plan was developed and implemented. The plan provides for the 'gapping up', coppicing or re-planting of hedges to provide habitats for wildlife and for the insertion of wide field margins of varying widths around arable fields. These margins provide habitats for many kinds of wildlife from wild flowers and insects to voles and small mammals. In turn these support a growing population of butterflies which feed and breed on the plants, of birds which feed on the insects and seeds and of hawks and owls which hunt the small mammals. An additional benefit is provided by the predatory insects which live in the margins and spread into the growing crops to prey on insect pests thus reducing the amount of insecticide spraying required.

The let farms

Four farms are let to tenants. These are Hartridge Farm (550 acres), Southridge Farm (564 acres), Bower & Warren Farm (660 acres) and Buckhold Farm (209 acres).

The farms toward the northern end of the Estate were

A modern tractor
and slurry spreader.
© Greenaway Collection

required to plough up the downland by the Wartime Agricultural
Committee during the Second World War and the land has been
retained as arable ever since. The dairy herds once seen on all
these farms have now gone and they all concentrate on arable
crops with small numbers of fattening beef cattle, sheep, outdoor
pigs, soft fruit and a livery.

Woodland

The Estate manages 2181 acres of woodlands as a commercial
business. A forester carries out all the establishment work with
the help of a small number of regular staff and by using contractors as necessary. The woods were severely damaged by the
hurricanes of the late 1980s and the replanting of the devastated
areas has only recently been completed. Historically, traditional
woodland planting has been practised with hardwoods for the
final crop with intermixed conifers as nurse trees.

Half the Estate woodland is either Ancient Semi-natural
Woodland or Ancient Re-planted Woodland and the Forestry
Commissioners' policy of only allowing the planting of native
hardwoods in such areas has required a change in the management policy. In 2001 the Estate employed forestry consultants to
develop a twenty year plan for the woodlands: the first ten years
to be detailed and the second ten years in outline. In accordance
with Forestry Authority guidance a Scoping Meeting was held
with all interested groups who were encouraged to provide information for the plan and to discuss their concerns. The bodies
represented included the local parish councils, English Nature,
English Heritage, West Berkshire Council and interested individuals. The final plan will address as many of their concerns as
possible and will take account of the environmental, wildlife,
archaeological and historical aspects of the woodland. Constraint
maps will be produced for each wood before work commences.

The Christmas tree
harvest near Childs
Court farm in 2001.
© Greenaway Collection

In general terms the plan will result in healthier woodlands
where trees are grown on suitable soils and at suitable stocking
rates. The decaying coppices will be cut and repaired.

Christmas trees

The Estate is one of the largest private producers of Christmas
trees in the country and these occupy some 536 acres. They are
managed by nine permanent staff with the assistance of casual
labour at busy times – particularly during the harvest which starts
in November when the total staff can amount to over forty. Some
150 000 trees are harvested each Christmas. The Estate, with three
other growers, owns a marketing company called Needlefresh
Direct Ltd. This company markets the majority of the group's
trees to supermarkets and garden centres.

Sporting

Organised pheasant shooting is an important Estate activity and
is the reason for the survival of many areas of otherwise uneco-
omical woodland and coppice. These areas are often of considerable wildlife value and highly valued by the community for their
beauty and interest. The Estate is divided into six shoots. Four
full time keepers are employed on the two main shoots and
during the season there are fifty days shooting. The four minor
shoots in the south of the Estate are let and have part time
keepers employed by the lessees. The Estate owns fishing rights
on the Pang.

Maintenance and Improvements

The cost of maintenance and improvements forms a major part
of Estate expenditure. Self employed tradesmen deal with minor
works but all the major projects are carried out by building contractors. In the last twenty years the Estate has undertaken over

twenty major rebuilding or extension projects and new building
and conversions of old farm buildings have added to the housing
stock. These conversions have included the conversion of Yattendon Court into fifteen flats in 1977, the conversion of Frilsham
Home Farm buildings into light industrial units, the conversion
of a cow shed at Childs Court Farm into a base for a company

Barn interior with conversion almost complete.
© Greenaway

Late 19th-century farm buildings at Frilsham Home Farm converted to offices and workshops.
© Greenaway Collection

Retirement homes in
Yattendon converted from
redundant farm buildings.
© Greenaway Collection

servicing children's parties and the conversion of Grade II Listed
cow sheds and boxes into cottages for retired staff. The latest
project has seen the conversion of a 17th century barn at Childs
Court to offices. In 1989 the Estate gave a site on the edge of
Yattendon village for twelve houses to be built by the NAC Rural
Trust under the 'Village Homes for Village People' scheme. The
aim of the scheme is to make affordable houses available to avoid
local young people being forced out by the high prices normally
obtained for country homes. The Estate recognised that without
the young people amenities such as the shop, post office and
school would close and the village would die as a working
community.

The light industrial units provide a valuable source of local
employment. The Frilsham Home Farm complex alone houses
amongst others: a company producing forms for NHS Trust
hospitals and also flight manuals for aircraft; a computer printer
servicing company; a company manufacturing light sensitive
filters; a diagnostic veterinary laboratory and a computer network company.

All these companies were either started by local people or
employ local residents.

Yattendon Village

The Estate owns virtually the whole of the beautiful village of
Yattendon including the local amenities of the shop and post
office, hairdresser, butcher, hotel, craft shop, blacksmith and

garage. The whole of the village square is listed Grade II and the cost of maintaining 'the Estate village' and the amenities is considerable.

Access to the Estate

'The Ridgeway' National Long Distance Path runs through the northern part of the Estate and is extensively used by the public. There are over 52 miles of footpaths, bridleways and by-ways on the Estate and these together with four Permissive Paths give access to most parts of the Estate. Ashampstead and Burnt Hill Commons are both owned by the Estate, but a formal agreement with Ashampstead Parish Council gives parishioners rights of access and use similar to common rights. In 1996 the Estate developed a Management Plan for the Commons in co-operation with the Parish Council and local residents. An annual meeting is held to discuss both commercial and voluntary work for the coming year.

Educational access to the Estate is managed via the Countryside Commission and the Pang Valley Countryside Project. Currently Frilsham Water Meadows are available and school and society visits can be made to Estate operations such as farms, woodland and Christmas tree areas.

Conclusion

The Estate advertises itself on its letter head and on its farm name plates as having carried out 'responsible farming since 1925'. I hope that the reader will share our opinion that the Estate takes its local responsibilities very seriously and is more than a merely commercial operation.

18 Some Pang Valley church restorations 1846–1912

John Sims

The church's restoration
In eighteen-eighty-three
Has left for contemplation
Not what there used to be
(John Betjeman, *Hymn*)

The 'restoration of churches', thundered the Revd Francis Close from his Cheltenham pulpit on the eve of Guy Fawkes Day 1844, 'is the restoration of Popery'. Three years later the archbishops and bishops ruled that altar flower vases were illegal.

These are reminders of the strong feelings which church restoration and furnishing could arouse in the 19th century. The purpose of this article is to give a brief background to the general activity of church restoration in the Victorian period before turning to look at the cases of four Pang Valley parish churches (Bradfield, Stanford Dingley, Bucklebury and Hampstead Norreys), both in terms of what was done and how it was influenced by the individual circumstances of each village.

In the nineteenth century there was a volume of church building and repair on a scale unprecedented since the fifteenth and early sixteenth centuries. Many churches were in a poor state due to the normal ravages of time and inadequate maintenance. There was a revival in the serious study of the Gothic style of the Middle Ages, which inspired the foundation of the Cambridge Camden (later Ecclesiological) Society in 1839 to promote the study of medieval church architecture and liturgy, to encourage the repair and internal re-arrangement of churches to bring them back to what was imagined to have been their original state, and to re-intoduce the appropriate liturgy. This linked with the Oxford (Tractarian) Movement, which advocated a return to the Catholic tradition of the Church emphasizing the central importance of the sacerdotal and sacramental elements as against the Protestant concentration on preaching and personal salvation. These two High Church movements proved a powerful force so that by the 1840s the spate of church restoration was well under way. In its early stages it was viewed with suspicion or worse by Evangelicals like Francis Close, but gradually the general principles came to be accepted by all parties in the Church. As a result, between 1840 and 1874 a total of 7144 churches – more than eighty per cent of the total number of medieval churches – had undergone restorations costing more than £500. In the Oxford diocese alone, the expenditure was £735111 (the equivalent of more than ten million pounds today).

The basic tenet was that Gothic and Christian architecture were synonymous and that Gothic achieved perfection in the Decorated style of the early fourteenth century. Consequently genuine medieval features of an earlier or later period, instead of being repaired, were often completely replaced, thus obliterating part of the visual evidence of the church's history. Chancels were fitted out with a properly railed in communion table and stalls for clergy and a choir. Post-Reformation structural alterations and fittings were, if possible, removed. The ubiquitous three-decker pulpits, galleries and rented or privately owned box pews in particular were anathema. Seating was provided in open benches, all or most of which were made free, since all were equal in the sight of God. In practice, of course, some were more equal than others. God had made them high and lowly and ordered their estate, and woe betide the villager who forgot this and presumed to sit nearer the front than the gentry!

In rural areas such as the Pang Valley, it is possible to identify four common factors which were likely to influence the nature of church restoration in a parish. These are the social structure, demography, changes of incumbents, and availability of funds.

For social structure, parishes may be divided into 'squire' and 'squireless'. Squire parishes had a single dominant landowner who was normally resident and usually lord of the manor. Squireless parishes had either one or several non-resident dominant landowners, or a group of relatively small landowners. Bradfield and Bucklebury were squire parishes, controlled by the Stevens and Hartley families respectively. Stanford Dingley and Hampstead Norreys were squireless parishes. In Stanford Dingley the principal landowners were W.H.H. Hartley of Bucklebury and Thomas Floyd of Frilsham. In Hampstead Norreys there was no dominant influence but a group of farmers with similar sized holdings.

Growth of population might exert pressure to increase seating capacity of the church if it had become grossly inadequate. Coupled with genuine concern for the spiritual needs of parishioners was anxiety to maintain social control and the need to compete with the Nonconformists. The following table shows the change in population in each parish between 1801 and the time of the restoration (Bradfield 1847–8, Stanford Dingley 1870, Hampstead Norreys 1879–80 and Bucklebury 1911–12), whether the population at the time of restoration was increasing or declining, and approximately what difference the restoration made to the seating capacity (figures vary).

	Bradfield	Stanford Dingley	Hampstead Norreys	Bucklebury
1801	678	133	855	1122
At restoration	1042 (1841)	169 (1871)	1378 (1881)	1136 (1911)
Per cent change	+54%	+27%	+61%	+1.25%
Trend	increasing	declining	declining after 1881	decline 1831–1901 increase from 1901
Old seating	270	160	250	400
New seating	500	180	292	350

Only in the case of Bradfield did restoration result in a substantial increase in seating capacity. The population there continued to increase throughout the century, even discounting the distortion attributable to the Union workhouse and the college, so that by 1901 it had outstripped both Bucklebury and Hampstead Norreys. The apparent size of demand at Hampstead Norreys is deceptive since much of the population was in outlying settlements and attended neighbouring churches.

General studies of church restorations have shown that a high proportion occurred within a few years of the advent of a new incumbent. The four Pang Valley parishes conform to that pattern. The date for initiation of restoration refers to when it was formally agreed by the Vestry or when fund raising started.

	Bradfield	Stanford Dingley	Hampstead Norreys	Bucklebury
Incumbent	T. Stevens	A. B. Valpy	H. D. Grantham	E. M. Thorp
Inducted	1842	1864	1876	1907
Restoration	1846	1865	1877	1911 initiated

There were three main ways of financing church restorations. A church rate could be levied. Until 1868 this was a compulsory rate levied on all, whether or not members of the Church of England. Hence it was unpopular and socially divisive. Comparatively few parishes resorted to it, and none of the four with which we are concerned did so. In the case of squire parishes, the squire might incur the whole cost; this happened at Bradfield and, partially, at Bucklebury. Otherwise it was a matter of soliciting voluntary contributions which might be supplemented by grants from the national Incorporated Church Building Society (ICBS) and the diocesan equivalent. These bodies, especially the former, tended to relate the size of grant to the increase in seating capacity. Hampstead Norreys was the only one of these four parishes to apply.

Having considered the general characteristics, we can now take a closer look at each parish in turn to see what happened.

Bradfield

The restoration of Bradfield church was a drastic remodelling which virtually amounted to rebuilding. It was essentially a one-man show, that man being the 'squarson' (squire and parson combined) Thomas Stevens. The Stevens family had been rectors since 1740 and lords of the manor and principal landowners since 1751. Thomas Stevens went to Oriel College, Oxford, in 1827 when it was the centre of the nascent Oxford Movement. Keble came to stay at Bradfield and in 1835 Newman preached at the dedication service of the chapel-of-ease at Buckhold. Stevens, however, was never a full-blown Tractarian but had a passionate interest in Gothic architecture. This was fuelled by the close friendship he forged with the architect George Gilbert Scott whom he met in the course of his work as an Assistant Poor Law Commissioner. In about 1838 they discussed plans for Bradfield church which came to nothing, probably because Thomas's father, Henry, was still rector and did not share his son's enthusiasm.

Bradfield Church before restoration.

In 1842 Henry Stevens died and Thomas inherited both the heavily mortgaged estate and the living. Undeterred by the rocky state of his finances, he determined to enlarge the church as a memorial to his parents, also arguing that the increasing population was outgrowing its capacity. No doubt his architectural enthusiasm was an additional motivator. Once decided, he moved fast. At a vestry meeting on 23 September 1846 he offered to undertake the whole expense without levying a church rate on condition that he should be allowed to have the works done under his own direction and control. Not surprisingly his offer was accepted, and a subsequent meeting endorsed the engagement of Gilbert Scott to prepare plans. The foundation stone was laid on 17 October.

The actual building work, carried out by Wheeler of Reading, probably did not start until the spring of 1847. It must have taken rather longer than planned because in October 1847 the new south arcade collapsed and had to be rebuilt. The church was re-opened with a service of consecration on 4 July 1848, although some work on the south transept continued into the following year. Essentially the south aisle was rebuilt, the north aisle was extended eastwards to provide seating for schoolchildren, a south transept was built over the Stevens vault and the chancel was hugely lengthened with an apsidal east end. Virtually all the windows were filled with stained glass by William Wailes of Newcastle, the leading firm of the time, and there was a wealth of stone and wood carving. The ironwork was made by the talented Bradfield blacksmith James Holloway. This was an expensive job. The cost of £7000 would have been much greater but for the use of local materials: the chalk came from the village chalk pit (now the Greek Theatre) and the timber from trees on the estate. Thus cost of materials and carriage was kept to the minimum.

The one fly in the ointment was the Revd John Connop of Bradfield Hall. The Connops, with 900 acres, were the only family which could challenge the pre-eminence of the Stevenses who owned well over 2000 acres. The Connops had put up a gallery pew in the south aisle which in 1809 had been confirmed by faculty to be their property. Connop insisted on retention of this pew despite its incongruity in the new church which was fitted throughout with open benches in the approved style. In its favourable review the *Ecclesiologist*, the influential journal of the Ecclesiological Society, described the Connop pew contemptuously as a 'flying sentry box'. Connop himself never used it, but each Sunday his unfortunate daughter had to sit in it perched up above the rest of the congregation. It was finally removed in 1858.

Gilbert Scott, never one for false modesty, described Bradfield as 'one of my best works'. In our own time John Betjeman has admired it as 'long drawn, mysterious and vast'. Although a destructive restoration, it resulted in a more architecturally distinguished building and a fascinating contribution to the history of its time.

Stanford Dingley

Here we have a very different story. Stanford Dingley was a small parish with no substantial resident gentry. The rector from 1830 to 1864, Charles Holloway, was described by Bishop Wilberforce as a good man but Low Church, and hence unlikely to be infected by a predominantly High Church enthusiasm for restoration. Of the two principal landowners, William Howard Winchcombe Hartley of Bucklebury probably lived mostly on his Gloucestershire estate after fire destroyed Bucklebury Manor. The other, Thomas Floyd of Frilsham, was absorbed with farming and country pursuits. His brother was rector of Frilsham where he probably worshipped, so he was unlikely to have had much interest in either church architecture or Stanford Dingley church. Consequently there was no impetus for drastic alteration to a church which was more than adequate in size for the population.

Things changed with the arrival of a new rector, Anthony Bird Valpy, in 1864. To his eyes the church, with homely dormer windows in the roof and its interior filled with box pews, a three-decker pulpit and a west gallery containing a barrel organ which only played four hymn tunes, must have appeared distressingly old-fashioned. The structure itself, apart from the eighteenth century brick chancel, was dilapidated. If there had been a

Stanford Dingley Church before restoration. By courtesy of the Rector and Churchwardens.

wealthy landowner as at Bradfield, the entire humble church
might have been pulled down and replaced with something more
seemly to mid-Victorian eyes. As it was, Valpy embarked on a
laborious five year fund raising exercise which eventually raised
£700. No application for a grant was made to the ICBS or the
Diocesan Church Building Society, possibly because a case could
not have been made for increasing seating capacity. Arthur Billing
of Reading was engaged as architect; the contractors were the
large London firm, Dove of Islington. The restoration took place
in 1870 with the church re-opening on 29 June.

The work carried out entailed re-roofing and removal of the
dormers, refacing the exterior (apart from the chancel) in flint,
repair of pillars and arches, removal of the ceilings, west gallery,
pulpit and box pews and replacement with open benches, all of
which were free. A new south porch and buttresses were built
and two new windows inserted in the south aisle to give the
additional light needed after removal of the dormers. In the
course of the work extensive traces of wall paintings were
uncovered. Much was saved, and some of the purely decorative
design embellished. Others, which modern preservation
techniques might have managed to preserve, were lost.
These included an 11 foot high St Christopher.

The most regrettable loss was Basden's House. This picturesque
lean-to structure on the south side to the west of the porch was
given by Sebastian Lyford in 1607 'for neighbours to sitt in' with a
small endowment for its upkeep. Valpy described it 'an unsightly
shed … an unsightly, barbarous looking place'. It was duly swept
away.

In 1902 Valpy's successor, E. H. Horne, supervised rebuilding
of the shingled belfry using a home-made crane and local labour,
and in 1905 Dr Lacy of the Garden House designed an incongrous
Gothic reredos and panelling for the chancel. Happily these were
later removed and the reredos re-sited as a screen at the west end
of the nave.

This is a case where shortage of money limited the amount
of restoration work which could be done. The old texture and
picturesque haphazard accretions over time were lost, but on
the whole there was relatively little harm done and the building
was made structurally sound.

Hampstead Norreys

Like Stanford Dingley, Hampstead Norreys was a squireless parish
but the pattern of principal land ownership was rather different.
Here there were four farmers with holdings of broadly similar
size: Luke Lousley at Manor Farm (742 acres), Thomas Dewe
at Haw Farm (651 acres), William Dewe at Wyld Court Farm

Hampstead Norreys
Church.

(635 acres) and Hayward Aldworth at Eling Farm (605 acres).
The vicar from 1843 until his death in 1875 was John Blissard.
Immediately on his arrival he erected a pew in the chancel for his
family, and minor repairs were carried out in 1852 and 1867–68.
Expenditure on the church fabric from 1840 to 1874 was only £350.
The erection of a vicar's pew at a time when the Cambridge
Camden's Society's onslaught on such objects was already in full
flow suggests that Blissard was a man of the old school who
would not be energetic in promoting new style restoration.

Blissard was succeeded in 1876 by Henry Grantham, evidently
a man of a very different stamp. Within a year of his induction he
had persuaded the vestry to resolve on restoration and to appoint
a committee for that purpose. Given the oligarchic nature of
power in the parish, a committee was inevitable but something
of a mixed blessing. Grantham told Archdeacon Pott that he was
fighting single-handed against ignorance and bigotry and Pott
acknowledged that Grantham had met with many difficulties.
When he visited to discuss the plans, he patronizingly described
the committee as 'sturdy Berkshire yeomen, but upon the whole
not a bad lot'. Evidently the church was badly in need of repair:
Pott described it variously as 'deplorable', 'wretched' and 'most
depressing to the Incumbent'.

The architect chosen was Arthur Baker of London. When
his plans were submitted with the application for a grant to
the Diocesan Church Building Society, the Diocesan architect
G. E. Street was critical. He disliked building a vestry on the south
side and recommended putting it under the tower; criticised
retention of a west gallery; and thought the estimated cost

£1800) excessive for the amount of work to be done. Street
was a very fine architect but in this case his judgement was faulty.
As the bells are rung from ground level, his proposal to site the
vestry under the tower was impractical and building it on the
south side would have been much less visually intrusive than it is
on the north. The gallery was needed because the alternative of
building a new aisle to replace its seating capacity would have
cost £400–£500 more.

The church was closed on 13 April 1879 and re-opened on
28 April 1880. The builder was Silver of Maidenhead and the final
cost was £1531 plus £325 for the chancel which was met by the
Marquis of Downshire, the lay rector. Grants were obtained from
the ICBS (£35) and from the Diocesan Church Building Society
(£100). The remainder of the cost was met by subscription and
many gifts were made of furniture and fittings.

As usual, the old pulpit and pews were swept away. There was
general repair to the fabric, reflooring, insertion of new windows
and addition of a vestry and organ chamber on the north side of
the chancel. Inside, the most drastic structural change was the
removal of a timber and plaster partition which separated the
nave and chancel and the substitution of a Gothic chancel arch.
In the course of this work the remains of a stone screen were
found but were removed. A number of wall paintings were
uncovered but only one was preserved. On the other hand, the
slab with a carving of a mounted knight, found being used for
flooring, was retrieved and placed on the wall.

As at Bradfield, privately owned faculty pews posed a problem.
Prior to restoration there were twenty-one seats in these. All
were surrendered except for ten contained in two pews belonging
to Luke Lousley of Manor Farm. These pews were repaired at his
expense and retained with their doors, albeit in cut down form.
'Pretentious and exclusive' was the verdict of the rural dean at
the re-opening service. Overall, however, seating capacity was
increased from 250 to 292 and the number of free seats from 229
to 282.

Like Stanford Dingley, this was a restoration where money was
tight and the cheapest options, such as a gallery for schoolchildren,
had to be adopted. Some needlesss destruction took place, probably because preservation would have entailed extra cost, and the
absence in both churches of any stained glass, in contrast to
Bradfield, reveals the lack of wealth.

Bucklebury

In April 1877, when the Hampstead Norreys vestry was resolving
to restore the church, the Society for the Protection of Ancient
Buildings was founded at the instigation of William Morris with

Bucklebury Church.

the purpose of halting the tide of destructive restoration. Its view
was that all parts of the structure and fittings should be preserved
as part of the historic growth of the church and that restoration
should be limited to repair and conservation necessary for that
purpose. In Bucklebury we have an example of the application
of SPAB principles.

Alone among the Pang Valley churches, Bucklebury remained
virtually unaltered throughout the 19th century. £400 was spent
on it between 1840 and 1874, most of which must have been
applied to renewal of the door and windows in the chancel which
was done at an unknown date round about 1850. Bucklebury was
a squire parish and it is here that we must seek the reason. The
owner from 1832 to 1881 was Winchcombe Henry Howard
Hartley. The manor house burnt down soon after he inherited
and he did not rebuild it. It is likely that he lived principally in
Gloucestershire at Lyegrove House, Old Sodbury, where he was
also lord of the manor; certainly he died and was buried there.
He may also have taken a relative lack of interest in Bucklebury
as a consequence of having been defeated in his attempt to
enclose the Common in 1835. No vicar would be likely to embark
on restoration without active support from the squire, who was
the lay rector, and the declining population offered no incentive
to do so.

After Hartley's death in 1881, Bucklebury was inherited by his
niece, Nina Webley-Parry. The Revd Edward Thorp came as vicar

in 1907 and it seems to have been his initiative, having gained
Mrs Webley-Parry's approval, to restore the church in 1911.

By this time attitudes to church restoration and in particular
the value of post-Reformation fittings were changing under the
influence of the SPAB. The 1899 *Kelly's Directory* mentions
Bucklebury's 'old-fashioned square pews, pulpit with sounding
board and western gallery'. Thorp accordingly approached the
SPAB who sent one of their approved architects, William Weir,
to report and make recommendations. In a further sign of the
times, the vestry meeting to discuss Weir's report was held on
the vicarage lawn and was advertised by printed notices. At this
meeting Thorp explained that he wanted to alter the seating so as
to get rid of the unseemly behaviour which went on at the back
of the church in the high box pews which made it impossible to
spot the culprits. Offences included reading newspapers, using
peashooters, defacing hymn and prayer books, and leaving behind
assorted litter (nut shells, orange peel, banana skins and football
coupons). The only opposition came from H. T. M. Wallis, son of
the former curate, who pleaded in vain for the pews to be left
alone and especially for the retention of the three-decker pulpit
on the grounds of rarity and historic sentiment.

The solution adopted was to remove the front block of
pews, which were eighteenth century deal, to substitute the
oak Jacobean ones from the back and to replace those with open
benches. The old oak benches in the north aisle, which had been
converted into deal box pews, were changed back to their original
state, and the three-decker pulpit was removed. The sounding
board was kept and a new pulpit was constructed out of old
carved oak from the Manor Farm pew on the south side of the
chancel which was removed. The Manor pew on the north side
was set back to improve visibility of the sanctuary, which was
raised by one step. The chancel was embellished with mural dec-
oration and striking stained glass all designed by Frank Brangwyn
who in his youth was apprenticed to William Morris. The church
was closed in August 1911 and re-opened on 17 February 1912. The
work cost £500, with Mrs Webly-Parry paying for the chancel.
The plastered walls were brushed down and limewashed having
been examined for traces of wall paintings.

This was a highly sophisticated restoration which successfully preserves the impression of an 'unrestored' church. Like
Bradfield, it was in the vanguard of contemporary fashion. The
contrast between the two vividly illustrates the revolution in taste
which occurred between 1846 and 1912.

Those who have made detailed studies of each parish will
be able to add to this brief account whose aim has been to set
individual restorations within a wider context and to indicate

how study of them can contribute to the broader history of each parish.

Sources

Basil Clarke Papers (Council for the Care of Churches)
Berkshire Archaeological Journal
The Ecclesiologist
ICBS files (Lambeth Palace Library)
Oxford Diocesan Papers (Oxfordshire Record Office)
Parliamentary Papers (Returns of Church Building and Landowners)
Transactions of the Newbury and District Field Club

19 The Didcot to Newbury Railway

Bill Peto

So you'd like to ride on the footplate of a steam locomotive
working a passenger train from Didcot to Newbury on its
journey to Southampton? I think you will find those 17½ miles
will be quite enough at this time of year. It will be bitterly cold
on the footplate and even colder on the return trip when the
engine may be running tender first. The tender is the vehicle
which runs behind the engine and carries – in this case – 4½ tons
of coal and 2500 gallons of water, but main line trains carry considerably more. Our engine will probably be an old 'Duke Class'
4–4–0 built in Queen Victoria's days and now almost worn out
and certainly past her best. She will have a cab giving little
protection from the weather apart from a canvas sheet attached
to the rear of the cab roof and supported by two pillars sticking
up from the tender. These sheets were introduced in about 1912
but only on engines where the driver requested them. However,
when the First World War broke out in 1914 all engines need to
hide the glare of the fire from German airships hovering in the
dark sky above. The enginemen then called them 'Zeppelin
Sheets' and some still do because names change slowly on the
Great Western Railway. During our day on the footplate you will
probably hear words such as 'whoa' for 'stop', 'the galloper'
instead of 'the express train', or 'put the engine away in the stalls'
instead of 'in the engine shed'. All these were common phrases
when cars had not yet appeared on our roads. The Zeppelin
Sheet may keep off a bit of rain but it won't keep out the cold.
Most people think an engine footplate is hot because
of the white hot fire in the furnace but the cold winds blowing
through the crack between the cab and the boiler quickly gets rid

The 'Comet' in Newbury
Station 1939.
© GWR Collection at
Didcot Railway Museum

of the heat from the fire and freezes the driver and the fireman –
and us on this occasion. I've had a word with the Great Western
Railway Company and they have been kind enough to issue a
footplate pass for you to ride on the engine from Didcot to
Newbury and back, but I must accompany you under an Act of
Parliament dated 1845 to ensure that you do not distract the attention of the driver or fireman as they go about their duties. So any
questions to me please! Your pass says you must travel on the
7.15 a.m. train from Didcot so I'll meet you at the station booking
office at 7.00 a.m. tomorrow morning after you have bought your
return ticket. The company requires you to have one – although
no one will look at it! See you in the morning!

You ask why I said 'booking office' and not 'ticket office' which
is the more usual term nowadays. 'Booking office' comes from
the days of the broad gauge railways back to 1837 before tickets
were introduced. You then paid your fare to the 'booking clerk'
who entered your particulars in a ledger (book) before you
boarded the train. You took whichever seat the guard told you to
– even if it meant sitting next to a drunk or to someone ridden
with fleas for the whole journey. The guard then locked you in
and it was too bad if the carriage caught fire, as they often did
since the wheels were large and rubbed against the woodwork.

You've arrived early this morning so we will make our way up
the stairs to the platform at once and see if the engine has arrived

The 'Comet' working a loose-coupled goods train mainly of coal wagons. Since she has no vacuum braked wagons she is restricted to a speed of 20 to 25 miles per hour depending on the line on which she is running. She once had a lovely brass dome on the boiler, but by the time this photograph was taken it had been painted over because it had reflected the sun into the driver's eyes at certain times of the day.
© Bill Peto

for our train. Here she comes through the early morning mist and, as I expected, she is one of the old 'Duke Class' which usually work the Newbury and Southampton line. She is the '3283 Comet' from Didcot Shed and she entered service in March 1899 since when she has run nearly one and a quarter million miles – equivalent to three and a half journeys to the moon! Her original tender was sold to the British Government in 1917 and was lost at sea when the troopship *Hunstrick* was torpedoed by a U-boat west of Gibraltar on her way to Salonika. A professional salver has told me that these engines and tenders will still be in quite good condition after 84 years under water and salvage with air bags and divers is quite practicable if anyone wished to do it.

'Comet' drops gently back onto our three coaches and our fireman jumps down onto the track to couple the leading coach to the engine and to connect up the vacuum brake and steam heating pipes. Notice that there is a lot of spare space on the arc name plate of the engine because 'Comet' is such a short word. Shortly before the 1939–45 war she was running around with two additional letters added at each end of the brass name plates. She was then named 'IN COMET AX'!

Keep your footplate pass handy and we will go and ask driver Bert East if he will allow us to ride on his footplate. He has the final say and he could refuse to accept the official pass if he wishes. Fortunately he is very friendly on this very cold morning and welcomes us to the footplate of 'Comet'. We must find a place to stand where we will not be in the way of the fireman when he is shovelling best Welsh steam coal through the firehole.

Keeping out of his way will not be easy in 'Comet's' very narrow cab. Yes, I know there are seats for the driver and fireman which they will not be using on the journey, but neither will we because the engine is not sprung like a passenger coach and the vibration will be very unpleasant – even when we are standing and holding onto something all the time. Not all drivers are keen on this old engine and I have heard one driver say 'She is not strong enough to pull the skin off a rice pudding'!

The driver and fireman have spent forty five minutes oiling all the working parts of 'Comet' and preparing her for the journey. We now await the blast from the guard's whistle and a wave of his green flag before the fireman checks that the signalman has lowered the arm of the signal and we move off on our journey. 'Right away, mate, the bobby's dropped the board' shouts our fireman in traditional railway parlance from the Victorian broad gauge days. Until 1874 the trains were signalled by the Railway Police and old names die hard on the Great Western.

Our driver gives three short blasts on the whistle to let the 'bobby' know that we have cleared the points on the main line and then we start pulling hard up the slight incline to Upton & Blewbury Station. As we leave Didcot we see the local football ground on our left with the short spur of railway above it where the Station Pilot engine stands while waiting to be used to attach or remove a van from another train. While waiting the engine crew have a free grandstand view of a football match on a Saturday afternoon. Occasionally a main line express engine fails in the Didcot area and then the Didcot Pilot has to spring into life and rush the delayed train up to London, but when our 'Comet' is the Station Pilot then the main line drivers try to limp on to Reading and ask for a replacement engine there.

We have four sand boxes on 'Comet' which are filled with fine dry sand. If the rails are slippery on uphill inclines the driver can blow a little sand in front of the wheels to stop them from slipping. This works equally well when leaves of any type are on the track in the autumn.

The smoke from our chimney streams back over Didcot where the local people are just beginning to get up.

It was in 1881 that the steam shovels and gangs of navvies started to build the track on which we are running towards Newbury. It was then a single track and was opened to traffic on Wednesday 12 April 1882. Four years later Didcot Station was burned to the ground when a careless porter spilled oil near the Waiting Room fire. It burned furiously from noon until nightfall and horse-drawn fire pumps came from Oxford, Harwell, Wallingford and Abingdon because Didcot did not then have a fire station of its own.

Navvies were men who had once built the Navigational Canals and who now roamed the country seeking work building railways. Each man carried his own pick and shovel and pushed his own wheelbarrow as he went from county to county seeking work. These men were a great nuisance to local people, particularly when they were kept for weeks waiting for their pay. This sometimes happened when the railway contractors had not been paid by the railway companies. They could buy neither food nor beer and sometimes turned very nasty – as happened at Sonning Cutting near Reading – and many a navvy was found on the wrong side of a hen house door. King William IV ordered the Great Western Railway Company to form their own police force to control their navvies. The policemen were based at the larger stations which became known as 'police stations'. Later, when town police forces were formed and learned from their railway colleagues, they called their bases 'police stations' too – and still do. In contrast, there were then no railways in Ireland and the Irish police called their bases 'police barracks'.

We have just reached the deserted station of Churn Halt which marks the top of the climb from Didcot and what a racket we made as the old 'Comet' struggled to haul her three coaches up the 1 in 106 gradient! We are both freezing cold, despite the red hot fire in the firebox, but the poor fireman must be very warm from his exertions shovelling coal to a greedy fire all the way from Didcot. Churn is a very deserted spot and there are so few passengers waiting to board or leave trains here that they only stop if prior notice is given to the guard that passengers wish to alight. Passengers wishing to join the train must wave their arm as the train approaches and signal it – just like a bus. The only passengers would be ramblers, people going to the rifle range, or – during the war years – people going to the military camps. A very young abandoned lamb was once found on Churn Halt and a kind hearted driver took it to Compton Station where the station master's wife reared it as a family pet!

Until the Second World War trains could only pass at stations because the track was single line. No train could move on the single line unless the driver had in his cab a train staff passed to his fireman by the bobby. It was impossible for more than one staff to be out of the signal box at any one time and so a head on collision was impossible, except in the very occasional case of human error. You will have noticed our fireman taking a big iron hoop with the staff attached as we passed by each signal box. He then read out to Bert East, our driver, what was printed on the staff – just to be quite sure that he had been given the correct staff for that section of the line.

The Company know exactly how long a train should take

between each signal box and the time of passing is entered by the bobby in his signal log. Now, all around Churn are the most lovely mushrooms growing wild in the fields, and many a driver would stop while his fireman jumped off the engine to pick a basket full for each of them. The train would then resume its journey – but rather later than scheduled. This problem would be solved by picking a third basket of mushrooms and passing them to the bobby with the compliments of the train crew. The time of passing would be slightly 'adjusted' in the signal log – and everyone was happy! There were also lots of rabbits in the same area, but I have never heard of drivers carrying a gun and shooting them – as they did regularly on some western Welsh branch lines!

During the Depression of the 1930s when the Jarrow March took place to bring the suffering of the unemployed workers to the attention of the government, train loads of rabbits were sent from west Wales to the north-east coast of England as cheap food for those out of work. They were transported in bogie milk vans which were branded 'for rabbit traffic only' – lest the smell of the rabbits should taint the milk on a future journey. By then, anyway, most milk was carried in 3 000 gallon glass lined tanks so the vans which carried milk churns were becoming surplus to requirement.

Most of the Didcot to Newbury line was like a switchback, slightly up or slightly down. Every day a small engine would work a goods train both ways along the line and would stop at all stations with a siding or goods yard and drop off a wagon or two and pick up one or two others. This little goods train has been known as a 'fly' since very early years. The origin of the name is unknown, but I would suggest that the train 'hopped' from station to station just as a fly does from item to item. One day a new guard was required to learn the route so he accompanied an experienced guard in his van on the Didcot to Newbury run. On arrival at one of the stations they applied the brake van's hand brake and one of the guards went forward and uncoupled those wagons that were to be left with the brake van while the engine did its job with the front wagons. This accomplished, the engine and wagons returned and set back to be coupled to the rear part of the train by the guard so that the journey could continue. All went well and the guard signalled to the driver to set off for the next station. He took off his hand brake and retired into the van to discuss football or something as the van started moving. It gathered speed and the two men soon realised that it was moving unusually fast. They soon realised that they were free-wheeling rapidly in reverse down the incline with several wagons while the engine was carrying on with the rest of the train in the opposite direction! Each guard looked at the other. 'Didn't *you* recouple our wagons to the front section of the train?' 'No, I thought *you* had done it!'. 'But I thought *you* had!'. They applied the hand brake and stopped the runaway wagons. It could have been nasty.

Through Hampstead Norreys we go, changing the staff again, and on through Hermitage where there used to be a nudist camp. It would have hardly been popular today with the temperature near freezing! A mile and a half further on we speed over Fisher's Lane level crossing and after another two and a half miles we shall be in Newbury on the West of England Main Line – and that is as far as our footplate pass will allow us to go.

Facts and Figures

- The Didcot, Newbury & Southampton Junction Railway was incorporated in an Act of Parliament dated 5 August 1873.
- The line connected to the Great Western Railway at Didcot and to the London & South Western Railway at Shawford Junction.
- A connexion to East Ilsley was planned but never built.
- The first sod was cut in Newbury on 26 April 1879.
- Didcot to Newbury opened on 12 April 1882.
- The service provided was four passenger trains and one goods train per day.
- Compton Station was rebuilt in 1902.
- The DN and SJR was absorbed by the Great Western Railway in 1923.
- The line was doubled in 1943 to cope with wartime traffic.
- The line closed to passengers on 10 September 1962.
- The line closed to goods traffic on 10 August 1964.

The Wildlife

20 The Pang Valley Countryside Project

Sally Wallington and Colin Esrich

Part one – Countryside Management in the Pang Valley

In the beginning …

From 1989 to 1993 the upper reaches of the River Pang were dry.
This was due primarily to the abstraction of 13.5 million litres of
water per day from a bore hole at Compton. The local parish
councils formed a pressure group called the Pang Valley
Conservation Trust and in April 1992, after intensive lobbying,
Thames Water PLC agreed to reduce water abstraction to five
million litres per day. The next summer the river returned.

This success was the catalyst for the creation of the Pang
Valley Countryside Project by the local community, with support
from local authorities and statutory agencies in January 1993.

The Pang Valley is an extremely attractive rural landscape
located within the North Wessex Downs Area of Outstanding
Natural Beauty and on the doorstep of the urban areas of
Reading, Newbury and Thatcham. The Pang rises near East Ilsley
and flows through a heavily wooded landscape characterised by
mixed farming with riverside grazing land, before reaching its
confluence with the Thames at Pangbourne. The valley has a
diverse landscape encompassing the river Pang, ancient woodlands, chalk downland, heathland, rolling farmland and small
villages. There are several Sites of Special Scientific Interest and
many Wildlife Heritage Sites.

However, over the past few decades the countryside has
come under increasing pressure – partly due to changes in farming
practices, rising demands from recreational users and a lack of

The River Pang.
© Pang & Kennet Valleys
Countryside Project

awareness and understanding of the natural environment. The increasingly diverse demands made on the countryside of the Pang Valley have implications for its wildlife, landscape and amenity value.

With these issues in mind the Pang Valley Countryside Project was set up with the aim of protecting and enhancing the natural beauty of the Pang Valley and helping people to appreciate the countryside. By working in partnership with farmers, parish councils, community groups, schools and other agencies we are helping to secure a diverse and thriving countryside, a working environment rich in wildlife.

The specific objectives are:
– To conserve and enhance the biodiversity of the natural environment and landscape in the Pang Valley.
– To promote environmentally responsible farming practices throughout the project area.
– To increase awareness of the countryside and environmental issues through education and interpretation.
– To involve all sectors of the community in caring for and appreciating the local environment and countryside.

Our managed countryside

The River Pang and the surrounding valley had been heavily influenced by human activities. Many important landscape and wildlife features are present today only because of past farmers and countrymen. Traditional farming methods provided many

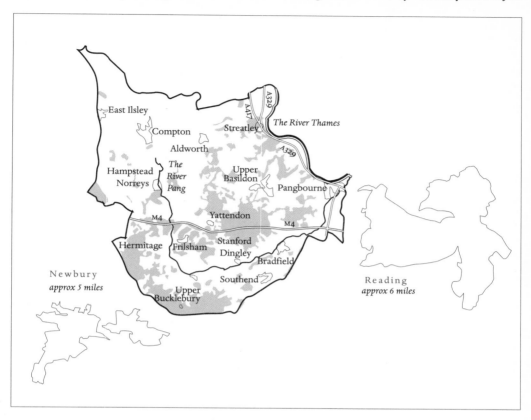

East Ilsley
Compton
Streatley
The River Thames
Aldworth
The River Pang
Hampstead Norreys
Upper Basildon
Pangbourne
M4
Yattendon
M4
Hermitage
Frilsham
Stanford Dingley
Bradfield
Newbury
approx 5 miles
Southend
Reading
approx 6 miles
Upper Bucklebury

The Project area now covers 160 km² and encompasses fifteen parishes within West Berkshire.
© Pang & Kennet Valleys Countryside Project

specialist habitats and landscape features, such as hedgerows, that were an inherent part of farming. Our wildlife has evolved to take advantage of the results of our past activities; barn owls nest in our barns, violets grow in coppiced woodland, insects live in old parkland and pollarded trees and our hedgerows provide vital wildlife cover and food sources.

Farming has moved forward at a dramatic pace to ensure that we can feed ourselves, but this process has meant the decline of many characteristic features of our countryside. Consequently coppiced woodland is left uncut, hedgerows are no longer laid, willows are left unpollarded and as a result the wildlife and conservation value of our countryside is reduced. We cannot turn the clock back but we must be aware of the changes taking place in the fabric of our countryside and start planning for the long-term future.

Over seventy-five per cent of land in West Berkshire is in agricultural production so working with farmers and landowners is key to a healthy and thriving environment for both people and wildlife.

This aspect of the Project's work is vital in helping to manage change in the countryside, particularly with the shift away from

Pang Valley landscape.
© Pang & Kennet Valleys
Countryside Project

agricultural subsidies towards agri-environment schemes. The
Project aims to help farmers make conservation an integral part
of farming and land management practice. The Project has con-
tacted and encouraged over fifty farmers and landowners within
the Pang Valley to take responsibility for the stewardship of the
countryside. Many have responded positively and with the Project's help, have carried out practical work and entered environmental grant schemes. Without the co-operation and help of the
valley's farming community the Project would have achieved
nothing. We have now made contact with most of the valley's
farmers and have worked with them to produce tangible results.
If you visit the valley you will find that work in long-term agreements and work carried out to date (2001) includes:

5 ponds restored
50 barn owl boxes erected
1 bat hibernaculum
173 willows pollarded
33 new willows planted
99 hectares of grassland managed with no chemical inputs
12 kilometres of field margins created to buffer hedgerows and
watercourses
23 hectares heathland restored
13 kilometres hedgerow planted and restored
1.6 kilometres of hedgerow layed
24 hectares of new broadleaved woodland
280 hectares opened for educational access
1 barn thatched and restored

Charcoal and woodland products

As well as encouraging farmers and landowners to undertake
environmental enhancements through various grants the Project
has sought to promote the management of small woodlands and
the reinstatement of coppice through the development of sus-

Charcoal production.
© Pang & Kennet Valleys
Countryside Project

tainable rural businesses – most notably Pang Valley Charcoal.
Julian Fawcett and Martin Wright set up their kilns in Rushall
Farm, Bradfield and worked with the Project by taking derelict
hazel coppice and turning it into charcoal. Over the years they
have perfected the art and sell around 15–20 tonnes per year of
high quality charcoal to local outlets.

This not only benefits the local environment but also globally
it helps to preserve habitats such as the mangrove swamps. Of
the 50–60 000 tonnes of charcoal used annually approximately
ninety-six per cent is still imported. This locally produced charcoal is a high quality, sustainable product, which lights easily,
without the need for firelighters or fuel and has not been transported halfway round the globe.

More recently Pang Valley Charcoal diversified to Pang Valley
Woodland Products and expanded the business to use local wood
from sustainable sources for the production of countryside furniture, milling and sawing timbers and lathes for traditional timber
framed buildings. This increased work has led to additional seasonal staff being taken on thereby further creating rural employment opportunities.

Local Community Action

The Project is keen to help local people improve their local environment and also to raise the environmental awareness of everyone
in the area. The most effective way of doing this is to get people

to participate. Through participation new ideas and skills are used and remembered. Few Pang Valley residents work in the country-side and many people are becoming increasingly divorced from their countryside environment. The volunteer work, walks and talks help to redress this imbalance and positively encourage people to explore and carry out practical work in their nearby countryside. Specific tasks in the area's villages have attracted further help and the Project is always open to suggestions or ideas from local parish councils. The Project has set up two conservation volunteer groups – Pang Valley Conservation Volunteers and the Bucklebury Heathlands Conservation Group and both are excellent examples of local people taking responsi-bility for and caring for their immediate environments.

The Pang Valley Conservation Volunteers (PVCP) have a roving brief and carry out a range of activities throughout the valley. Where farmers are involved in major conservation schemes the volunteers will often go along to provide a helping hand. In this way farmers and the local community are brought closer together.

The Bucklebury Heathland Conservation Group (BHCG) con-centrates on maintaining the heathland habitat on Bucklebury Common. In their formative years the Project provided much help and assistance but this group has clear work parameters and is now entirely autonomous calling on the Project when specific expertise or practical help is needed.

These two volunteer groups have made a significant contribu-tion to the countryside in their area. More volunteers are always needed, as there is plenty of work to do. Volunteers also help out by undertaking survey work. In the Pang Valley we have been working on a project with local people from a number of parishes to assess the areas' hedgerows and a team of volunteers has been brought together to monitor and maintain the barn owl boxes throughout the valley.

A number of Parish Councils contribute to the Project and this relationship has developed further with the establishment of a Parish Council representatives meeting. This acts as a forum for the exchange of ideas and the development of community based projects.

In conjunction with the Kennet Valley Countryside Project there is also a membership group – Friends of the Pang and Kennet Valleys – which further enables local people to get involved through walks, talks, events and to assist with fundraising for local projects.

Effective local partnerships

The Pang Valley Countryside Project is a partnership of local farmers, parish councillors, local authorities and government

Pang Valley Conservation
Volunteers clearing
ragwort from a SSSI
meadow.
© Pang & Kennet Valleys
Countryside Project

agencies who all wish to implement the Project aims and in doing so achieve their own objectives too. The co-operation the Project receives enables the work to be implemented on private land, tapping into expertise where necessary. Importantly the local involvement of the Project's steering committee and close liaison between the Project and parish councils empowers the local people to make decisions regarding the environment.

The Pang Valley Countryside Project is a partnership currently funded and supported by: the West Berkshire District Council, the Environment Agency, the Lord Illife Family Charitable Trust, English Nature, the Englefield Estate, local parish councils, the John Simonds Trust, the Friends of the Pang and Kennet Valleys, and the Farming and Wildlife Advisory Group.

The future of the Project relies on funding to ensure the continuing success. The PVCP provides the funding partners with a practical body able to implement their countryside policies 'on the ground'. By involving the local community the Project is helping to carry out West Berkshire's Local Agenda 21 and will be a key delivery mechanism for Biodiversity Action Plans and the new programmes of the North Wessex Downs Area of Outstanding Natural Beauty. All concerned recognise that conservation is an ongoing process that requires regular input if it is to achieve real long-term gains.

The Project now has the confidence and respect of local landowners, this allows us to address environmental problems in greater depth. We will use the next three years to further raise the environmental awareness of farmers and landowners to promote the use of practical solutions to potential environmental problems. For example we will be returning to the river to work towards supporting the viable population of key species such as the watervole, which could become extinct on the Pang by 2005 if urgent action is not taken. This can only be achieved by working closely with all of the riparian owners along the Pang.

The project is in its eighth year and has seen many achievements and this success is due to the support and involvement of the local community and by working in partnership with agencies and other organizations. What started as a few people concerned about their local river has grown into a highly innovative and successful countryside management project delivering real long-term benefits for the community on biodiversity, landscape and environmental education. We are extremely grateful to all the people who have given their enthusiasm, time, and commitment over the years, without which little could have been achieved. It just goes to show that if you really care about your local environment, miracles can happen.

Part two – Environmental education in the Pang Valley

The promotion of environmental education has always been one of the main aims of the Pang and Kennet Valleys Countryside Project.

In the Pang Valley the John Simonds Trust for Education in the Countryside, based at Rushall Farm, Bradfield, was already catering for large numbers of school children when the Project was set up in 1993. It seemed a logical step therefore for the two organisations to unite and work together to deliver environmental education in the Pang Valley. Nearly ten years on and the partnership has achieved massive success, so much so in fact that it now stands as one of the foremost providers of environmental education in the south of England.

The educational aims of the Pang Valley Countryside Project are:
– To provide a high quality curriculum based education service for schools.
– To promote a love and understanding of the countryside.
– To encourage leadership, self-confidence and mutual respect in young people.
– To develop understanding between town and country.

These aims are met in a number of ways: holding training sessions for teachers, reaching children through an educational website and by occasionally visiting schools. Of most significance however is the leading of school visits to farm and countryside sites in the Pang Valley. The Pang Valley is an ideal place for children to explore and learn about the environment in safety. Its excellent location means that it is accessible to schools from as far away as London and Oxford whilst being only a short coach trip away for those in Reading and Newbury.

Because the Project owns no land of its own it is immediately apparent just how vital the support of local farmers and land-owners is to the success of the education work. By allowing access to their land (often under the terms of the Countryside Stewardship Scheme) people like Graham Childs, Lord Iliffe, Tim Billington, William Cumber and Lord Benyon have done a great deal to facilitate environmental education in the Pang Valley. After all, can there be a better way to understand farming than by visiting a working farm or to study rivers than by putting on a pair of waders and getting into a beautiful chalk stream teeming with aquatic life? First hand experiences that take place in a meaningful context are precisely what make environmental education such a powerful tool.

Thanks to the co-operation of landowners, schools coming to the Pang Valley can choose from a variety of working farms and countryside sites to visit, four of which also offer safe access to the River Pang. Other resources available include a fully acces-sible pond dipping platform, ancient woodlands, hedgerows and meadows, camping and bunkhouse style accommodation and fully accessible toilets, hand washing and picnic facilities. The Pang Valley Countryside Project supplies all the necessary educational equipment for visiting schools.

In addition to the school visits, many church and youth groups use the site at Rushall Farm during evenings and weekends. The eighteenth-century threshing barn there (affectionately known as the Black Barn) has become a real focus for the community, a place where people come for celebration and worship.

Besides the sites themselves, the success of the educational work has always depended upon the quality of the educational staff. Alex Fowles was the first Education Officer followed by Colin Esrich. The education officer's job is to organise school visits, train staff, be responsible for health and safety, liaise with schools and help to lead the visits. There is also an assistant Education Officer and up to seven trained, part time staff who help to lead visits, all employed by the John Simonds Trust. Having such a large team reflects a strong belief in the impor-tance of building good relationships with visiting children and ensures that health and safety is never compromised.

School visits to the Pang Valley are usually based around the geography or science elements of the National Curriculum.

Pond dipping.
© Pang & Kennet Valleys
Countryside Project

Areas commonly studied include: modern farm systems, sustain-ability and environmental change, woodland management and ecology, fieldwork techniques and pond and river studies. Children are encouraged to learn key skills and acquire knowledge and understanding in the different areas through investigative, hands–on activities. During their visit the children are also encouraged to see the value of maintaining a living, working countryside which is essential for providing us with healthy food and as an important part of our heritage. In addition to the larger groups, many GCSE and A-level students come to the Pang Valley and to the River Pang in particular to carry out their practical fieldwork activities.

As with the wider work of the Pang and Kennet Valleys Countryside Project, the success of environmental education has also been the result of working through partnerships. In addition to the John Simonds Trust, the Pang Valley Countryside Project has developed close working relationships with several other key partners including the Environment Agency, the Iliffe Family Charitable Trust, the Englefield Estate and several local farmers and landowners. The support of the Farming and Wildlife Advisory Group and the funding from West Berkshire District Council have also been of fundamental importance. By harnessing

Stream dipping.
© Pang & Kennet Valleys
Countryside Project

the combined effort and financial resources of other organisations, the level of service provision has gone far beyond what could have been achieved by the Project working alone. As a result, the education service has delivered far-reaching benefits and real value for money.

Since it began in 1993 the environmental education service of the Pang Valley Countryside Project has been used by over 30 000 students. Current figures reveal that almost 6 000 schoolchildren of all ages and abilities, from nursery to university, visit the different sites each year. With the emphasis placed on sustainability and management/care of the environment in the new National Curriculum (2000), the value of the service to schools looks set to become even greater over the coming years.

The work in the Pang Valley is complemented by exciting initiatives taking place in the Kennet Valley. Educational projects for primary schools have included barge trips on the Kennet and Avon Canal and interactive theatre workshops. Secondary schools meanwhile, have benefited from a new education pack on sustainability (complete with CD ROM) and the opportunity to take part in a national scheme working with businesses in the food and farming sector.

The education work of the countryside projects is not just

Adults on a
conducted walk.
© Greenaway collection

limited to young people. Adult education in the two valleys is
thriving thanks to an extensive programme of guided walks and
talks. Designed to raise awareness and understanding of the
countryside and its management these walks and talks cover
a range of subjects and are very well attended.

Regardless of what is specified in the school syllabus however,
other changes at societal and global level make education about
the environment an imperative. The Earth is suffering significant
environmental damage and it is our actions and behaviour which
are the cause. The fact that so many young people have such little
connection to the natural world, and neither empathy nor respect
for those who live and work in the countryside should be of concern to us all. As long as attitudes remain so negative or even
apathetic then our behaviour will continue to cause harm.
Promoting better understanding, respect and care for each other
and our environment is perhaps the challenge of all education
but environmental education in particular. It should be a source
of pride for those living and working in the Pang Valley that so
much of this valuable work is taking place here.

References

To find out more about environmental education in the Pang and Kennet Valleys contact the Project office for school visits, guided walks, talks and events or visit the projects websites on www.rushallfarm.org.uk and www.futureinyourhands.co.uk

Pang Valley Countryside Project
The Old Estate Office
Englefield Road
Theale
Berkshire
RG7 5DZ

Phone 0118 930 5335
Fax 0118 930 5336

21 Coombe Wood – a site of special scientific interest

Malcolm Storey

Introduction

Coombe Wood in Frilsham comprises almost 20 hectares of semi-natural woodland. It is one of the most biologically interesting of several such areas within the Yattendon Estates holding. The wood was first notified as a SSSI (Site of Special Scientific Interest) by the then NCC (Nature Conservancy Council – now EN, English Nature) in 1985. It also falls within the North Wessex Downs AONB (Area of Outstanding Natural Beauty).

This description is based on surveys carried out on visits made in 1996 and 1997. Forestry operations since then may have made some of the descriptions obsolete.

Most of the site is mature semi-natural broad-leaved woodland, undulating across two small west-sloping valleys. A bracken-covered clearing at the south-west corner leads into large old birches. There is also a rather uninteresting conifer plantation.

Although there is no running water on the site, at least during the summer, there is a damp marshy area at the top of the southern valley which runs down to a ditch. There are also a number of varying-sized depressions, some quite deep, which are presumed to be swallow holes.

Dead wood is present in the form of stumps and short pollards, small fallen wood and some large fallen logs. Several interesting insects breeding in dead wood have been seen and it is likely that others remain to be found.

The site is bounded to the north by the embankment of the M4. To the east and west it is surrounded by fields and the

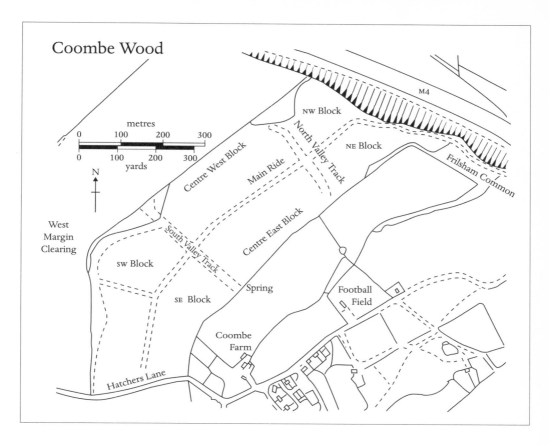

Coombe Wood

Based upon the Ordnance Survey Map with the permission of Her Majesty's Stationery Office.
© Crown Copyright
MC100036335

Christmas tree plantations of Yattendon Estates, except that the north east corner connects to Frilsham Common.

Just south of the SSSI, the hoverfly *Brachypalpoides lenta* was seen feeding on hawthorn blossom . This is a particularly beautiful species with a cherry-red abdomen. It breeds in dead wood. Hopefully it also occurs on-site.

The compartments

The wood is bisected by a narrow north–south ride which is in turn intersected by two broad sunny east–west rides which conveniently creates six blocks of woodland.

1 *South-western block*

This compartment slopes gently to the north-east. It is old coppice with some multi-stemmed ancient coppiced Sessile oaks under Sessile oak and ash standards. The canopy is roughly 20 metres high. Towards the western end, birch appears and there are occasional wild cherry .

Some of the oak trunks have the 'Barnacle' lichen. This is an old forest species requiring clean air which is now very rare in

Berkshire. Humphrey Bowen, in *The Flora of Berkshire*, (1968), included it in his list of Berkshire species which were 'recorded in the nineteenth century but appear to be extinct now.' It doesn't have a real English name, but it's one of the first lichens people learn and is often referred to as 'that lichen that looks like barnacles'. Unfortunately another lichen (*Pyrenocollema halodytes*) which actually grows immersed in the shells of barnacles on the seashore, probably has a better claim to the name.

The under-storey is approximately 2–4 metres high and consists of hazel, holly, hawthorn (*Crataegus monogyna*) and sycamore with the occasional field maple. It is sparse over most of the area, except towards the east.

Near the main ride the flora is quite diverse with primrose, red currant, dog's mercury, bugle, yellow pimpernel and wood sedge. Further away from the ride, the ground flora is sparse with honeysuckle, a few small sprigs of bramble, many oak seedlings, and three kinds of Buckler ferns. The lower two-thirds is well covered in bluebells and bracken, merging into the bracken-covered clearing.

The compartment has a fair amount of dead wood, though mostly small pieces, but there have been recent falls, mostly birch, towards the bottom of the slope.

A large depression near the main ride is presumed to be a swallow hole.

2 South-eastern block

The ride along the southern border of the SSSI bends around into this compartment to peter out in a patch of buckler ferns. These are mainly false male-fern. This species is restricted to more acid sites than the much commoner male fern. It is often found on the acid soils on the higher ground surrounding the Pang Valley. The false male fern is sometimes called the scaly male-fern. Elsewhere in the compartment most of the ferns are the true male fern and this probably indicates that the soil or ground water is more acid at this spot. The rest of the eastern section of the compartment is ash woodland with abundant bluebells in the ground flora. The slightly larger western section is drier and less interesting.

In the eastern section, the ground flora is dominated by bluebells in the spring with the bare leaf litter visible in places and buckler ferns in damper parts. The trees, mainly ash with some oak and birch, are not very large. Many of the ash trunks have patches of barnacle lichen on the north side of their bases.

The scrub layer is well developed at 3–6 metres, being mostly hazel with some honeysuckle and forming an above-ground network. This is one of the key habitat requirements for dormice and these may be present, although they apparently have not been searched for.

A few very old oak stumps and a good quantity of more recent fallen wood provide habitat for fungi and deadwood insects. One of these is the cranefly, *Ctenophora pectinicornis* (Diptera: Tipulidae). The *Ctenophora* craneflies are about the same size as the more familiar *Tipula* craneflies that live in every garden, but fly more strongly and more purposefully. This, combined with their black and shiny appearance make them quite wasp-like and this specimen was at first mistaken for a large ichneumon wasp as it flew around the base of a large ash trunk. The species breeds in dead wood.

3 *Centre west block*

A rather uninteresting plantation of introduced conifers.

4 *Centre east block*

This comprises the adjacent sides of two valleys with the watershed between. One side is mature Beech woodland with large old trees, some fallen wood and little ground flora on a south west facing slope. The other side is a darker and colder north-facing slope.

5 *North-west block.*

Light airy woodland with a fairly gappy canopy, rather overgrown with Bramble. There was little in the way of shrub layer, but at ground level, there were patches of Great Wood-rush.

6 *North-east block*

Again, light airy woodland with a fairly gappy canopy. The trees are mostly Sessile Oak, with a few Beech and Birch. There is an uneven age structure with many trees of the same age, planted in rows, circumferences: 62.5 inches, 67.5 inches, 75 inches, 81 inches (oak), 81 inches (beech) My impression was that the older trees were nearer pure Sessile oak, while the younger ones (approximately 28 inches circumference) had more hybrid characters. Again, several oak trunks have the barnacle lichen. Heavy deer grazing has prevented regeneration from the oak and beech stumps. There was very good germination of oak seedlings following the bumper acorn crop in 95, but the deer will probably remove these.

By the way of dead wood there were a few cut stumps, short pollards ranging from a few cm to 1.5 metres high and some fallen branches but no large fallen pieces.

The shrub layer is poor with a few isolated hazel and holly.

At ground level, except for a bare ring of approximately one

metre around bases of the larger trees, much of the compartment is an almost pure monoculture of Great Wood-rush. This
species often shows such luxuriant growth in Pennine woodlands
but it is most unusual in Berkshire. There is bracken on the
bottom half of the slope and the top area and also bramble
patches, which will provide a valuable nectar source for summer
insects as long as the canopy remains open.

Patches of disturbed ground (mammal activity and forestry
operations) in this compartment support a variety of herb species
including foxglove, heath speedwell and slender St John's wort.

Near the field on the south-eastern border, the woodrush stops
abruptly and a much richer ground flora has developed. This
could be due to either a change of soil or to fertiliser drift from
the adjoining field.

7 *Clearing at western margin*

This large clearing has a good show of Bluebells early in the year.
The ground flora also includes creeping soft-grass, nettle, goose-
grass, ground ivy, dog's mercury, greater stitchwort, wood sorrel,
bugle, yellow pimpernel and a patch of very erect, shuttle-cock
shaped male ferns. By high summer it is smothered in dense
bracken.

A few very large standing birches grow at the southern end
and along the eastern margin a number of them have fallen providing valuable deadwood habitat.

There are several depressions which are presumed to be swallow
holes, although may be the result of human disturbance.

The Rides

Main Ride

A muddy patch at the Southern end of the main ride supports
water starwort and remote sedge. From here a grassy track
gently slopes SW–NE. It is more or less bare along the wheel
tracks. Above, the hazel understorey and sessile oak overhang,
but only at one or two points do they meet to provide a bridge
for tree-living species, such as dormouse if these are present.

There is a well-developed herb zone on each side mainly of
creeping soft-grass, with some yellow archangel on the south
side, and primrose, bugle, nettle, bluebell, and yellow pimpernel
in the spring, all overtaken by bracken and buckler ferns in the
summer.

The central section of the track comprises a warm sunny track
rising out of the first valley and followed by shady coolness as it
descends into the second valley.

Finally it rises again and bends to run atop a small ridge parallel to the M4 embankment as it leaves the wood and sets off across Frilsham Common.

Track in Southern Valley

This shady, grassy track slopes from south-east down to north-west. The top is steep and, apart from a small flat platform, the footing is difficult. Further down the slope soon lessens while the ground gets softer and damper until you come to a seepage area. Although no running water was seen during the visits, a few stoneflies were present in June 1996. This common species has aquatic larvae which are normally found in ponds and slow streams. Here they apparently survive on the surface of the mud and amongst wet leaves. There are one or two clumps of thin-spiked wood sedge below the seep where a small ditch runs down the track. This is a locally common species in the damper wood-lands of the Pang Valley. Unfortunately it often grows in shade where it is a shy flowerer; it must then be recognised from its wide leaves.

As it approaches the intersection with the main track, the ground becomes drier and more level, until the junction itself which is quite firm and dry where the ground has been made up. There is a grassy clearing which is probably the best spot on the site for wildflowers and for butterflies and other sunshine-loving insects. The rare parasite fly, *Subclytia rotundiventris* was found here. The larvae of parasite flies are internal parasites of insects. They grow within their host consuming its tissues from within, but avoiding vital organs until they are full grown, so that the host continues to live. Eventually, the full grown parasite larva bursts out of the host, killing it, and pupates. This biology inspired the *Alien* series of science fiction films. In the present species, shield bugs assume the John Hurt role, especially the birch shield bug. This has also been found at the site, indeed this shield bug is as common as its foodplant, birch. A single plant of pale sedge, quite scarce in this area, grows under the oak tree on the eastern corner.

Below the main track, the ditch reappears alongside a broad herb-rich bank where common spotted-orchids flower in early summer. The narrow buckler fern grows nearby. This fern needs a damp habitat, even by fern standards, and an acid soil. It is quite uncommon in the modern countryside where so much marginal land has been fertilised or drained for agriculture or development. The ditch continues among sedges down a wide and grassy track until finally disappearing into the woodland.

Being well lit and damp, this was the most botanically interesting ride.

Track in Northern Valley

This ride was much less interesting. It is rather drier and much of it is quite heavily shaded. Few plants apart from grasses were seen.

The oak jewel beetle breeds in dead wood. One individual was swept from low vegetation which was mainly composed of great woodrush, but of course it may have fallen from trees above. It was found rather late in the season (13 October 1996) by Martin Harvey.

Conclusion

This essay results from a handful of visits during 1996–7 including only one during a not very fruitful fungus season. A fully detailed report and species list has been prepared and may be obtained from the author. Even so, the list of species encountered (especially fungi and animals) must be considered to be very preliminary. The complete species list for Coombe Wood would be likely to run to several thousand species compared to the two hundred or so species found during my visits.

References

Bowen, H.J.M. *The Flora of Berkshire* (1968)
NCC SSSI Notification document (1985)

Acknowledgements

Martin Harvey visited the site with me on 13 October 1996. He added several interesting records including the oak jewel beetle (*Agrilus pannonicus*)

I would like to thank Yattendon Estates for permission to visit Coombe Wood.

22 Water meadows in the Pang Valley

Dick Greenaway

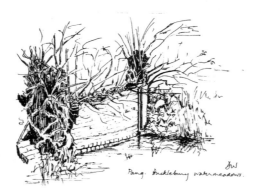

Pang. Bucklebury watermeadows.

What are water meadows?

Water meadows are grass fields in river valleys which have been provided with a complex system of channels, drains and control structures which allow the surface of the field to be covered with a moving sheet of river water for a given period and then drained dry.

Water meadows are *not* simply any wet and undrained field alongside a watercourse, although such fields may have provided the impetus and sparked the idea of artificially flooded fields.

In the medieval period and before, the meadows or meads were a very important resource and valued much higher than ordinary arable land. Their location in low lying parts of the landscape where the water table was close to the surface and where winter floods often covered them with water produced lush crops of grass and herbs. The community relied on making hay from this source to feed the horses, plough oxen and breeding stock through the winter. Sometimes more than one cut could be taken if the season was long enough and the weather warm and dry. After the hay making the animals could be turned out on the meadows to fatten until the weather broke. The surplus stock would then be slaughtered and salted down or sold at market. Retained animals would be moved back to their owner's paddocks or closes for the winter.

At some time, probably in the fifteenth century, farmers began to emulate the natural flooding. Fitzherbert, writing in 1523, in his book *The Boke of Surveying and Improvements* recommended the value of flooding in fertilising the land with sediments and filling

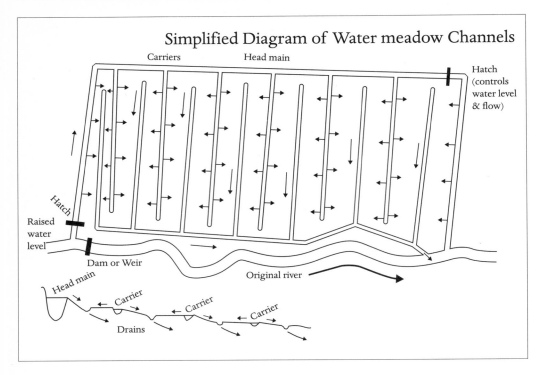

Simplified Diagram of Water meadow Channels

Carriers
Head main
Hatch (controls water level & flow)
Hatch
Raised water level
Dam or Weir
Original river
Head main
Carrier
Carrier
Carrier
Drains

in uneven areas with the added value of killing the moles which spoiled the pasture. He claims that the best situation for a flooded meadow was immediately downstream of a town. When we think of the lack of sanitation in a medieval town where every-man's chamber pot was emptied into the street, it is easy to understand where the nutrients came from! Sheep were the main beneficiaries of the water meadow system. Wool was the single most important product of Tudor farming. Huge fortunes were made from the backs of sheep. The glorious churches of the Cotswolds and other well drained areas of Britain were paid for by men who produced and exported wool to mainland Europe. Later on the sheep flocks became an essential part of mixed farming allowing heavy crops of wheat and barley to be obtained from otherwise impoverished soils.

When and where did they originate?

Irrigation is an ancient practice. Irrigation channels have been identified in the Middle East associated with civilisations which flourished many centuries BC, but the earliest reference yet found in Britain is in Fitzherbert's book of 1523. However, he is confident in his advice and seems to consider it an established practice, so it does not seem unreasonable to place the adoption of flooding in the late 1400s. No secure claim has been made for the first place of use, but it is most likely to have been in the south of England.

Maintenance of water-
meadow at Charlton
All Saints near Salisbury
in 1935.
© Rural History Centre
The University of Reading

What were water meadows used for?

The main function of a water meadow system was to advance
the growing season of grass and herbage and thus allow a greater
number of sheep to be kept. The medieval stock or sheep farmer
had a perennial problem in feeding his animals at the end of the
winter, especially if spring was delayed. In addition, poorly
nourished ewes produced a poor lamb crop and thus the output
of wool and mutton dropped. Wool was more important than
mutton and no one with any sense of value ate lamb.

How were water meadows used?

By flooding the grass fields in late winter the farmer obtained an
early crop of grass and herbs. Firstly, the water was likely to be
slightly warmer than the ground chilled by the winter, especially
if the river was spring fed, and so the water raised the temperature of the soil and encouraged growth. Secondly, the water
contained suspended nutrients – as mentioned above. The combination of the two caused a sudden burst of growth in the grass.
Once the meadows were dry the sheep were turned onto the
meadows to graze during the day and then moved to the arable
fields for the night. A new area was enclosed for each night with
portable hazel hurdles and the 'folded' sheep fertilised the soil
with their droppings before being moved back to the water
meadows the following morning. At the end of the spring, when
grass was available in the ordinary drier pastures, the sheep and
their lambs were moved off the water meadows and the grass
and herbs allowed to grow to provide one or more hay crops. It
was found that grazing the damp meadows after about May
exposed the sheep to liver fluke and foot rot.

Flooding could be arranged in two ways. The cruder method

was simply to dam the stream at the downstream end of the meadows and allow the water to back up and cover the land. However, this water would be static and it was found that this method tended to produce coarse grass and poor quality herbage. A better method was found to be flooding from upstream with a moving film of water. This was known as 'floating downwards' as opposed to the cruder method of 'floating upwards'.

Floating downwards involved raising the level of the water in the river at the upstream end of the meadows and then conducting the water through small channels in the surface of the meadow from which it spilled to cover the whole surface before being collected by draining channels and returned to the river downstream of the dam. The amount of sediment water can carry depends on the speed of the water. The greater the speed the larger the volume. As the speed drops suspended silt is deposited, so as the water moved slowly over the meadow surface it deposited a continuous rain of silt – far better than the single deposit of standing water. Also, the water was shallow. Some of the upper parts of the plants would show above the surface and continue to receive light and oxygen and thus prevent the plant being killed. Although the principle is simple the surveying and engineering required to design and build an effective water meadow is quite sophisticated and many water meadows are extremely complex and required great skill to build, operate and maintain. The men who did this work were known as 'watermen' in the Pang Valley and as 'drowners' in south Wessex. 'Waterman' became a family name – there are ten listed in the Reading Phone Book. One of their principle skills was to know when to stop! If the water stayed on the grass too long the finer herbage would be killed, if not long enough then the benefits of the water meadow would not be realised.

Such a system obviously involved major capital expenditure and the elaborate systems are usually found on large estates. However, the benefits could be great with claims for four times the quantity of hay being made from a field after floating than was available before. Also, stocking rates were much higher, in Wiltshire as many as 500 pairs of ewe and lamb were carried per acre. On the down side, the rent demanded for 'watered land' could be as much as five times that for 'unwatered'.

Water meadow flora

The regular sequence of flooding, grazing, flooding, hay making, grazing and flooding produced a specialised and very rich flora. It should be remembered that the 'pre-herbicide' farmer did not consider hay to be the product of a single species of grass. The Pang Valley meadow described in the appendix to this essay contains twelve species of grasses. In fact, the modern continental farmer still includes herbs in his hay. In addition to many types of grass the meadow would contain many sorts of flowering and non-flowering plants such as agrimony, cow parsley, cuckoo flower, meadowsweet, ragged robin, fritillary, clover, buttercups, plantains, sorrel and many others. A list of the species found on our example site is included in the appendix.

Along the river channel itself would be willows, alders and sallows – all of which would be put to good use for basket making, for clog soles and for thatching spars. There would also be reeds, sedges and rushes and these could also be used for basket making and for making rush dips to light cottages.

When did they go out of use?

Water meadows gradually went out of use with the decline in the demand for sheep and wool. They were expensive to maintain and were badly affected by the great agricultural depression in the late nineteenth century. For a while they were used to fatten beef cattle, but the heavy animals broke down the channel sides and poached the soils turning the luxuriant meadows into poor quality badly drained grassland. In the 1970s many of the old meadows were ploughed up to grow subsidised cereals. Water meadows finally disappeared from use in the early 1900s. The last local survivor that I am aware of was at Midgham on the Kennet.

Pang Valley water meadow sites

There are many examples along the Pang Valley and two of them are available for educational access. These are 'The Dairies' at Tidmarsh on Englefield Estate land and 'Frilsham Water meadows' near Frilsham Mill. Access to these sites must be arranged via the Pang Valley Countryside Project. The Project has produced very useful sets of information for each site. In addition to these sites there were others at Tidmarsh downstream of The Dairies, at Marlston – linking to the set at Frilsham – and between Bucklebury and Stanford Dingley. There are indications on aerial photographs that there may have been others at Bradfield, at Maidenhatch and at Everington.

What signs can be seen on the ground?

The most obvious sign of a water meadow are the blocks of long parallel ridges and shallow ditches which once carried the water. These can easily be confused with the ridge and furrow caused by medieval and post-medieval ploughing, but if found near a watercourse they are likely to be a water meadow. Even when ploughed out they can be seen as alternate strips of light and dark soil in a freshly harrowed field. Sometimes the remains of the control

The Dairies Water meadow
at Tidmarsh. Photograph
by Aerofilms.
© The Environment
Agency

sluices, or 'hatches', can be found in the banks of the river and in
the channels themselves. An unusually straight river channel with
a winding ditch running roughly parallel may indicate the artificial
'header' channel and the course of the original stream. Examples
of this exists between Bucklebury and Stanford Dingly and again
between Frilsham and Bucklebury at Marlston.

Documentary sources for information on water meadows

The best sources of information for identifying water meadows
are the superb Ordnance Survey First Edition Large Scale plans.
These were made in the mid to late 19th century – soon after the
hey day of water meadows but while they were still in existence –
and they show in detail all the channels, sluices, hatches and
bridges. Field names can be a help – but as 'The Dairies' shows –
not always definite. Aerial photographs – particularly if taken in
the winter – often show up the patterns of ditches very clearly.
Estate maps and documents are another useful source. These
may be only available in the local estate office, but many County
Record Offices have early maps and plans.

The Future for water meadows

It is difficult to see a future for large areas of water meadows.
Selected sites have been re-constructed – for example The
Environment Agency and the National Trust re-built two meadows
on the National Trust estate at Sherbourne in the Cotswolds and
are planning to recreate another site at The Vyne near Basing-
stoke. Land owners adopting the Countryside Stewardship

Scheme are encouraged to preserve and recreate water meadows and are offered the highest payment rates for doing so. A few sites have been designated Sites of Special Scientific Interest (sssis) and should receive care and maintenance. Other sites like 'The Dairies' and 'Frilsham Meadows' will be retained for their botanical, historical and educational value, but the remainder are likely to remain poor quality grassland unless drained and 'improved' as monocultures. Nevertheless, in their day they were, as described by Oliver Rackham, the 'supreme technical achievement of English farming'.

Sources

Bettey, J.H., *Rural Life in Wessex, 1500–1900* (1977)
Countryside Stewardship, Countryside Agency
Muir, Richard, *The New Reading the Landscape* (2000)
Pang Valley Countryside Project, The Englefield Estate 'The Dairies'
Rackham, Oliver, *The History of the Countryside* (1986)
Taylor, Christopher, *Fields in the English Landscape* (1975)

Appendix

Species recorded by theBerkshire, Buckinghamshire and Oxfordshire Wildlife Trust on a Pang Valley Water Meadow.

Meadow & Hedgerow Flowers

yarrow	greater (rats tail) plantain	agrimony
meadow buttercup	cow parsley	creeping buttercup
lady's smock (cuckoo flower)	common sorrel	common mouse ear
broad leaved dock	creeping thistle	prickly sow thistle
spear thistle	common chickweed	goosegrass (cleavers)
red clover	cut leaved cranesbill	stinging nettle
doves foot cranesbill	germander speedwell (birds eye)	
meadow vetchling	thyme leaved speedwell	ragged robin
tufted vetch	black medic	

Wet Meadow & Waterside Plants

marsh foxtail	lesser spearwort	marsh thistle
water figwort	great willowherb	water betony
floating sweet grass (flote grass)	common comfrey	common valerian
yellow flag	greater water grass (reed sweet grass)	
brooklime	watercress	

Grasses

creeping bent (fiorin)	crested dogstail	meadow foxtail
cocksfoot	sweet vernal grass	sheep's fescue
false oat grass	Yorkshire fog	soft brome
wall barley	barren brome	Timothy

Reeds, sedges and rushes

hairy sedge	soft rush	great pond sedge
common reed	jointed rush	smooth meadow grass
compact rush		

Tree & shrub   Alder

23 Moor Copse Nature Reserve

Sally Oldfield

Moor Copse nature reserve, situated near Pangbourne, is a place rich in wildlife, character and natural beauty. The reserve, which actually consists of three woodland copses, a meadow and a stretch of the River Pang, is owned and managed by the Berkshire, Buckinghamshire and Oxfordshire Wildlife Trust (BBOWT).

The reserve covers 27 hectares and forms part of the Sulham and Tidmarsh woods and meadows SSSI (Site of Special Scientific Interest). Visitors can park off the A340, just south of Tidmarsh. Much of the woodland is very wet and wellingtons are recommended all year round. Although somewhat inconvenient for human visitors, the wet nature of the woodland is extremely beneficial for wildlife. Of particular interest is the alder-carr (wet woodland dominated by alder trees) since this type of habitat is rare in southern England.

Visitors to Moor Copse can explore the woodland using the winding pathways known as 'rides'. These have been created not only to allow access for people but also for the benefit of sun-loving wildflowers, butterflies and other insects. Taking the path leading from the car park, you will be guided through Hogmoor Copse, one of the three copses that make up the reserve. Common spotted orchids and the occasional twayblade can be seen here in early summer, growing under the coppiced hazel.

Opening out onto the banks of the River Pang, the path then provides you with a walk along a beautiful stretch of this healthy chalk stream, and it is easy to see why the view is said to have inspired Kenneth Grahame to write the classic *Wind in the Willows*.

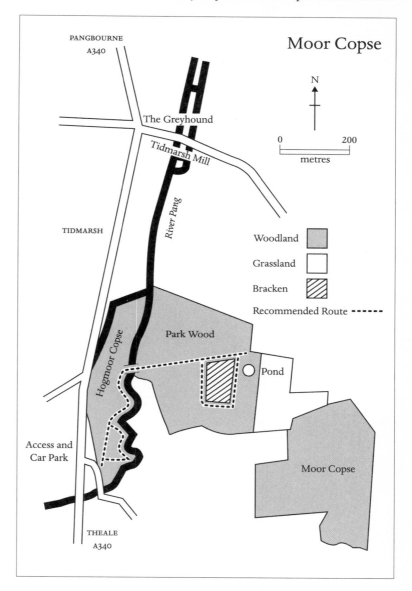

The River Pang is one of the cleanest rivers in the Thames Basin
and supports a wide range of plant and animal life. Look out for
kingfishers, banded demoiselle damselflies and even the scarce
scarlet tiger moth. However, the one animal to really keep an eye
open for is the elusive water vole. Starring as 'Ratty' in the *Wind in
the Willows*, this animal is now thought to be the most endangered
mammal in Britain. Its numbers have undergone a drastic decline
due to loss of habitat and predation by American mink. The river
bank habitat in Moor Copse reserve provides an ideal home for
water vole and it is hoped that their numbers will increase here.

Crossing the bridge brings you into Park Wood, which in spring is carpeted with bluebells, primroses and other wildflowers. Wetland plants such as yellow flag iris and water mint thrive in the damper areas.

Beyond Park Wood lies Five Acre Field and beyond that is Moor Copse, the woodland after which the reserve was named. BBOWT is managing Five Acre Field by grazing it with ponies at the appropriate times of the year. The aim of this is to gradually increase the diversity of wildflowers found in the meadow.

The nature reserve as a whole is being managed to maintain the wide variety of different habitats that exist here, which all support a diverse range of wildlife. Different species of plant and animal are adapted to survive under different conditions and the management of Moor Copse reserve reflects this. Some parts of the woodland are left undisturbed, allowing trees to mature and die naturally, creating plenty of dead wood habitat which is so important for woodpeckers, bats, fungi and many invertebrates. However, in other parts of the reserve coppicing is taking place.

Coppicing is an old woodland management technique, used commonly over the centuries to produce useful timber products. Trees (most often hazel) are cut down to almost ground level and then allowed to re-grow. This results in a number of fast-growing, straight stems, instead of a single trunk. The stems are excellent for use in fencing, as well as hurdle and charcoal making. Coppicing is also beneficial to wildlife, as the effect of cutting down trees means that sunlight reaches the woodland floor, allowing wildflowers to grow. As the coppiced trees grow, they create a dense scrub-like environment which attracts nesting birds and small mammals.

The practice of coppicing has declined in recent years, but overgrown coppiced hazel can be seen in many woods today, indicating how these woodlands were managed in the past. In order to restore coppicing at Moor Copse, BBOWT has had to overcome certain problems, the most difficult being that posed by deer.

Muntjac and roe deer are frequently seen at Moor Copse but, although a delightful sight for visitors, they are not such good news for conservation. In high numbers, deer can cause serious damage in woodlands. Muntjac are Asiatic deer which escaped from Woburn some years ago and now breed so successfully in England that they have reached very high densities. Muntjac love to feed on the fresh new shoots of young coppice, and as a result often kill the trees completely. Therefore to enable coppicing to take place at Moor Copse, BBOWT have had to take steps to exclude deer from certain parts of the nature reserve. That is why, as you walk round the reserve, you will come across a seven foot high fence. The fence has an access gate in it to allow people through and several much smaller gates at intervals to provide access for badgers.

A visit to Moor Copse reserve is an enjoyable and rewarding experience for those with a keen interest in natural history, as well as those looking for a pleasant walk in the countryside. Perhaps most importantly, however, this nature reserve is being managed primarily with wildlife in mind and will continue to provide a much needed sanctuary for our local wildlife, both the scarce and the common, for generations to come.

BBOWT is happy to answer enquiries about Moor Copse, or any of its other 90 nature reserves. We also provide advice on wildlife conservation issues. BBOWT is one of 46 Wildlife Trusts working across the UK to achieve the shared aim of securing a better future for wildlife.

Please contact us at BBOWT
Hasker House
Woolley Firs
Cherry Garden Lane
Maidenhead
Berkshire SL6 3LJ

Tel 01628 829574
Email bbowtberks@cix.co.uk

24 Ashampstead Common: The Origin, History and Future of a Wooded Common

Dick Greenaway

This essay sets out to tell the story of the commons of Ashampstead Parish in Berkshire, to explain their origins and their importance to the community around them in the past and to put forward ideas for continuing this importance into the future.

Ashampstead parish is dry country and as a result was settled late compared with the surrounding parishes. This lack of water is due to the geology and to the soils. The underlying rocks are soft and porous chalk which often breaks the surface. On top of chalk the Ice Ages left a complex mixture of soils. Some of these are fertile, some less so, but they are all porous. The result of this porosity is that the parish has always lacked surface water. Except along the southern edge there are no springs, and nowhere are there streams. Wells have to be dug to depths in excess of thirty metres (one hundred feet) to reach the water table. The soils, although fertile given modern farming techniques, were less attractive to primitive agriculture. Although they overlay chalk they tend to be acid, heavy clay mixed with flints. As a result of these two factors – the lack of water and the difficult soils – people appear not to have been attracted to them until population pressures and lack of more easily worked land forced their use.

In the centuries after the collapse of Roman rule, in the period commonly called the Dark Ages and lasting from the fifth century AD to about the tenth century AD, the size of the population was held down firstly by what appears to have been a period of plagues and secondly by the disruptions caused by wars and invasions. These culminated in the Danish Wars of the late ninth century in which King Alfred of Wessex was finally victorious. This victory and the subsequent settling of the Danish army in the north east lead to a period of stability and population growth which was not disrupted in the south of England by subsequent invasions and changes of ruling dynasty. As a result the population could not be fed from the existing farmland with the current farming technology and settlement of less favoured areas became necessary.

All this is not to say that no one lived in the parish during these early periods. There is evidence that people were in the area during the Mesolithic (approximately 5000 BC – approximately 2500 BC), Neolithic (approximately 2500 BC – approximately 1900 BC) and Bronze Ages (approximately 1900 BC – approximately 500 BC). They were probably attracted by the easily available flints which they used to make tools. A Mesolithic flint core has been found on Ashampstead Common, discarded when it became too small to hold while removing flint blades. A Neolithic stone axe was found near Pykes Hill and a Bronze Age scraper near Childs Court. Small areas may even have been cultivated since a broken Neolithic hoe blade has also been found on the edge of Ashampstead Common. However, there is no sign of settlement and the impact of these people on the landscape is likely to have been small. No evidence has been found for any occupation during the Iron Age, Roman or Saxon periods except for one very worn Roman coin.

The very name 'Ashampstead' is a late form and appears as 'Ashden' ('the valley of the ash trees') in the *Domesday Book* (1086). It only becomes 'Esshamstead' ('settlement by the ash trees' in 1212). It appears therefore, that the parish was settled and its boundaries defined not long before the Norman Conquest in 1066, probably in the early tenth century, by people moving west from Basildon.

The ongoing parish hedgerow survey is providing evidence for how this settlement took place. It is plain from the makeup of the hedges and particularly from the plants in the hedge bottoms, that the road network was established before the land was cleared. Most of the roadside hedges contain plants such as bluebells and yellow archangel which if found in woods would mark the woods as ancient secondary woodland. The fields behind the hedges were cleared leaving a strip of woodland along the roadside which was then managed to form a barrier and a boundary but which allowed the original woodland plants to survive in the hedge bottom.

The same evidence, combined with place and field names, can be used to identify the original clearings. For example, 'Stubbles' means 'cleared land'. The element 'pightle or 'piddle' which is common in the field names of the parish, has the meaning of 'a field cleared from woodland'. Readers who remember Rudyard Kipling's stories will be intrigued by 'Pokes Piddle' near Childs Court Farm with its echo of 'Pooks Hill' in *Puck of Pook's Hill*.

By combining all these elements it seems that settlement grew from a focus around the present village of Ashampstead and spread southward along the flatter land and gentler slopes until by the early thirteenth century it had reached the present northern edges of Ashampstead and Burnt Hill Commons. The clearance had included a gap driven between Ashamstead Common and Basildon Common in the valley bottom alongside the ancient north-south road from Aldworth to Bradfield. This gap was appropriately named 'Breach Field'. One should not be surprised at this rate of clearance. The European settlers of New England started work in the mid seventeenth century. Using similar tools to those available to the medieval farmers they had cleared vast swathes of woods similar to Berkshire woods by the mid nineteenth century.

Small private paddocks were cleared along the side of the road eastward out of the village and their names, which include 'Close' or 'Pightle', illustrate their ownership and origin. The situation in the early thirteenth century is shown on the map opposite.

Primitive farming and early society, and indeed all farming up to the early twentieth century, required large quantities of timber and wood. The two terms are deliberately used to mean two different materials even though both are derived from trees. 'Timber' infers large units. We refer to 'timber beams' and 'timber framed houses' whereas 'wood' implies smaller items such as 'wooden poles', 'wooden handles', 'firewood', etc. The need for timber and wood in its various sizes for building, for fuel, for tools, for fencing and all the other requirements of society in ages when transport and metal were expensive and plastic not yet invented, meant that not *all* the land could be cleared for farming. Substantial areas had to be left wooded and then intensively managed to provide for the needs of the community. These areas can also be identified by their flora.

It is worth pausing in the story at this point to consider the concept of Ancient Woodland Indicator Species. In the second half of the last century a considerable amount of research was carried out by environmental scientists and academics – notably by George Peterken, Max Hooper and Oliver Rackam – on the botanical make up of woods and hedges known from documentary evidence to be ancient. From this research came the often abused 'Hooper's Hedge Hypothesis' by which the age of a hedge can be estimated from the number of species of hard

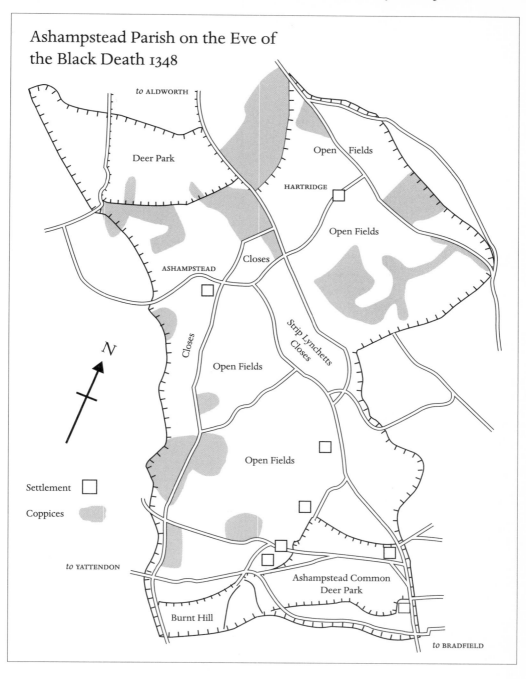

Ashampstead Parish on the Eve of
the Black Death 1348

to ALDWORTH

Deer Park

Open Fields

HARTRIDGE

Open Fields

Closes

ASHAMPSTEAD

Closes

Strip Lynchetts Closes

Open Fields

N

Open Fields

Settlement

Coppices

to YATTENDON

Ashampstead Common
Deer Park

Burnt Hill

to BRADFIELD

Based upon the Ordnance
Survey Map with the
permission of Her
Majesty's Stationery
Office.
© Crown Copyright
MC100036335

wood shrubs in a thirty metre length. The research also produced
a list of plants most often associated with ancient woods and rare
or absent in woods resulting from abandoned farm land or from
plantations. Typically these are plants which are poor at spreading
their seed or which are at the northern edge of their natural
range. These plants spread slowly and once destroyed rarely

return unless deliberately reintroduced. The prime example of such a plant is the bluebell. The plant spreads by bulb division and by seed. However, its seeds are small and heavy and so drop close to the parent plant. Bluebells are able to use none of the clever distribution techniques used by plants such as burdock, which stick their seeds to animals coats, or sycamore which provides its seeds with wings, or dandelions whose seeds have fluffy parachutes. Some bluebell seeds may be spread in mud stuck to human or animal feet, but in general the rate of spread is as little as a metre a century. The list of 'Ancient Woodland Indicator Species' is used by English Nature and other naturalists and landscape historians, in conjunction with other evidence, to identify woodland which has been in existence since at least 1600. If a wood was in existence in 1600 there is a very good chance that it has been there much longer. This is not to say that it is a direct descendant of the primeval forest. The intensive management of woodland will have altered the makeup of all woods so that they will little resemble the 'wildwood'. However, their ground flora will be rich and special and not found elsewhere.

To return to the main theme. Areas of retained woodland will have taken two main forms, the first being 'coppices'. These were wooded areas in which the trees had been cut off at ground level and allowed to shoot into multiple stems which were harvested at short intervals, typically eight to ten years, to produce sticks, poles, stakes and small logs. The 'coppice stools' were often interspersed with 'standards'. These were trees which were allowed to

An early twentieth-century coppice with standards after coppicing the hazel. The cut hazel is stacked to the right of the picture.
© Greenaway Collection

Above
Mr Ben Palmer, woodman
of Ashampstead Common,
making hurdles.
© Greenaway Collection
Right
Mr Ben Palmer
with a gate hurdle.
© Greenaway Collection

grow to a large size before being cut as timber to provide planks
and beams. This particular management regime, with its lack of
ground disturbance and its cycles of years of shade followed by
years of sunlight, encouraged the growth of plants such as bluebells, wood anemones, primroses and early purple orchids which

benefited from the suppression of coarser plants by the years of shade. By recording woods with these plants it is possible to estimate which were the uncleared woodland areas. These areas are also shown on the map on page 209.

The second class of uncleared land was the 'wooded common' into which class Ashampstead and Burnt Hill Commons fit.

The term 'common' gives rise to more misunderstanding than most words in the English language. Land shown on the Ordnance Survey map as ' common' will be understood by many people as 'land owned by the community to which everyone has a right of access'. This understanding is fundamentally wrong. 'Commons' took many forms – common fields, wood commons, common grazing, heath commons etc. – the fundamental concept being that they were areas of land (or water) which were *owned* by one person or group but on which *other specified individuals or groups* had particular rights. For example the owners or tenants of specific houses in the Manor of Ashampstead had the right to graze their cattle (among other rights) on land owned by the lord of the manor of Ashampstead. Not every resident of the manor had that right, only the specified residents. Even then their rights were closely controlled. For example, they could only graze that number of animals on the commons in summer which they could house on private land over winter.

Commons were often on poor land and this is certainly true of Ashampstead's commons. The northern part of Ashampstead Common itself is mainly on Berkhamstead soils. These are soils that were on the surface during the Ice Age and were badly leached of their nutrients. The southern part is on Winchester soils which are somewhat more fertile. Burnt Hill Common is on Frilsham Beds which are mainly infertile wind blown sands. Nevertheless the commons were an important resource for the commoners. The grazing allowed the more fertile fields to be shut up for a hay crop in the summer – thus providing food to over winter the cattle, particularly the plough oxen. The bracken provided a source of bedding for animals, furze and fallen wood provided fuel. In addition the open space provided a playground for the community. Authors such as William Cobbett, writing in the 1820s during the destruction of many commons, and the poet John Clare , writing at about the same time, explain in lyrical terms how important the commons were to the community.

Such was the status and function of commons. Additionally, in the case of the commons of Ashampstead parish we find that they had an unusual episode in their early development. About 1240 they seem to have been used as a deer park and to have had a substantial bank with an inner ditch constructed around their perimeter.

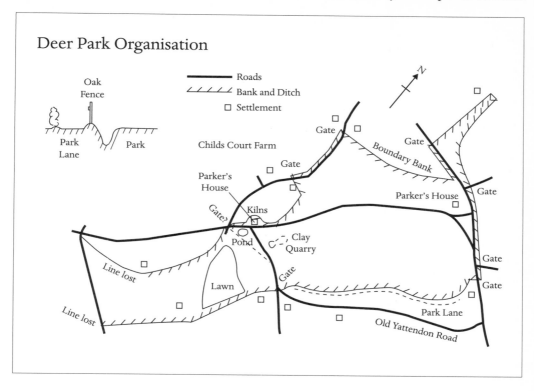

Deer Park Organisation

Deer parks were a medieval status symbol – almost the ultimate status symbol – because they produced venison. Venison was a product literally beyond price since the law did not permit it to be sold. Parks were also a method of demonstrating wealth and social status through conspicuous consumption. They were very expensive to create and very expensive to maintain. The Ashampstead Common park – if such it is – would class as a small park, yet its park pale consisted of a deep ditch and a steep bank topped with a 1.5 metres (five feet) high fence of split oak palings which can still be traced for about 5.6 kilometres (3½ miles). This was no small enterprise for a community equipped with little more than metal tipped wooden shovels. Even today it would be a major undertaking with the help of mechanical excavators. The slightness of the resources is demonstrated in a poignant way by noting the frequent minor changes of direction of the park pale which were probably made to avoid major trees – something that later park pales do not do.

One should not think of deer parks as the scene of Hollywood style hunts with huntsmen on horseback blowing horns and waving banners. The hunts were closer approximations to a modern pheasant shoot. The luckless deer, usually fallow, were bred and fed by the parkers and then driven into open areas called lawns where they were shot from stands by archers and crossbowmen. Animals were also killed by professional huntsmen to supply the owner's table and gifts of live animals could be made by the owner to stock a friend's park.

The evidence for a park on Ashampstead Common relies on evidence on the ground and on documentary evidence. In 1246 the prior of Poughly Abbey near Chaddleworth (West Berkshire) brought an action in the court at Reading against one John of Bagpuize (Kingston Bagpuize near Abingdon) and a number of Ashampstead commoners. The prior claimed that he was being prevented from exercising his right of common pasture in a wood in Ashampstead by a fence erected by John and his colleagues. The court found against him because the jury maintained that the prior's property in the manor did not carry right of common in the wood. Nevertheless, it seems that the prior prevailed at some time in the future because one of the houses on the common, which may have been for the park keepers, was named 'Maggots Hall', or more correctly 'St Margaret's Hall', and Poughly Abbey was dedicated to St Margaret. That Ashampstead's commons were the wood in question is made more likely by the fact that John also had a manor in Bradfield (known later as 'Buckhold alias Childs Court') and a possible ancestor – Ralph of Bagpuize – is recorded in Domesday as holding a manor in 'Ashden'. The de Somerys are reported to have enclosed a park in Bradfield at a date unspecified in the thirteenth century and they would appear to have been the overlords. It is even probable that the manor boundaries of Ashampstead and Buckhold did not coincide with the parish boundaries and that Ralph and John's manor included the southern part of Ashampstead parish. Finally, the only other candidate for a deer park in Ashampstead parish is the de la Beche park to the south of Aldworth. However, the licence for the creation of this park still exists and it was not granted until 1335.

The physical evidence is convincing even though the park outline is of an unconventional shape. Firstly there is the surviving bank with its ditch on the *inside*. Despite six hundred years of weathering this is still an impressive obstacle along the southern side of the Common. Its date is confirmed by some eleventh–thirteenth century AD pottery kilns incorporated in it at one point and by the size and obvious antiquity of yew trees growing on it.

Then there is its layout. A candidate for a parker's house overlooks the eastern entrance from a high vantage point and a second one overlooks both the western entrance and an artificial pond which may have been created to water the deer. Deer poaching was a major problem for medieval deer park owners and all parks had resident wardens. The parkers not only monitored and tended

The thirteenth century
Deer Park Boundary Bank
and Ditch.
© Greenaway Collection

A modern example of the
type of fence that would
have stood on the crest
of the bank. (Moccas Park,
Herefordshire).
© Greenaway Collection

the deer, they also combated the poachers. Both candidates for
'parkers houses' appear to be of suitably early dates and both are
sited in commanding positions.

Close by the pond is an open area which would be a good
candidate for a 'lawn'. Finally, along the south side, where the
pale survives best, there is a second lesser bank paralleling the
main bank and a few metres distant. This is a typical 'Park Lane'
which allowed easy access to the split oak fence for maintenance
purposes. The arrangement can be seen more readily on the map
on page 209.

Early houses cluster along the edges of the park with their
gardens ending at the bank. One of these must have been of
particular antiquity since the bank and ditch were routed
carefully around its edge.

Use of the land as a deer park would not preclude its continued
use as a wood common. In many well documented parks it is

Mrs Sparks & Mrs Hancock's   Ashampstead Common
Just before demolition   May 1932.

A possible parker's house –
demolished in the 1930s.
© Greenaway Collection

clear that common rights were not extinguished by the creation
of a park. Grazing of commoners animals, coppicing and collection of bracken could go on without unduly disturbing the deer,
and the park pale would keep the commoners animals in as well
as the deer.

It is impossible to say with certainty when the deer park ceased
to function. Many parks – particularly the smaller ones – were
short lived. One possible cause for its demise could have been the
arrival of the Black Death (bubonic plague) in 1348 which killed a
very large proportion of the population – as much as fifty per
cent in some places – and took aristocrats as well as peasants.
After the first horrendous years the plague reoccurred at intervals
until at least the eighteenth century. Its impact on society and its
organisation was sweeping. No longer were there masses of poor
labourers who could be compelled for life to be tied to their lords
and to their manors. Labour was scarce and expensive. The change
was largely responsible for the end of the feudal system of duties
and services and the creation of a market economy. The reduction
in the population was also responsible for stopping the clearance
of marginal land, and in many cases considerable areas of cultivated land reverted to grassland and to woodland. These areas
too have their distinctive flora and land forms which can be
recorded and mapped.

The reduction in the size of the labour force coincided with
the growth in the wool trade. Large areas of land were turned
over to sheep grazing. The downland to the north of

Ashampstead became particularly famous for sheep and East – or 'Market' – Ilsley became one of the premier sheep markets in the country. Sheep were grazed on the downs by day and penned at night on arable fields. When the wool trade declined cereal growing took over and high yields could only be achieved with the heavy dunging of penned sheep and this became their prime function. The penning was done using portable woven hazel hurdles. These had a very short life and many thousands were required. As mentioned in the essay on water meadows, it was reported in 1793 that 'in general the size of the hurdle is about four feet six inches (1.35 metres) long, three foot six inches (1.05 metres) high, made chiefly of hazel, with ten upright sticks; and fifteen dozen of them, with a like number of stakes and wriths, to confine them together, will enclose a statute acre of ground and will contain twelve or thirteen hundred sheep therein very commodiously'. Considering how many tens of thousands of sheep were kept, the demand for coppiced hazel must have been enormous. It seems that some marginal farm land was deliberately planted with hazel to provide for the demands of the hurdle makers. These areas too can be identified by their ground flora – particularly by the absence of bluebells. Indeed, little patches of hazel seem to have been planted wherever they could be squeezed in – alongside roads and tracks and in many odd corners.

Nevertheless, despite the changes to society, there continued to be a class of semi-independent cottagers and rural craftsmen who got their living from their skills and from small scale husbandry. To them the commons were still important as places to graze their animals, gather materials for their crafts, fuel for their homes and bedding for their animals. Indeed, the area along the old Yattendon Road was known as the 'Land of Milk and Honey' because the commoners grazed their goats and pastured their bees there. This way of life finally expired only in the mid twentieth century and Tim Culley describes its last days in his essay on farming in the valley. For a local example we could look to Ben Palmer who lived on Burnt Hill Common. He described himself as a woodman and got his living from making hazel hurdles. He coppiced areas of the commons for his materials and in addition rented a strip of land in a nearby field which he ploughed with a single furrow plough pulled by a donkey. During busy times on the farms he would take casual work to help out. His way of life cannot have been very different from that of commoners eight centuries previously.

The commons were used for other less rural activities. They were extensively quarried – as the various pits and hollows show. Possibly the first quarrying was for the clay to supply the pottery industry mentioned above. Later it was discovered that by ploughing large amounts of frost weathered chalk into the acid clay of the fields it was possible to create a much more fertile soil. Many woods and the fields themselves still have major pits showing what a vast quantity of chalk was used for this purpose. Some of the smaller and shallower pits were probably the result of gravel winning for road making. The age of the trees now growing in the bottom of the pits indicate that digging probably ceased in the mid nineteenth century.

As the traditional uses of the commons declined they were put to other uses. A Doctor Watney bought the Buckhold Estate in the late nineteenth century and this then included the commons. He introduced exotic species of trees to give the area a park like appearance. He was responsible for the magnificent wellingtonias and cedars that still survive, and for the many less obvious exotics that can be found by careful searching. The commoners objected strongly to this activity and pulled up as many of the saplings as could be found. During the Second World War both commons were used by the military as camping grounds and their hut bases can still be found together with less obvious relics such as deformed trees and bark carvings.

All this activity over so many centuries obviously had a major impact on the natural history and in particular on the botany. By mapping the indicator species it is possible to identify the effect of the settlements around the edges of the commons. On the map opposite I have plotted the areas of very dense bluebells and the areas of dense dog's mercury. Bluebells and dog's mercury exist in other areas but these are the particulary dense areas. The reason for choosing bluebells as an indicator of stability is explained above. Dog's mercury however, has the opposite connotation. It is usually identified with anciently disturbed land which has been subsequently abandoned. This certainly seems to be the case on the commons as the densest areas are directly located in areas of obvious human activity such as the quarry and areas around sub-stantial pits. The division is illustrated in the photograph on page 239. Combining these plots with the location of entrances through the deer park pale it is possible to estimate which group of commoners were exploiting which area of common. This also is shown on the map opposite by the broad arrows.

The later use of the commons by the military can also be detected by the distribution of nettles. These plants require a high level of phosphate which is often supplied by human waste and their distribution ties in well with the known locations of latrines and cookhouses.

Modern society has no immediate use for the commons as lands of milk and honey, although all historians know the

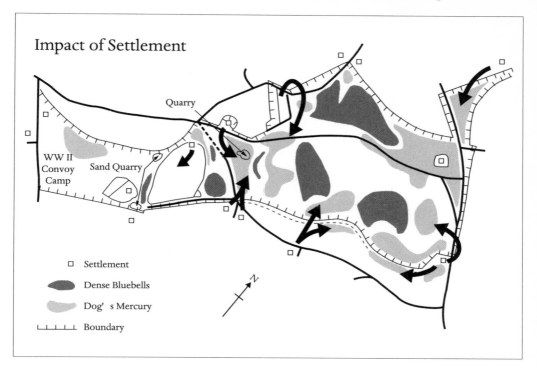

Impact of Settlement

□   Settlement

     Dense Bluebells

     Dog's Mercury

⌞⌟⌞⌟⌞⌟   Boundary

impermanence of 'golden ages'. Present society sees them as recreational areas and areas from which occasional crops of timber trees can be harvested. Yet their beauty and interest is the result of centuries of active use and without management they will fairly rapidly decline to much less interesting mixed woods of sycamore and ash, seamed by muddy tracks used by pony riders and occasional walkers. To resist this trend a management group has been set up consisting of the land owners, the parish council and the people who live on and around the commons. The group has the documented intention of actively working on the commons to maintain and enhance their interest and value as sources of commercial timber, as rich wildlife habitats and as sources of delight.

In my personal opinion this work rightly devolves to the community in its widest sense. It is not something the community should expect others to do for it. The landowner should not be expected to engage in coppicing to no economic purpose, nor should the local wild life organisations be expected to fund the management of private woodland and political and administrative organisations should not be expected to intervene uninvited. However, all these organisations working together *with the local community* can maintain and enhance an area to everyone's benefit. At the same time the community will develop a local and personal pride in their environment and a deep knowledge of the landscape within which they have made their homes. As it develops, this pride and awareness will spill over into other aspects of living so that the natural world is no longer seen as a source of objects to be used and discarded. Rather it will be seen as something to be respected and nurtured and used with care and with thought for the future. Without direct local involvement pride in and understanding of the area cannot grow and any outside operations will be merely short term palliatives.

To develop this pride a programme of work has been developed which is within the capacity of local volunteers and which emulates the activities which created the rich environment of the commons. Areas of hazel are being coppiced to reintroduce the cycles of sunlight and shade, three small glades are being cut and cleared each year to simulate the effects of summer grazing, a wide sunlit glade is being created to encourage different levels of undergrowth which in turn will encourage plant and insect life and thus the butterflies and birds that depend on them. For their part the landowners are developing a twenty year forestry management plan for all their woodland. This is being done in conjunction with the Forestry Authority and after consulting the local communities and specialist organisations such as English Nature and English Heritage. As far as the commons are concerned this will extend and improve the earlier local management plan. The landowner will continue to carry out the heavier tasks beyond the capacity of volunteers by removing larger trees when necessary and by organising their thinning operations to cause as little damage as possible. Thinning causes open areas which will be allowed, wherever possible, to restock by natural regeneration rather than by replanting. In some areas the desire to maintain a rich diversity of trees may require some replanting, but this will be done with suitable local species. An area around the quarry will be left untouched by any operation to develop in its own way. Standing and fallen deadwood will be retained as homes and breeding grounds for invertebrates since a healthy invertebrate population is the foundation for a healthy population of so many other species. The local Wildlife Trusts play their part by providing the technical expertise and assisting with the long term planning. The third element of the group, the parish council, plays its part by being the link to the political organisations. Without higher level political support local groups can find it difficult to attract the attention of resource providing organisations. Without this total community involvement the work will not succeed and our society will be the loser. With this total involvement the environment, society and the individual are enhanced.

References

The Commons of Ashampstead Parish, a Management Plan & an Environmental and Historical Study, Yattendon Estate/Ashampstead Parish Council (1996–2002)

Greenaway, Dick, On-going Surveys of Woods and Hedges

Rackham, Oliver, *Trees and Woodland in the British Landscape* (1976)

Rackham, Oliver, *The History of the Countryside* (1986)

Tate, W. E., Domesday of English Enclosure Awards & Acts (1978)

Victoria County History

25 Pang Valley Flowers

Margot Walker

Ampibious Bisort
(pensicaria)

Marsh Marigolds

Along the Pang Valley you will find water meadows, acid-clay
woods, woods on chalk, fields of clay and flints and even some
sand, so the distribution of plants is varied and interesting. In the
river itself there are obviously *water* plants. In recent times the
Upper Pang has dried up after years of drought but it is amazing
how the plants recovered when the river flowed once more.
Growing in the water is water forget-me-not; the name is not an
ancient one – Shakespeare never used it and it is thought that
Coleridge popularised it in a poem written in 1802. Another blue
river plant is brooklime, whose leaves can be eaten like watercress
and indeed in the seventeenth century, diet drinks were made of
it. There were commercial watercress beds widely spread
between Stanford Dingley and Bradfield. Floating on the river
itself is water-crowfoot, covering large areas with white flowers,
and common and least duckweed can make the surface of the
water solid. The latter came from America in the seventies and is
said to have spread eleven miles in three months on the Kennet
and Avon canal. Another river plant is amphibious bistort, with
spikes of deep pink flowers above oblong leaves like an aquatic
orchid. At the edge of the stream grow water mints; 'the savour
or smell of the water mint', wrote Gerard, 'rejoiceth the heart of
man'. Common, rough and Russian comfrey have all crossed and
grow by streams in quantity. Marsh marigolds have been seen this
year (2000) on Frilsham common.

Turning to the *woods*, the first signs of new life in January, are
the pale green leaves of the honeysuckle, whose stems always
twine clockwise. Later come the two wood violets, one with a

Wood Spurge

dark spur and one with a light. The woodspurge, beloved by the poet Rossetti, has bright yellow-green flowers and was described by a nineteenth century herbalist as 'a clever juggler balancing on his upturned chin, a widely branched series of delicate green saucers'.

Much less common is toothwort, a parasite growing on the roots of hazel. It has a flower like an orchid with protruding purple stigmas, is flesh-coloured, cool and clammy and called the corpse flower in the north of England. More cheerful are the little white strawberries. The barren strawberry is the earliest to bloom and can be distinguished from the wild strawberry by the marked gaps between the petals.

The wood anemone, an abundant gregarious flower, grows mostly in dry woods. Another spring flower, often overlooked, is goldilocks, the wood buttercup with stem leaves deeply divided into narrow segments. Everybody knows dog's mercury, which carpets the woods and is so called because plants not used medicinally were thought to be inferior and were often called 'dog'. Male and female flowers are on separate plants.

Wood Anemone

By May the woods with dappled shade will be carpeted with bluebells. Gerard Manley Hopkins describes them as 'coming in falls of sky colour, washing the brows and slacks of the ground with vein-blue'. Growing with the bluebells is the early purple orchid, smelling of cats and sadly much rarer than it used to be. Its food is stored in two root tubers, a firm one filling up for next year and an old one supplying its present need. The shape of the tubers has given the plant various vulgar names. Ophelia's garland was woven with 'long purples that liberal shepherds give a grosser name'. A gruel made from the dried tubers was called saloop and was sold in the coffee shops of London in the eighteenth century. There are still wild daffodils in the woods between Chapel Row and Stanford Dingley.

A garden escape growing on the edge of Cray's Copse, Frilsham and on Ashamstead Common, is the green alkanet which has bright blue flowers with white eyes, like a large forget-me-not. It has never spread widely as the four nutlets of the fruit just divide and drop to the ground near the parent plant. The name is derived from the Arabic for henna and it is possible that it was introduced to this country for making a cheap dye from the roots. One of the prettier woodland colonists is the yellow archangel nettle. Geoffrey Grigson thought it must have been called 'archangel' from its angelic quality of not stinging. Another woodland carpeter, later in the summer, is the enchanter's nightshade, a romantic name for a singularly unattractive little spotty pink flower, really only interesting botanically because it has two of everything – stamens, petals, sepals

Yellow Archangel

Yellow Pimpernel

Betony

Bugle

and fruits. More showy in July is the six foot tall spire of the purple foxglove, used medicinally since the nineteenth century as digitalis, the heart stimulant.

A plant of *chalky woods*, with many names , is the stinking iris or gladdon or roastbeef plant; more noticeable in winter with its orange seeds, whereas in June you have to look closely for the inconspicuous slatey-blue flowers. You only have to snap a leaf to understand the origin of its reputation as 'stinking'. The Solomon's seal, with its slender greenish-white bells hanging down in clusters of two, three or four, is no longer a common plant. The sixteenth century herbalist, Gerard, observed that an application of the fresh root 'taketh away in one night or two… any bruise, black or blew spots gotten by women's wilfulness, stumbling upon their hasty husbands' fists'. The wood sanicle, belonging to the same family as cow parsley, is frequent in chalk woods; it has small tight white heads like little balls and minute white flowers.

Damp woods have their own flora. An early flower is the small white wood sorrel, whose leaves close up when the sun gets hot. Its Berkshire name is 'cuckoo's victuals' ; in the Middle Ages it was called 'Alleluia', because it appeared at Easter. For the very botanically minded and for those who like peering into wet ditches, there is the water starwort, which flowers in the spring. Easier to see is the violet flowered bugle, in bloom from May to June; it has an erect spike and at any one time only a third of the flowers are out. Common in boggy woods is the male fern – so called for its robust appearance, in contrast to the more delicate though quite similar lady fern. The bog stitchwort, a weak strag-gling version of the snowy white hedge stitchwort, described by the poet, Edward Thomas, as the whitest flower on earth, is fairly common. A more appealing flower is the yellow pimpernel with oval leaves, flowers like a five-pointed star and stems like threads. When it has finished flowering, the corolla drops entire onto the ground.

Wood clearings yield many interesting plants. In spring the sweet woodruff carpets calcareous or base-rich ground. It has leaves in whorls up the stem like little ruffs and small white flowers. When dried it exudes the sweet scent of new mown hay, coming from the essential oil coumarin. Both the yellow agrimonies grow in wood clearings; the fragrant one, with larger sweet smelling leaves is much less common and usually found only on acid soils. In late summer clearings are dotted with rich red betony, with its tiers of nettle-like flowers; it's second name in Latin is officinalis, implying that the plant was used medicinally.

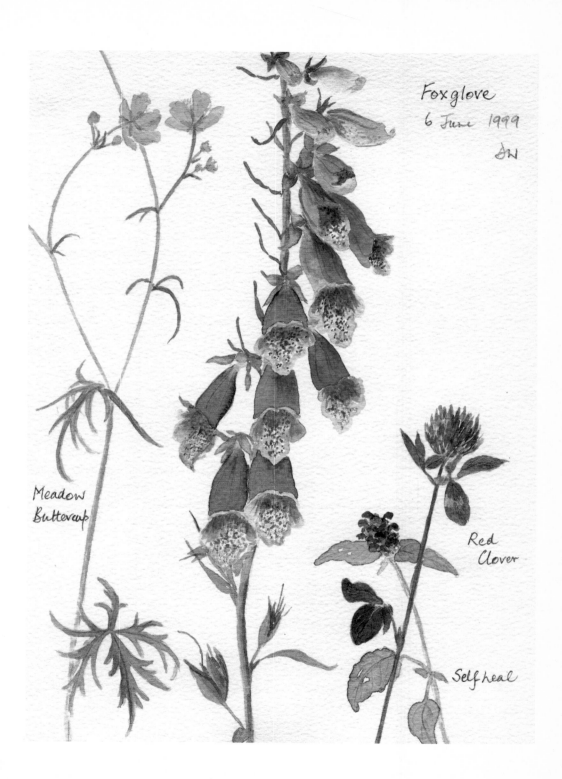

Foxglove
6 June 1999
SN

Meadow
Buttercup

Red
Clover

Self heal

Sneezewort

White Bryony

Pineapple Weed

Now the rosebay willow-herb fills the woods with colour; it has loose spikes of pinkish purple flowers and later on narrow seed pods that split to show the plumes of long silky hairs attached to the seed. This plant spread over the country in the nineteenth century with the coming of the railway and it grows well on ground burnt by fire; it was notable on bomb sites after the Second World War.

Leaving the shade of the woods for more *open grassy places*, we find in April one of the most refreshing sights of spring – primroses and cowslips in abundance and with them the false oxlip. The deliciously scented cowslip has not the most elegant of names, as cowslip is the polite form of cowslop. The primrose comes in two forms, the pin-eyed (with pistils uppermost) and the thrum-eyed (with stamens uppermost). Later on in June there are the pinky-mauve spotted orchids and devil's bit scabious, which belongs to the teasel family. It has a short root stock, believed to have been bitten off by the devil. The oddly-named sneezewort, which has an overall greyish effect often grows with it.

Waste ground hosts many different plants. One of the most exuberant is the Himalayan balsam or policeman's helmet. Unmistakeable, six foot high, with flowers ranging from palest pink to dark purple, leaves with red teeth and capsules that go off with the noise of rifle fire, and it is spreading at an alarming rate. Less agressive is the wild mignonette with flowers in conical racemes which smell faintly. Much more aromatic is the pineapple weed, a common alien with conical green heads looking like and really smelling of pineapples. The giant hog-weed is another menace. It grows up to ten feet high, with flower heads up to four feet across and has become naturalised along the roads and rivers and should not be touched as it can give a dangerous rash. If there is anything to climb, you will find the beautiful flowers of the greater convolvulous.

Turning to the *hedgerows*, the first flower to appear is the snow-drop, not a native plant, but abundantly naturalised. Its leaves are able to pierce anything that comes in its way. The next flower to bloom is the purple or white sweet violet, our only fragrant violet, with heart-shaped leaves which grow very large after flowering. Later on comes the blue-violet ground ivy with an aromatic scent coming from the underside of the leaf. Everyone knows the glossy yellow celandine on the bank. It is a very vari-able plant, the stamens numbering between twenty and sixty; there should be eight petals, but sometimes there are six and sometimes ten. If you pull one up you can see the little bulbils at the base and realize why the plant is also called pilewort. In April the wild arum appears frequently in the hedgerow; it has many names including lords-and-ladies and cuckoo pint. The arrow-

Solomons Seal

Daffodil

shaped leaves are either a dark green or with purplish-black spots and the spadix is also purple or – more rarely – yellow. Later there is a conspicuous spike of fleshy scarlet berries.

In summer, the white bryony, the only English member of the cucumber family, climbs the hedges. The root, which is long and thick and supposed to be shaped like a child's body and thought to be like the true mandrake, was sold in more credulous times to barren women. Nothing in the hedge smells so good as the honeysuckle.

Growing amongst the hedge parsley is the goat's beard, a 'clock plant' closing at mid-day; the beard is the long silvery pappus. Every year the tall white flowered hemlock increases its territory along the road; this umbellifer has an evil-looking purple spotted stem and a foetid smell. Its foliage is poisonous and it was this poison that Socrates used to end his life. Another hedgerow plant is tansy with yellow button heads and spicy smelling leaves. The pale yellow snapdragon or toadflax is known to all country children. It was once a weed found in flax fields and looked not unlike flax itself until the flowers opened. Both the deep scarlet corn poppy, which is the commonest poppy in the south, and the pale poppy, smaller and weaker, grow in the hedgebanks in high summer, now that they have been ousted from the corn by weedkillers.

There are interesting hedges in the area, containing a wide variety of species indicating the age of the hedge. There are spindle trees, familiar to all in the autumn, with their orange-coated seeds inside coral pink fruit; the wood is used for making spindles and skewers, hence the name. There are wayfaring trees, with flat-topped clusters of creamy-white flowers with a sickly smell. There are field maples, alder buckthorn with black fruit, yellow berberis and spiraea, red stemmed dogwoods and apple trees.

The last flower to bloom in the valley – and in every other valley in the country – is the ivy, beloved of romantic poets and bees alike. Shelley wrote of the 'yellow bees in the ivy-bloom' but he did not describe the greenish yellow petals and the showy bright golden stamens. Ivy scrambles everywhere but only flowers when the stems emerge into the light.

There are many other local flowers not even mentioned – the numerous species of speedwell, the vetches, the hawkweeds, known botanically as the 'yellow perils', the grasses, sedges and many more besides – but space forbids.

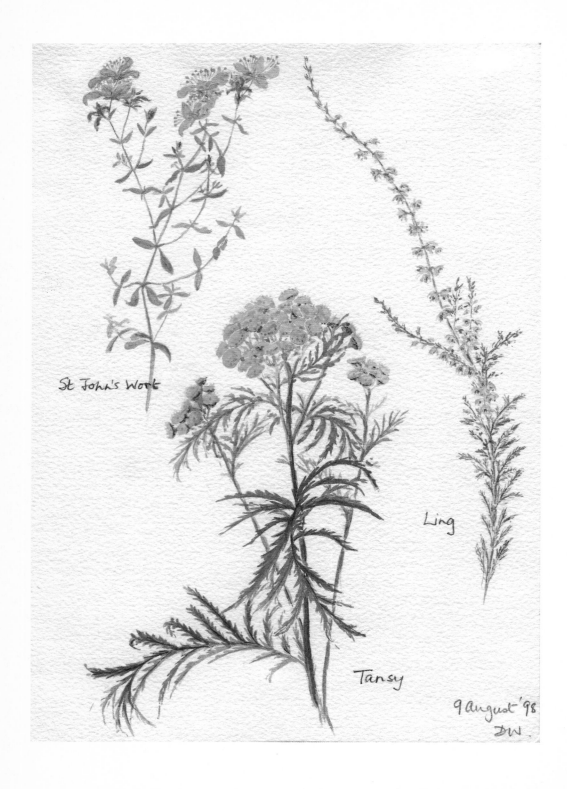

St John's Work

Tansy

Ling

9 August '98
DW.

Spearmint

Marjoram

Wild Basil

Blackberry

DW

1 September 1998

26 Nature's Numbers

Margot Walker

No need to be a mathematician to understand nature's numbers and they can add considerably to our interest in flowers. Felicity Palmer was a good botanist with an enquiring mind and would have been interested in the mathematical functions and patterns of plants. UNESCO nominated the year 2000 as World Mathematics Year and mathematicians have been working on numerical phenomena.

One of the most architectural and common shapes to be found in plants is the circle, represented by the dense spherical heads of the alliums (onions), the lilac and white heads of the drumstick primulas, the blue globe thistles and the round leaves of the smoke bush.

We are all familiar with the triangular shape amongst flowers, either their growth habit or the shape of their flowers or leaves. We all know the conical flowers of lilac and the strikingly triangular buddleias; trilliums have triangular flower parts, one of the acacias and one of the penstemons have triangular leaves. Many plants bear the eponymous name pyramidal, like the pyramid orchid.

We need to learn the word fractals, which is used for shapes which are repeated on an increasingly smaller scale. The purple leaved cow parsley is a good example; if you look closely you will see the leaf stalk divides into three and these divisions are repeated time and time again until the edge of the leaf is reached. Ferns provide another example and also fennel.

Self-similarity is a form of mathematical echo, clearly demonstrated by the grey artemisia. The leaflet is obviously a leaf in miniature and the leaf itself looks like a miniature shoot, the shoot a miniature branch, the branch a scaled-down plant. The same similarity can be seen in junipers, mountain ashes and ferns.

Another extraordinary sequence in flowers is called the Fibonacci system. Nothing new about this, as it was invented by Leonardo of Pisa in the year 1202. He was a great mathematician and traveller who came across the then newfangled number notations invented by the Hindus and Arabs; he wrote an epoch-making book and the western world owes its current system of arithmetic to him. He was given the nickname 'Fibonacci' (Son of Bonaccio) by the eighteenth-century French mathematician Guillaume Libri and it stuck and most people assume it comes from the thirteenth century. From him we learn that nature has its favourite numbers – one, two, three, five, eight, thirteen, twenty-one, thirty-four, fifty-five, eighty-nine etc; each term from three onwards is the sum of the previous two. You will find these numbers if you count petals, sepals etc. For example lilies have three petals, buttercups have five, delphiniums eight, marigolds thirteen, asters twenty-one, and most daisies have thirty-four, fifty-five or eighty-nine. The Fibonacci sequence also accounts for the spiral patterns in sunflowers; if you count the spirals in the head of a sunflower the answers are always Fibonacci numbers.

We can now go out into the wild and into our gardens, start counting, look at our plants afresh and appreciate the contribution mathematics makes to the interest in flowers. Or shall we just admire them for their beauty?

Further reading

'Stewart, I., *Life's Other Secrets*, The Penguin Press (1998)
Chelsea Flower Show 2000, 'Nature's Numbers', Sparsholt College (2000)

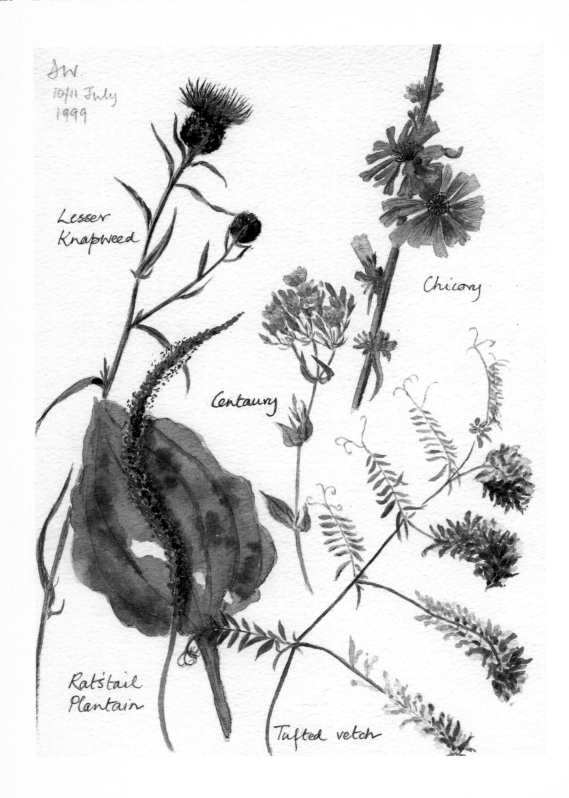

JW.
10/11 July
1999

Lesser
Knapweed

Chicory

Centaury

Rat'stail
Plantain

Tufted vetch

27 Wild Flowers in Frilsham

Dorcas Ward

This is a record of the wild flowers found within the parish of Frilsham in 1998–9. It was part of a wider wildlife survey of the parish, initiated and masterminded by Felicity Palmer. Two hundred and forty wild plants in flower were observed and identified.

The Survey

It was a strictly amateur survey, carried out with no claims to botanical knowledge other than that obtained from a rural childhood and the standard reference books (eg. *The Collins Guide to Wild Flowers*, which, to put this list in context, illustrates over 1300 species). A good many sub-species have probably been included in more generic classifications. It excludes grasses, sedges and ferns.

Almost all the flowers recorded were seen beside public roads or rights-of-way, with minimum trespassing into woods, meadows or Christmas tree plantations. A few flowers, previously associated with arable land, were only found as garden weeds.

The Changes

It is a commonplace that changes in agriculture, road maintenance and other land usage are diminishing the variety and quantity of our wild life. Probably there was much more in previous centuries. But over two hundred wild flowers, many in abundance, suggests that considerable richness remains. A comparison with a botanical list made thirty five years ago seems to show that some of the most attractive flowers (such as both corn and marsh marigolds) have disappeared recently. But others have increased (such as mallows which were spectacular in 1998). One purpose of this record is to provide a benchmark against which future changes can be monitored.

The Record

After a short list of flowering trees, all other flowers are listed in alphabetical order of their English name and are recorded as 'abundant', 'frequent', 'occasional' or 'rare' against twelve locations. Flowers are recorded under 'other' if found in the parish but outside these locations. The format of the record means that locations are fairly approximate and may include more than one type of habitat. For instance, a lane may run through both woods and fields, through both damp and dry patches of soil.

Hatchers Lane (or Hatchetts Lane) also known as Rectory Hill	88 species
Dragon Hill (the lane up past Hawkridge House)	51 species
Frilsham Common, south of Coach Hill, including the allotments	97 species
Frilsham Common, north of Coach Hill, including the football ground	88 species
Coombe Wood	94 species
Hawkridge Wood, incl Whitmoor Copse and meadow below Gamekeeper's Farm	74 species
Wellhouse Lane	38 species
The churchyard	41 species
The chalkpit	80 species
Hermitage Road (south verge of the road from Yattendon)	71 species
Valley Road (Brocks Lane) past the church	104 species
Yattendon Road (past the Potkiln and Magpie Farm)	112 species

Based upon the Ordnance Survey Map with the permission of Her Majesty's Stationery Office.
© Crown Copyright
MC100036335

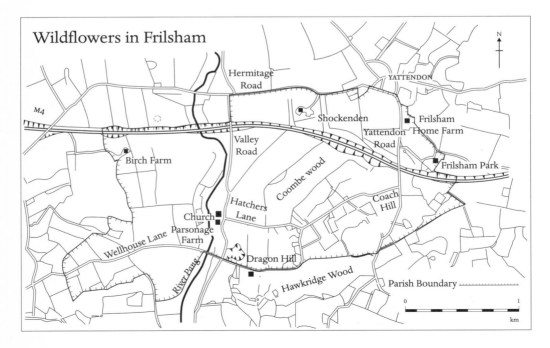

Wildflowers in Frilsham

Frilsham Wild Flowers 1998–99

flower	when	Hatchett's Lane	Dragon Hill	Frilsham Common	Frilsham Common*	Coombe Wood	Hawkridge Wood	Wellhouse Lane	Churchyard	Chalkpit	Hermitage Road	Brock Lane	Yattendon Road	other locations
Apple – naturalised	Apr			o									o	
Alder	Apr				f				f					
Blackthorn	Mar, Apr	o	f	o		la				o			o	
Cherry plum	Mar												o	
Cherry	Apr	o		o	o	o							o	
Elder	May–Jun	o	o	o		o	o		f	f	f	f		*f* along Pang
Gorse	Jan–Dec			f	f	la						o		
Horse Chesnut – white & red								f		o		o		
Larch – Japanese	Mar			o										
May – hawthorne	May	f	o	o					f	f	f	o		
Privet	Jun									o				and behind Shockendon
Rhododendron	May, Jun				o	o								
Rowan (berries)	Jul			o										
Spindlewood (berries)	May (Sep)										o			
Sycamore	Apr, May			o										
Willow – 'Pussy'	Mar			o		o								
Agrimony	Jun–Aug,	o								o	o	f	f	
Alkanet – green	May–Jul				o		la			o				
Barren strawberry	Mar–May	o	f					f						
Bedstraw – hedge	Jun	f			la	f		o	o		o	o		
Bedstraw – heath	Jul			o										
Bedstraw – marsh	Jun				o	f								
Betony	Jul, Aug				lf							o		
Bilberry	May			o	o									
Blackberry	Jun–Sep	o	o	f	la	a	o	o	a	o	f	f		
Black Medick	Aug			?					a		f	f		Gardens (seed heads)
Black Nightshade	Oct													Burntbush lane
Bluebells (*incl. a few white ones*)	Apr, May	f	f	la	a	a	a	f	f		f	f		
Bluebells – spanish	*May*								o			0		
Bristly ox tongue	Aug									o		o		
Broom	Apr, May				o	o								

abbreviations for frequency

a abundant (carpets)
f frequent (lots)
la locally abundant
o occasional (some)
r rare (only one or two)

further explanation of locations

Hatchett's Lane also known as Rectory Hill
Dragon Hill includes School Lane
Frilsham Common includes the allotment meadow
*Frilsham Common** north of Coach Hill including the football ground
Hawkridge Wood includes 'Cray's Meadow' below Gamekeeper's Farm
Brock Lane or Valley Road leading past the church to Everington cross roads

Frilsham Wild Flowers 1998–99

flower	when	Hatchett's Lane	Dragon Hill	Frilsham Common	Frilsham Common*	Coombe Wood	Hawkridge Wood	Wellhouse Lane	Churchyard	Chalkpit	Hermitage Road	Brock Lane	Yattendon Road	other locations
Bryony – black (fruit)	Aug	o												
Bryony – white	May–Jul						o			la		la		
Buddleia	Aug								o					
Bugle	May	o	o	o		f	f/a							
Bugloss – small	Aug			o										
Budock	Jul				o	o	o					o		
Buttercup bulbous	Apr, May		o					0		f	f	o		
Buttercup – creeping	May–Aug	a	o	a	a	la	a	o	f	a	f	a	f	
Buttercup – meadow	May–Aug	f	o	f		o	o				f	f	f	
Calamint – common	Sep							o						
Campion – bladder	Jun								o	o	o			
Campion – red/pink	Apr–Aug	o		o		o						o		
Campion – white	May–Oct		o	o	o	o		o		o	f	f	o	
Catsear – common (?Also recorded as Hawkbit)	Jun–Jul	f		o	o			f					f	
Catsear – smooth	Jun			o							o			
Celandine – lesser	Feb–May	f	a	f	f	o	f	f	la		o	f	f	riverside, Burntbush lane
Celandine – greater	May, Jun		o					o						River(Pang)side
Centaury – common	Jul, Aug					o					o			
Charlock (wild mustard)	May–Aug			o	o									Field N of motorway
Chicory	Jul										r			
Chickweed – water						o								
Chickweed (common)	May–Jul			o	o	o			o		o	f	f	Burntbush lane
Chickweed – mouse ear						o								
Cinquefoil (potentilla) – creeping	Jun–Aug	o	o		o		o		o			la	f	
Cinquefoil – spring	Apr	o	o											
Clover – red (pink)	May–Aug	o		o	o	o			f	lf	o	o	f	
Clover – white	May–Aug	o		f	a	f	f		f	a	o	la	o	
Coltsfoot	Feb, Mar					o			f				la	
Comfrey	May, Jun											o		by the Pang
Convolvulous (Field Bindweed)	Jun–Aug	a						o			a	a	a	
Convolvulous (Great Bindweed, Bellbine)	Jul–Aug			o	f	o		o	f		o	o		
Corncockle	Jun						r							
Corn Spurrey	Aug			o										
Cow parsley	Apr–May	a	a	f	f		f	a	f		a	a	a	riverside, Burntbush lane
Cow wheat	Jun–Aug			f	la									(round football field)
Cowslip	Apr, May		o			o	o	la	o			o		

flower	when	Hatchett's Lane	Dragon Hill	Frilsham Common	Frilsham Common*	Coombe Wood	Hawkridge Wood	Wellhouse Lane	Churchyard	Chalkpit	Hermitage Road	Brock Lane	Yattendon Road	other locations
Cranesbill – cut leaved	May–Oct	f		o	o	o						o		riverside
Cranesbill – dove's foot	May–Aug	o		f		o			o			o		riverside
Cranesbill – longstalked	Jun											o		
Cransebill – small flowered	May, Jun, Oct			o								o		
Creeping Jenny *(some may have been* Yellow Pimpernel)	May, Jun			o	o	f	la							
Cress (hairy & greater bitter)	Apr, May			o		o			o		o	o		
Cress (common wintercress)	May										o			
Crow garlic	Jun, Jul	la								o	o			
Cudweed– Marsh (–Wayside)	Sep													beyond Magpie Farm
Daisy	Apr–Oct	f	f	f/a	a	o		f	f	a	f	a	o	
Dame's violet	May–Jul										o			
Dandelion	Apr–Oct	f	f	f	f	o	f	f	f	f	f	f	f	
Deadnettle – red	Feb–Oct	o		f		o					o	o		a in field w of Yattendon Rd
Deadnettle – white	Apr–Oct	f	f	f	o		o	f	f	f	f	f	o	riverside, Burntbush lane
Dock	May–Jul	o	o	o	o		o	o		a	o	o	o	
Dock – clustered	Jun, Jul			o	o	o								
Dog's mercury	Feb, Mar			f	f	a	f							woodlands
Dogwood	Jun			o							o			
Enchanter's Nightshade	Jul		o	f		f						o		
Evening primrose	Jul, Aug											r		
Fat Hen	Jul									a				
Feverfew	Jul, Aug			o										
Field madder	Jul													beyond Pang
Fogwort – common	Jun, Jul					r								
Fleabane	Jul, Aug					a			f					
?Fools parsley	June											o		
Forget me not	Apr–Jul		f	o	o	f	f		o			o	o	riverside
Forget me not – water	Jun						o							(in the Pang)
Forget me not – wood	May–Aug			o		o						o*		(woods near motorway)
Foxglove	May–Aug	o		o	la	la	a		o	o				

abbreviations for frequency

a abundant (carpets)
f frequent (lots)
la locally abundant
o occasional (some)
r rare (only one or two)

further explanation of locations

Hatchett's Lane also known as Rectory Hill
Dragon Hill includes School Lane
Frilsham Common includes the allotment meadow
Frilsham Common* north of Coach Hill including the football ground
Hawkridge Wood includes 'Cray's Meadow' below Gamekeeper's Farm
Brock Lane or Valley Road leading past the church to Everington cross roads

Frilsham Wild Flowers 1998–99

flower	when	Hatchett's Lane	Dragon Hill	Frilsham Common	Frilsham Common*	Coombe Wood	Hawkridge Wood	Wellhouse Lane	Churchyard	Chalkpit	Hermitage Road	Brock Lane	Yattendon Road	other locations
Fumitory	24/5 Oct								o			r		a beyond Magpie Farm
Garlic mustard (hedge garlic)	Apr–Jul	a	f	a	f	f	f	f	o	o	o	f	f	
Goat's beard – lesser	May–Jul	f	o		o	o					o	o	o	
Goldilocks	Apr		la											
Goosegrass	May, Jun	a	o		f	f	f		o	o	f	f	f	
Ground elder	Jun, Jul		f	f			f	f	la			o		
Ground-ivy	Apr, May	f	f		f	f	f				o	f	la	Burntbush lane
Groundsel	Mar–Oct	o		o							o	o		beyond Pang & Magpie Farm
Hairy Tare	Jun			o						la		o	la	
Hawkbit (?greater and lesser)	May–Jul			o	o				f			o	f	
Hawkbit – autumn	Aug			f	f					f				
Hawksbeard – smooth	Jun, Jul			a					o			f	f	
Hawksbeard – beaked						o								
Hawksbeard – spiny											o			
Hawkweed – leafy	Jun–Aug		o		f						o			
Hawkweed – mouse ear	May, Jun	o						o			o	o		
Hedge mustard	Jul–Oct			o	o									behind Yattendon
Hedge parsley	May–Aug	f	f	o	o		o	f			o	f	f	
Hemlock	Jun–Aug					o				f	f	f	o	
Herb Bennet (Wood Avens)	May–Aug	f	f	o	o	o	o	o				f	o	
Herb Robert	May–Oct	f	f	f	f	a	f						a	
Hogweed	May–Aug	f	o	f	o	o	o	a		f	f	a	a	
Honesty	Apr, May							o	f			o		
Honeysuckle	Jun–Aug	o				o	o							
Hop (male & female)	Aug											o		
Horehound – black (Stinking Roger)	Jun										f	f		
Ivy								f			o	o		
Knapweed – greater	Jun–Oct										f	la	o	
Knapweed – lesser (Hardhead)	Jul, Aug	o				la				o	f	la	o	
Knotgrass	Aug					o					o			
Knotweed – Japanese	Aug	la								o				
Lady's smock (cuckooflower)	Apr, May	la	o					f						
Ling (heath)	Aug		o											
Lords and ladies (berries)	Apr, May	o	f			o	o				o	f		
Lucerne	Jul, Aug									o		r		
Mallow – dwarf	Jul							o						
Mallow – common	Jun–Oct						f			f		o		
Mallow – musk	Jun–Aug											o	f	

flower	when	Hatchett's Lane	Dragon Hill	Frilsham Common	Frilsham Common*	Coombe Wood	Hawkridge Wood	Wellhouse Lane	Churchyard	Chalkpit	Hermitage Road	Brock Lane	Yattendon Road	other locations
Mallow – tree	Jul–Aug										o			
Marestail	May	o												
Margarite (moon daisy or ox-eye daisy)	May–Jul		o	o		o	f			la		o	f	
Mayweed – scentless	Jun–Oct	f				la				a	f	f	f	la beyond Pang
Mayweed – stinking (chamomile)	Jun													Burntbush Lane
Meadow vetchling (yellow)	Jun, Jul	o					o		f	la	f	la		
Melitot – common	Jul, Aug				f	la						o		
Michaelmas daisy	Sep								o					
Mint – corn (?whorled?)	Jul				o									
Mint – spear	Aug								o					
Mint – water	Aug					la								in the Pang
Mugwort	Jul, Aug				o	o			f	f	f	f		
Mullein – great	Jul								o				o	N of motorway
Mustard – black	Aug										o			
Nettle leaved bellflower	Jun					r								
Nipplewort	Jun–Oct	f	f	f	o	o	o			o		f	a	
Orache – spear leaved	Aug	f								a	f			
Orchid – Common Spotted	Jun		r			o	o		o					
Pansy – field	May, Aug					o								Fields N of motorway
Pansy – Heartsease	May													behind Yattendon
Pennycress – common										f				behind Yattendon
Persicaria – (Redshank)	Jul, Aug		o			r			o					f in gardens
Persicaria – pale	Aug		o	la										
Pignut	Jul, Aug		o	la					o		f			
Pimpernel – scarlet	Jul, Aug			f										beyond Pang
Pimpernel – yellow	May–Aug		o	o	la	o								
Pineapple mayweed	Aug								o					
Plantain – Ribwort	May–Aug	f	o				o		f	a		f	f	
Plantain – ratstail	Jul–Aug	o	f	f	o				o			f	o	
Poppy – Corn (red)	Jun–Oct		o				o		o	o		o	o	

abbreviations for frequency

a   abundant (carpets)
f   frequent (lots)
la   locally abundant
o   occasional (some)
r   rare (only one or two)

further explanation of locations

Hatchett's Lane also known as Rectory Hill
Dragon Hill includes School Lane
Frilsham Common includes the allotment meadow
Frilsham Common* north of Coach Hill including the football ground
Hawkridge Wood includes 'Cray's Meadow' below Gamekeeper's Farm
Brock Lane or Valley Road leading past the church to Everington cross roads

Frilsham Wild Flowers 1998–99

flower	when	Hatchett's Lane	Dragon Hill	Frilsham Common	Frilsham Common*	Coombe Wood	Hawkridge Wood	Wellhouse Lane	Churchyard	Chalkpit	Hermitage Road	Brock Lane	Yattendon Road	other locations
Poppy – Welsh (yellow)	May, Jun								o					
Prickly Lettuce	Jul										o			
Primrose	Feb–May	o	f	o	f	f	f		f					
Ragwort	Jun–Aug	f		o	o	la				f	f	f	f	
Ragged Robin	Jun					r	o							
Rape	May, Jun			o						o	o			
Red Bartsia	Jul, Aug			o					o		o			beyond Pang
Rest Harrow	Jun–Aug									o	o			
Rose – dog	May–Jul	f		o	f	o	o	o		f	o	f	f	
Rose – field	Jun	o	?	o								o		
Saxifrage – meadow	May							la						
Scabeous	Jul–Oct	o		f			f			o	f	o		
Selfheal	Jun–Aug				f	o	a		o	o		o	la	
Shepherd's purse & Shepherd's cress	May–Oct			o						?		?		fields N of motorway
Silver weed	Jun–Aug	o				o								
Smooth hawksbeard	Jun		o						o			o		
Snowberry	Aug	o										o		
Snowdrop	Jan, Feb	la		o		la			a		f	o		
Sorrel – common	May–Jul	o	lf	o							f	o	o	
Sorrel – sheep's	Jun			o								?		
Sow thistle – smooth	May–Aug	f		o					f	f		f	o	
Sow thistle – prickly	Jun–Oct	o		o	f	o				o		o	o	
Sow thistle – corn	Jun–Jul								o			o		beyond Pang
Spearwort – lesser	Jun–Aug				f	o								
Speedwell – bird's eye	Apr–Oct	f	f	la	f	o	f	f	f			f	f	Burntbush Lane, Brock Lane
Speedwell – common field	Apr			o								o		f in fields w of Yattendon Road, N of motorway
Speedwell – ivy	Mar			f					f					garden weed
Speedwell – thyme leaved	Jun					o								
Speedwell – wood	May	o			o	o	o							
Spurge (woodspurge)	Mar–Oct	f		f	a	f	la					o		
St John's Wort – common	Jun–Aug	f	o	f	o	o	o		o		f	f		
Stinging nettle	May–Aug	o	f	f	f	f			f	f	f	f		
Stitchwort – greater (Starwort)	Apr–May	a	a	a	f	a	f	a		o		f	f	riverside, Burntbush Lane
Stitchwort – lesser	Jun–Aug		f	f	f	o	f					o	f	
Strawberry	Apr–Jun	o	o	o										
Tansy	Aug–Oct									o				beyond Magpie Farm
Teasel	Jul, Aug					o		o					o	beyond Pang

flower	when	Hatchett's Lane	Dragon Hill	Frilsham Common	Frilsham Common*	Coombe Wood	Hawkridge Wood	Wellhouse Lane	Churchyard	Chalkpit	Hermitage Road	Brock Lane	Yattendon Road	other locations
Thistle – creeping	Jun–Aug	f		o	o	f	o	o		a	f	f	f	
Thistle – marsh	Jun–Aug				f	o								
Thistle – musk	Jul													beyond Pang
Thistle – spear	Jun–Aug			f	f	o			o	f	f	f	o	
Thistle – welted	Jun, Jul					o	o			f				
Thistle – yellow star	May									o				
Toadflax – common	Aug						o							
Tormentil	Jul, Aug			la	o	o								
Trefoil – bird's foot (both greater & 'eggs and bacon')	Jun–Aug		o	f	o	la	f			f	o	f	f	
Trefoil – Hop (& Black Medick?)	May–Aug	o		o	f	a				f	f	o	o	
Trefoil – common yellow	May, Jun	o		f	f	f				a		o	f	
Vetch – bitter	Apr, May	la												
Vetch – bush	May–Oct	f	o	o			o			o		o		
Vetch – common	Apr–Jul	f		o	o	o				o	a	f		
Vetch – narrow leaved	May, Jun	o	o	o	o							o	o	
Vetch – tufted	Jul			o										beyond Pang (a by motorway)
Violet – Dog	Apr, May	f	f	f		o	o					f		
Wallpepper (yellow stonecrop)	Jun											o		
Water cress	Jun					la								by the Pang
Water Crow's foot	May–Jul					la	o							by and in the Pang
Weld	Aug									f				
Wild Angelica	Aug					o								
Wild Basil	Jul, Aug									f		o		beyond the Pang
Wild Carrot	Aug									o	f	f	f	
Wild Clematis (Travellers Joy, Old Man's Beard)	Aug										o	f		
Wild Marjoram	Aug									o				
Wild Parsnip	Jul, Aug										f	f	o	
Wild Radish	May–Aug		o							o				beyond Pang, N of motorway

abbreviations for frequency

a abundant (carpets)
f frequent (lots)
la locally abundant
o occasional (some)
r rare (only one or two)

further explanation of locations

Hatchett's Lane also known as Rectory Hill
Dragon Hill includes School Lane
Frilsham Common includes the allotment meadow
*Frilsham Common** north of Coach Hill including the football ground
Hawkridge Wood includes 'Cray's Meadow' below gamekeeper's farm
Brock Lane or Valley Road leading past the church to Everington cross roads

Frilsham Wild Flowers 1998–99

flower	when	Hatchet's Lane	Dragon Hill	Frilsham Common	Frilsham Common*	Coombe Wood	Hawkridge Wood	Wellhouse Lane	Churchyard	Chalkpit	Hermitage Road	Brock Lane	Yattendon Road	other locations
Willowherb – broadleaved	Jun–Aug	f	o	o		o	o		o					
Willowherb – pale (?)	Jun–Aug					o								
Willowherb – shortfruited(?)	Jun–Aug					o								
Willowherb – great (Codlins and Cream)	Jul, Aug	f			o	o		o	f					
Willowherb – Rose-bay	Jul, Aug	o		o	la				a			o		
Wood Anemone	Mar–May	o	f	o	f		o					o		
Wood Sage	Jul–Oct	o		o	f		o					f		
Wood Sorrel	Apr, May			f	f									
Woody Nightshade	Jun–Aug	o						o	o	o	o	o		
Woundwort – hedge or wood	Jun–Aug	f	o	o	o	f	f		o		f	f		
Yarrow	Jun–Aug	o		o				o	o	f	f	f		
Yellow archangel	May	o	o			o	f							Burntbush Lane

A very ancient ash coppice stool surrounded by blue-bells and other Ancient Woodland Indicators in an ancient woodland relic hedge on Ashampstead's parish boundary bank.
© Greenaway collection

The clear edge to the undisturbed bluebell area is shown in this photograph.
©Greenaway collection

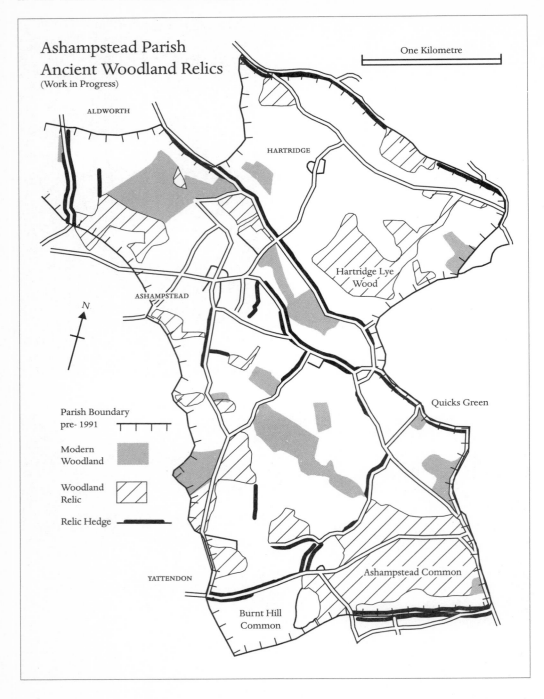

Diagram of woodland
relic hedges and bluebell
copses/woods within
parish boundary. Includes
settlements and roads.

28 Hedges – why bother?

Dick Greenaway

Hedges are a nuisance. They have to be cut and the cuttings puncture your tyres. Surround the patch with larch lap and paint it green! But hedges *do* make a difference. Get to somewhere where you can see a decent chunk of your area and look at the field pattern. Then mentally remove the hedges. What you have left is not Berkshire or south Oxfordshire. Possibly parts of Yorkshire, but not 'Oxon or Berks'. So hedges are important in giving landscape an identity. Of course they also have the severely practical function for which they were originally designed of keeping stock in and intruders out. But in addition to that they provide a record of the development of the landscape and are very important homes, routeways and sources of food for the local wildlife – particularly for birds, small mammals and insects. For example, it has been estimated that fifty per cent of British plant species (flora) live in hedges, and that fifty per cent of British butterflies are associated with hedges. A quarter of bird species considered as important under the UK's Biodiversity Action Plan are closely associated with hedgerows for nesting and feeding.

Hedges are almost an eco-system in their own right. The nectar and pollen of hedgerow species feeds the early insects, which in turn feed the nestlings of birds nesting in the hedges. The fallen leaves and deadwood in the hedge bottom are eaten by invertebrates – which, in turn, are eaten by hedgehogs and so on. A species rich hedge in autumn is a veritable larder of winter food with scarlet hips and haws, pink spindle berries, black dogwood berries, wild cherries and wayfaring tree berries and blue black sloes with the fluffy white, seed bearing old man's beard

A burst of blue as bluebells
respond to increased light
in an experimental coppice
area on Ashampstead
Common.
© Greenaway collection

Pang Valley Conservation
Volunteers coppicing an
over-age hazel coppice.
© Greenaway Collection

The hedge as a source of food.

Clockwise from top left
Spindle berries
Briar hips
Old Man's beard-seeds
Wayfaring free berries
Holly berries

draped over all. Late ripening ivy berries fill a hungry gap in late winter. These are illustrated on page 241.

Because this importance was recognised and because hedges were disappearing at an alarming rate, legislation was introduced to control their removal. In the 1980s some 5000 miles of hedges were being removed every year as farmers rearranged their farms to suit the use of ever larger machinery and as towns expanded and roads were widened to accommodate a growing and increasingly mobile population. The current regulations are The Hedgerow Regulations 1997. They set out the historical and wildlife criteria for defining an important hedge and how they are to be protected by the planning processes. The criteria are complex and it is not proposed to go into them in detail, but they define an important hedge and describe the method for surveying a hedge to record the important features. Basically, an important hedge is species rich in both the shrubs that make up the hedge and in the ground flora. It has standard trees scattered along it and forms the boundary of a site known to be ancient. It is also accessible to the public by being alongside a road or a path and forms an important visual element in the landscape. It is valuable as a connexion between habitats and it will link to other wildlife habitats such as woods or ponds. Few hedges will have all these features, but the degree to which they have them defines their importance.

Hedges go back a long way. The name comes from an Anglo-Saxon word 'hege' and 'old hedges' are mentioned in many early boundary descriptions, some of which date from the eighth and ninth centuries. Many of these boundaries – still lined with hedges – can still be identified. Hedges go back even further than that. Roman writers on agriculture give instructions on the planting and maintenance of hedges, and give the impression that it was an established practice in the first century BC.

Hedges were formed in three basic ways. Firstly, they were created by a process called 'assarting'. This was the clearing of a patch of woodland to form a field leaving a narrow strip of the wood as a shaw or shelter belt between the new field and the existing fields. Over the years this strip could be nibbled away by ploughing until it became narrow enough to be managed as a hedge. But it would still contain all the ground flora of the original woodland. These are particularly valuable hedges. Secondly, hedges can be planted. Records of planted hedges go back at least to Tudor times and show that mixtures of several species were commonly used when planting a new hedge . The hedge bottom of a planted hedge will contain the ground plants of the field being sub-divided. These will not be the woodland species – bluebell etc. – but may contain dog's mercury as a sign of anciently disturbed land. The heyday of planted hedges was after the Enclosure Acts were passed in the late 1700s and 1800s when millions of acres of open field were divided up with straight hedges. Many companies were founded to supply hedge sets for these. Thirdly, hedges can be self sown. A fence put up in an open area reasonably close to a source of seed will soon acquire a hedge as birds, which have fed on the local berries, perch on the fence and deposit seeds with their droppings.

By mapping the species contained in a hedge – both the shrubs and the ground flora – it is possible to see how the landscape developed. In my own parish of Ashampstead many of the road-side hedges contain a woodland ground flora of bluebells, wood anemones etc. – all plants which, if once destroyed never return. These plants are recognised by English Nature as Ancient Woodland Indicator Species and can be used to identify ancient woodland relic hedges as well as ancient woods. As the map on page 242 shows, it is clear that many of the roads around the parish were cut through woodland and the fields developed alongside them later – leaving a strip of woodland and an undis-turbed strip of land to become an ancient hedge. In some parts of the parish, notably in the north east, the whole area appears to have been cleared and the roads to have developed from tracks crossing the open fields since they contain only field flora in the hedge bottoms. The same technique indicates that the parish boundary was marked out through woodland. We are fortunate in having most of the original boundary bank around the parish. Parishes are thought to have been defined in the ninth or tenth centuries and Ashampstead's banks are massive in places and still crowned with hedges containing ancient coppice stools. Coppice stools are the still living stumps of hedgerow trees that were deliberately cut off at ground level so that they would produce many stems. Repeated cutting keeps the stool alive almost indefi-nitely and results in strikingly shaped stumps. The very richness of the woodland ground flora in the hedges on the boundary banks also indicates clearly that they are derived from woodland. The length of bank separating us from Streatley along the Southridge road is well worth a visit in May or early June when it is covered in bluebells, aenemones, woodruff, dog's mercury, yellow archangel and many other flowers.

There are ways to estimate the age of hedges, but they have to be used with care and supported by several sources of evidence. 'Hooper's Hedge Hypothesis' was developed by Dr Max Hooper after many years of studying hedges known to be ancient. He proposed that a 30 metre length of hedge would acquire a new hardwood species for every century of its existence. This has been interpreted as meaning that by counting the number of species you can estimate its age. This is not what he proposed and obviously only works if the hedge started with one species! It does not apply to hedges formed from woodland or to hedges planted with more than one species. Elm in a hedge can cause problems. Elm spreads by suckering and can rapidly take over an ancient species rich hedge turning it into a single species hedge.

This is why the hedge bottom plants are so important, because they can indicate the degree of reliance which can be placed on Hooper's Hypothesis for that particular hedge. It is very sad to see Countryside Stewardship officials advocating spraying off the hedge bottom before replanting and gapping up thus destroying this evidence and reducing the beauty, utility, historical and wildlife interest of the hedge. It was not considered necessary in the past – why should it be now?

To really estimate the age of a hedge you need other evidence in addition to the species count. The best source of evidence comes from early maps. Early maps held by some of the large estates can give a great deal of detailed information. Other sources of early maps are the local Record Offices – in our case the Berkshire Record Office in Reading. In Berkshire the first map of real use for hedge studies is the survey by John Rocque published in 1761. This is sufficiently detailed at 2 inches to the mile to show individual hedges and these are shown with a special hedge symbol to differentiate them from un-hedged boundaries. However, one must not expect such an early map made with primitive equipment to match a modern map. Nevertheless, used with care and tied in to features such as roads, churches and surviving old houses, the maps can be used to confirm the existence of a modern hedge in 1761. Pride's Survey of 1791 seems mainly to be cribbed from Rocque and does not add much. The first really detailed and accurate surveys in many parishes are the Tithe Award Maps of the 1840s and these are superb. They are directly comparable with modern mapping but do not indicate whether a boundary was hedged or merely fenced. Without doubt the best maps are the First Edition *Ordnance Survey Large Scale Maps* (about 1850–80) which clearly show hedges with every standard tree in the hedge! In the opinion of many people involved in landscape studies these are the best maps ever produced by the Ordnance Survey. By using a combination of evidence from early mapping, from early documents and from field study it is possible to make a case for the age of a hedge, but it should be remembered that the age can rarely be more than an estimate. It is not unusual to see dates for hedges quoted to a year in local history studies. Given the uncertainties described above these will almost never be sustainable!

The Council for the Protection of Rural England (CPRE) are currently sponsoring a nationwide study of hedges and the local Wildlife Trusts are providing volunteers and training and co-ordinating the results. The intention is to provide the planning authorities with a database of information about hedges which will allow them to make informed judgements when dealing with applications for hedgerow removal. It will also provide a bench-mark against which future studies can be measured to estimate the changes taking place in our countryside, and of course it will provide a valuable source of information to the landscape historian.

So hedges really are better than larch lap or barbed wire – even if they do have to be cut!

Sources

British Trust for Conservation Volunteers (BTCV)
Brooks, Alan, & Agate, Elizabeth, *Hedging – a practical handbook*
The Countryside Agency, *Hedgerows of England*, (May 2000)
Rackham, Oliver, *The History of the Countryside*, London (1986)
The Stationery Office Statutory Instrument 1160, *The Hedgerow Regulations* (1997)
Taylor, Christopher, *Fields in the English Landscape*, London (1975)
Thomas, Eric & White, John, T., *Hedgerow*, London (1980)

29 Pang Valley Birds

Tim Culley

The Pang Valley provides a varied habitat of woodland, gardens, riverside meadows and open fields. Its birds fall into three main groups and the ones that you will see in the valley will largely depend on the time of year. The groups consist of the residents that stay with us all the year round – robins, blackbirds, chaffinches, rooks and jackdaws; and two classes of migrants, winter migrants and summer migrants. These are completely different in origin and come for completely different reasons. The winter migrants come to us from Scandinavia, Germany and Russia to enjoy our relatively mild winters and these are birds like the redwings and fieldfares. They are often seen in groups foraging on fallen apples or hawthorn berries. The summer migrants are the swifts, swallows, martins, chiffchaffs, warblers, and white-throats. These come from their winter quarters in Africa to rear their families on the abundant food in our valley.

In winter a garden bird table situated near some bushes or trees for cover will draw all the classes of tits – coal tits, blue tits, great tits, marsh tits and long tailed tits. A peanut feeder will attract greenfinches, spotted woodpeckers and nuthatches. Less welcomely it will also attract their enemy the sparrowhawk. A puff of feathers and he is gone with a bird in his talons.

A winter walk along a footpath through open fields should show rooks and jackdaws in groups searching for food in grass or arable fields. Carrion crows are usually alone or in small family groups. The crow's call is a jerky, rasping 'keenght' or 'kaaah' – often repeated three times. But everyone knows the old saying to distinguish the species! 'If you see a rook on its own it's a crow and if you see a flock of crows they are rooks!' If the sun shines at any time in the winter skylarks will rise to a hundred feet singing loudly. They are common in the valley.

A new resident in the valley is the buzzard. They nest in local woods and can be seen looking for carrion in open fields or, in groups, soaring just for fun. You can often hear their 'mewing' even if you cannot see them. An even more recent resident is the red kite. These were re-introduced into the Chilterns in 1988 and are increasingly common in the valley as they quarter the fields looking for food. Look out for a large bird with a markedly forked tail.

When walking in woodland you need to listen as well as look. Well camouflaged birds are difficult to see, but their song or their alarm call will give them away. Robins maintain a territory in the winter as well as in the spring and they can be heard singing their song when other birds are silent. The blackcap sings between April and June and has a very pretty loud song but since he always sings from the middle of a dense bush he is likely to be completely invisible.

Of the three owls in our area the one most often heard is the tawny owl with its 'tu whit to woo'. They live in the woods and can be heard all the year round. The little owl, or screech owl, feeds by day but is not often seen. The barn owl is making a slow come back and only seems to be seen in car head lights at night as a ghostly white bird gliding at the road side.

Of our summer visitors the first to arrive is the chiffchaff and his name provides his complete repertoire. It is exciting when first heard because it is one of the first signs of spring at the end of March or early April, but it soon becomes monotonous! The chiffchaff is soon followed by the garden and willow warblers. These are very small brown birds with a sweet melodious song. The quality songsters come next, the now rare nightingale in hazel woods, the black cap in woods or thick scrub and the whitethroat in hedgerows.

The swallows and martins arrive in April and are first seen feeding on insects over rivers and open water but they soon take up residence. The swallows prefer the inside of sheds and barns for nest sites while the martins nest under the eaves. The swift is the last to arrive and the first to leave. They commonly nest under the slates of old roofs where there is just enough space to squeeze through. Unlike swallows and martins they never rest on telephone wires – they even sleep on the wing.

Two other rarer summer insect eaters can sometimes be seen in the valley. The cuckoo – once a common bird – is increasingly rare all over the world as its winter habitats in Africa are destroyed. Nevertheless it would not be summer without the call of the cuckoo. Even rarer is the nightjar. It spends its summer on heath land and areas of open heath have almost disappeared in the valley. Great efforts are being made to recover the heath land on Bucklebury Common where you may be lucky enough to hear its chirring song on a warm summers evening and to see its ungainly flight against the darkening sky.

If you are interested in getting to know birds start with a garden bird book and a feeding table and you will be surprised how quickly you learn. I have attached a list of the birds seen in the countryside and in the gardens around Frilsham between 1997 and 2000. You may find it interesting to see how many of these you can see for yourself and whether you can add to the list!

Frilsham farmland and riverside bird survey 1997–2000

name of bird	time of year	frequency	breed in locality
black cap	summer	common	yes
blackbird	resident	common	yes
buzzard	resident	common	yes
chaffinch	resident	common	yes
chiff chaff	summer	common	yes
coot	resident	common	yes
cormorant	resident	common	no
crow – carrion	resident	common	yes
cuckoo	summer	common	yes
dove – collared	resident	common	yes
dove – rock	resident	common	yes
dove – stock	resident	common	yes
dove – turtle	summer	rare	no
duck – mallard	resident	common	yes
duck – tufted	resident	common	yes
falcon – hobby	summer	occasional	yes
field fare	winter	common	no
finch – bull	resident	common	yes
finch – gold	resident	common	yes
finch – green	resident	common	yes
flycatcher – spotted	summer	common	yes
goldcrest	resident	common	yes
goose – canada	resident	common	yes
grebe – little	resident	common	yes
gull – black headed	resident	common	no
gull – great black backed	resident	common	no
gull – herring	resident	common	no
hammer – yellow	resident	common	yes
hawk – sparrow	resident	common	yes
heron – grey	resident	common	yes
jackdaw	resident	common	yes
jay	resident	common	yes
kestrel	resident	common	yes
kingfisher	resident	occasional	no
kite – red	resident	occasional	no
lapwing	resident	common	yes
lark – sky	resident	common	yes
linnet	resident	common	yes
magpie	resident	common	yes
martin – house	summer	common	yes

Frilsham farmland and riverside bird survey continued

name of bird	time of year	frequency	breed in locality
moorhen	resident	common	yes
nut hatch	resident	common	yes
owl – barn	resident	occasional	no
owl – little	resident	rare	yes
owl – tawney	resident	common	yes
partridge – English	resident	common	yes
partridge – redleged	resident	common	no
pheasant	resident	common	yes
pigeon – wood	resident	common	yes
pipit – meadow	resident	common	yes
plover – ringed	not known	rare	no
red wing	winter	common	no
robin	resident	common	yes
rook	resident	common	yes
snipe	winter	occasional	no
sparrow – hedge	resident	common	yes
sparrow – house	resident	common	yes
starling	resident	common	yes
swallow	summer	common	yes
swan – mute	resident	common	yes
swift	summer	common	yes
thrush – mistle	resident	common	yes
thrush – song	resident	common	yes
tit – blue	resident	common	yes
tit – great	resident	common	yes
tit – willow	resident	common	yes
wagtail – grey	resident	common	yes
wagtail – pied	resident	common	yes
warbler – willow	summer	common	yes
white throat	summer	common	yes
woodcock	resident	common	yes
woodpecker – green	resident	common	yes
wren	resident	common	yes

Frilsham farmland and riverside bird survey 1997–2000 continued

	name of bird	time of year	frequency	breed in locality
*seen in Frilsham gardens	brambling*	winter	occasional	no
	dunnock*	resident	occasional	not known
	gull – common*	not known	occasional	no
	redstart*	summer	occasional	no
	siskin*	summer	occasional	no
	sparrow – tree*	resident	common	not known
	tit – coal*	resident	common	not known
	tit – longtailed*	resident	common	yes
	tit – marsh*	resident	common	yes
	treecreeper*	resident	occasional	not known
	woodpecker – spotted*	resident	common	not known

30 Ashampstead, Berkshire: parish garden bird survey

Dick Greenaway

The origin of the Project

Early in 2000 I saw the results of a survey of garden birds carried out in Frilsham Parish at the initiative of Felicity Palmer of Coombe Farm. I was impressed by the quality of the information that had been gathered by people who would not have called themselves 'bird experts'. It occurred to me that it would be interesting and useful to emulate the Frilsham survey in Ashampstead, particularly since we were in the first year of the new millenium. In addition to the general interest of the project the survey would act as a benchmark against which to measure future surveys.

In April 2000 I put a short note in the parish magazine suggesting the project and rapidly had twenty volunteers. Each month throughout the year we completed our forms and the information grew. This report is the result.

The survey method

I shamelessly cribbed the recording form from Frilsham making only minor changes. We employed a new form each month and examples of the forms are included at the end of this essay in case anyone would like to crib from us!

Monthly collection allowed me to keep up with the data flow rather than having to analyse a whole year's worth of data at the end of the project.

I gave a score to each week's sightings. For example, a bird seen very frequently during the week was recorded 'FF' and scored four, a bird seen a few times was recorded 'F' and scored three, a bird seen occasionally was recorded 'o' and scored two and, finally, a bird but rarely seen was recorded 'ʀ' and scored one. This is a crude system but gave a reasonable idea of the regularity with which each species was seen.

I entered the scores into an Excel Spreadsheet which allowed me to sort the scores into sequence and to produce charts – a picture is worth a thousand words.

The Recorders

The recorders were well spread around the parish, but I grouped them into four areas for comparison. The village was well covered and some detailed patterns are obvious as a result, Ashampstead Green had two recorders and Ashampstead Common and Quicks Green one each. Each site was named by post code which enables grid references to be obtained. The four areas also represented four different landscapes. First the village with its tight pattern of houses and enclosed gardens. Then the Green surrounded by woods. Next Drift Barn at Quicks Green which is almost surrounded by arable fields and finally the common with a mixture of woods and arable fields.

In addition to recording the birds they saw in or over their gardens the recorders described their gardens. The object of this was to see if there were particular features that corresponded to a wealth or to a dearth of birds. This proved particularly interesting.

The Analysis

The weekly scores were totalled for each bird species at the end of the year and an average monthly score calculated. This score was then used as the measure of 'commonness' and the whole list was sorted into sequence using this score. The resulting list is shown on the chart included at the end of this essay.

To examine the effects of the four different landscapes I produced separate tables and charts for each area. They do, indeed, show marked differences. Over all blackbirds were the most common – as they are nationally – but this varied from area to area. On Ashampstead Green blue tits edged ahead. Crows came in second place at Drift Barn ahead of wood pigeons which were in second place elsewhere and this clearly reflects the arable fields around the house.

Commentary

It will probably be claimed that my analysis is crude and that more could be obtained by a more skilled statistician and this is probably true. Nevertheless, I believe the survey to have been of considerable value if only for the sustained interest it generated and for the bench mark of raw data it has provided for future surveys.

I will leave it to the reader to look at the charts and to draw his or her own conclusions, but a number of points have occurred to me.

– We recorded sixty one species in or over our gardens.
– The single greatest factor in determining 'richness' seems to be the presence or absence of cats. The gardens which exclude cats have an abundance of birds, those – like my own – where cats regularly roam have markedly fewer birds.
– Feeding also makes a major difference. Gardens with bird tables which are kept supplied all the year round have more species.
– The most common species are the blackbird and the wood pigeon. This matches the national bird survey results.
– There is a colony of collared doves in Ashampstead village which do not seem to be seen at the other sites.
– Sparrows are rare and almost confined to Ashampstead village and to Ashampstead Green.
– There is a mistle thrush in the centre of Ashampstead village which sometimes travels as far as the Green! Song thrushes are much more common than expected.
– Red kites rarely stray south to Ashampstead Common.

Conclusion

I believe everyone who took part in the survey enjoyed the effort. I am sure that those of us who were not particularly 'birdy people' at the start completed the year with a greater awareness of the wealth of bird life around us and are now probably able to do better than 'little brown job' when asked to identify a bird. I would include myself in this category.

I would recommend a survey of this sort to any other community – rural or urban – it is valuable and great fun!

ASHAMPSTEAD PARISH GARDEN BIRD SURVEY
RECORDING SHEET - one column per week

Name ....   **Address** ....

Month   *APRIL 2001*   **Post Code** ....
SYMBOLS
FF=4 days/ week or more.   F=fairly frequently.   O=occasionally.   R=rare.   N=nesting

Species	Week 02-08	09-15	16-22	23-29		Other species	Week 02-08	09-15	16-22	23-29	
Blackbird											
Blue tit											
Great tit											
Wren											
Chaffinch											
Dunnock											
Robin											
Song thrush											
Mistle thrush											
Green woodpecker											
Wood pigeon											
Collared dove											

Please note any other birds seen flying over head - eg. geese, herons, buzzards, kites - and any other sightings of interest.

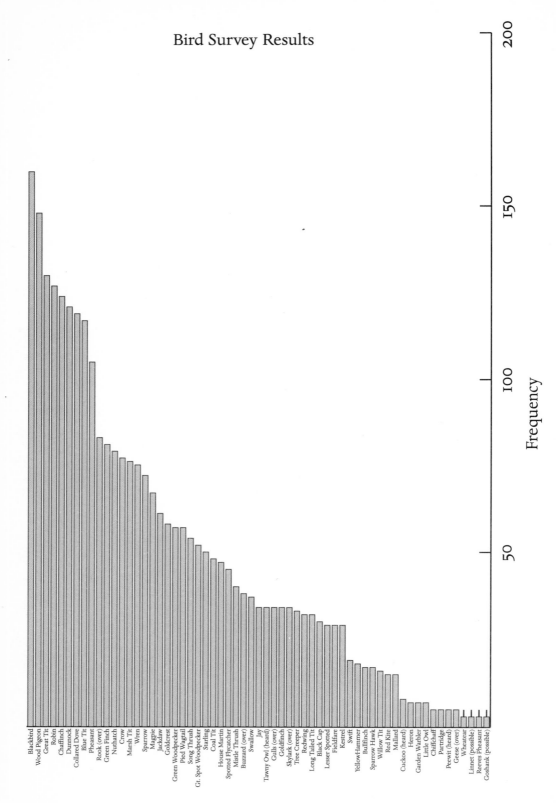

Bird Survey Results

Index

*Numbers in bold refer to illustrations, entries in single
 quotes refer to chapter titles*